It is Philippe Van Parijs' conviction that the Marxist tradition can be kept alive as an essential ingredient of Left-wing thinking, but only providing dutiful conservation gives way to ruthless recycling: the discarding of encumbering elements, and the reshaping of the remainder, using the latest intellectual technology. The essays collected in this book examine the structure and potential of historical materialism as a general theory of social change, they draw the lessons of the failure of Marxist crisis theory, and show how a rejuvenated notion of exploitation can illuminate the analysis of the class structure of welfare state capitalism or the assessment of international migration. They explore and advocate a 'capitalist road to communism', that expands the realm of freedom while bypassing socialism, and they develop those aspects of the Marxist project that converge, at the deepest level, with political ecology.

Studies in Marxism and social theory

Marxism recycled

Studies in Marxism and Social Theory

Edited by G. A. COHEN, JON ELSTER AND JOHN ROEMER

The series is jointly published by the Cambridge University Press and the Editions de la Maison des Sciences de l'Homme, as part of the joint publishing agreement established in 1977 between the Fondation de la Maison des Sciences de l'Homme and the Syndics of the Cambridge University Press.

The books in the series are intended to exemplify a new paradigm in the study of Marxist social theory. They will not be dogmatic or purely exegetical in approach. Rather, they will examine and develop the theory pioneered by Marx, in the light of the intervening history, and with the tools of non-Marxist social science and philosophy. It is hoped that Marxist thought will thereby be freed from the increasingly discredited methods and presuppositions which are still widely regarded as essential to it, and that what is true and important in Marxism will be more firmly established.

Also in the series

Marxism recycled

Philippe Van Parijs

CAMBRIDGE
UNIVERSITY PRESS

EDITIONS DE LA MAISON
DES SCIENCES DE L'HOMME

Published by the Press Syndicate of the University of Cambridge
The Pitt Building, Trumpington Street, Cambridge CB2 1RP
40 West 20th Street, New York, NY 10011–4211, USA
10 Stamford Road, Oakleigh, Melbourne 3166, Australia
and Editions de la Maison des Sciences de l'Homme
54 Boulevard Raspail, 75270 Paris Cedex 06

First published 1993

Printed in Great Britain at the University Press, Cambridge

A catalogue record for this book is available from the British Library

Library of Congress cataloguing in publication data
Van Parijs, Philippe, 1951–
Marxism recycled/Philippe Van Parijs.
     p.   cm. – (Studies in Marxism and social theory)
Includes index.
ISBN 0 521 41802 X
1. Marxism. 2. Historical materialism. 3. Capitalism. I. Title. II. Series.
HX44.5.P37 1993
335.4 – dc20   92–23166   CIP

ISBN 0 521 41802 X hardback
ISBN 2 7351 0536 9 hardback (France only)

For my fellow Septembrists,
in deep gratitude for a decade
of exceptional intellectual stimulation

Contents

ix

Acknowledgements

1 From contradiction to catastrophe

This chapter grew out of a paper presented in Oxford in December 1978 at Charles Taylor's Historical Materialism seminar, which consisted in a discussion, with G. A. Cohen, of the central theses of the latter's (then forthcoming) *Karl Marx's Theory of History*. An earlier version appeared in the *New Left Review* (London) 115, May–June 1979, 87–96. I am particularly grateful to Jerry Cohen, Steven Lukes, and Rom Harré for stimulating discussions.

2 Marxism's central puzzle

This chapter grew out of part of a paper on 'Marxist causation' presented at the 1981 meeting of the September group. An earlier version appeared in German in *Analyse und Kritik* (Berlin) 4 (2), 1982, 197–210, as part of a special issue devoted to a discussion of G. A. Cohen's *Karl Marx's Theory of History*, and in English in *After Marx* (T. Ball and J. Farr eds.), New York and Cambridge: Cambridge University Press, 1984, 88–104. I am very grateful to Terry Ball, Jerry Cohen, Jon Elster, John Roemer, Robert van der Veen and Erik Wright for their comments on the first draft. Some of the points made in this chapter were further clarified in 'The shifting primacy puzzle. A rejoinder' (*Analyse und Kritik* 5, 1983, 223–30), in which I responded to G. A. Cohen's 'Reply to four critics' (*Analyse und Kritik* 5, 1983, 195–222).

3 A rational reconstruction by way of obituary

This chapter grew out of a paper presented at the Economics Departments of the Universities of Louvain-la-Neuve and Cambridge and at the Communication and Cognition seminar at the University of Ghent. It first appeared under the title 'The falling-rate-of-profit theory of crisis. A rational reconstruction by way of obituary', in *Review of Radical Political Economics* (New York), 12 (1), Spring 1980, 1–16 and was reprinted in *History of Economic Thought* (Mark Blaug ed.), London: Edward Elgar, 1990, 126–44. An abridged French version forms a section of Jacques Attali, *Les Trois Mondes*, Paris: Fayard, 1981, 106–17. I am grateful to my audiences and referees, to Phil Armstrong, Johannes Berger, Sue Black, Jim Devine, Michel De Vroey, Ernst Fahling, Heiner Ganssmann, Jacques Gouverneur, Bob Rowthorn, and above all to Andrew Glyn and John Roemer, for many useful comments.

4 Why Marxist economics needs microfoundations

This chapter is a slightly revised version of a reply to Patrick Clawson's 'A comment on Van Parijs's obituary' (*Review of Radical Political Economics* 15 (2), 1983, 107–10). It was first published under the title 'Why Marxist economics needs microfoundations. Postscript to an obituary' in *Review of Radical Political Economics* 15 (2), 1983, 111–24. I am very grateful to Joseph Chung, Philippe De Villé, Jim Devine, Michel De Vroey, Heiner Ganssmann, Andrew Glyn, Jacques Gouverneur, Makoto Itoh, Alain Lipietz, Jim Lindsey, Angelo Reati and John Roemer for stimulating discussions. To get a fair picture of the debate, one would of course need to read Clawson's arguments as he stated them himself, not just my restatement of them.

5 Exploitation and the libertarian challenge

A Dutch version of this chapter was presented at the University of Antwerp in March 1986. It was first published as chapter 5 of *Modern Theories of Exploitation* (A. Reeve ed.), London and Beverly Hills: Sage Publications, 1987, 111–31. (Spanish translation in *Zona Abierta* (Madrid) 51/2, 1989, 87–114.) I am grateful to John Baker, Sue Black, Jean Cartelier, Terrell Carver, Michel De Vroey, Andrew Glyn, Jacques Gouverneur, Erik Oger, Andrew Reeve, John Roemer, Ian Steedman and Robert van der Veen for fruitful discussions and useful comments on an earlier version.

6 A revolution in class theory

This chapter grew out of a comment on Erik O. Wright's framework for class analysis which I presented at the international seminar 'Recent developments in class theory and class analysis' held in Amsterdam in April 1985. It was presented at the annual meeting of the Dutch Association of Political Scientists (Amersfoort, June 1986) and at the 1987 meeting of the September Group. It first appeared in *Politics and Society* 15, 1987, 453–82, and was reprinted in *Debates on Classes* (Erik O. Wright et al.), London: Verso Books, 1989, 213–41. I am particularly grateful to Leo Apostel, Sue Black, Johannes Berger, Sam Bowles, Mino Carchedi, Jos de Beus, Michael Krätke, Mary Nolan, Adam Przeworski, Ian Steedman, Robert van der Veen, Jenny Walry and Erik Wright for useful comments and discussion.

7 Marxism and migration

This chapter is based on the commentary I presented at the Ethikon Institute conference on ethical aspects of the transnational migration of people and money (Mont Saint-Michel, October 1989), subsequently published as 'Citizenship exploitation, unequal exchange and the breakdown of popular sovereignty' in *Free Movement* (Brian Barry and Robert Goodin eds.), Hemel Hempstead: Harvester Wheatsheaf, 1992, 155–66. I thank Brian Barry, Bob Goodin and the other participants in this particularly successful meeting for their useful comments.

8 A capitalist road to communism (with Robert J. van der Veen)

Early versions of this chapter were presented at a discussion group in Manchester (May 1983), at the 1983 meeting of the September Group and at a seminar at the Freie Universität Berlin (May 1984). The final version was written, jointly with Robert van der Veen, in the course of my stay as a visiting lecturer at the University of Amsterdam in the Spring of 1985. It was originally published in *Theory and Society* 15 (5), 1986, 635–56, and is reprinted here by permission of Kluwer Academic Publishers. (German translation in *Umbau des Sozialstaats* (M. Opielka and I. Ostner Hrsgb), Essen: Klartext, 1987, 167–76. Spanish translation in *Zona Abierta* (Madrid) 46/47, 1988, 19–45.) We are particularly grateful to Rod Aya, Heiner Ganssmann, Norman Geras, Andrew Glyn, André Gorz, Staf Hellemans, Cornelia von Kleist, Michael Krätke, David Purdy, Ian Steedman and 'Titanic', to all our colleagues in the September Group (especially Jerry

Cohen, Jon Elster, Adam Przeworski and Erik Wright), to three anonymous referees and to each other, for stimulating discussions and comments from which the final version has benefited 'greatly. Because most of
these people, to put it mildly, remain rather critical of our central idea,
they can hardly be held responsible for whatever the reader may find
objectionable, indeed scandalous, in this chapter.

9 Universal grants versus socialism (with Robert J. van der Veen)

An earlier version of this chapter was presented at the 1986 meeting of
the September Group. It was originally published in *Theory and Society* 15
(5), 1986, as a reply to the comments by Johannes Berger, Joseph Carens,
Jon Elster, Alec Nove, Adam Przeworski and Erik Wright on the original
version of chapter 8 above, and is reprinted here by permission of Kluwer
Academic Publishers. (A Spanish translation appeared in *Zona Abierta*
(Madrid) 46/47, 1988.) We are very grateful to Ian Gough, Gérard Roland
and all members of the September Group (especially Hillel Steiner) for
useful comments on an earlier draft.

10 In defence of abundance

This chapter is a much revised version of a paper discussed at the
Universities of Amsterdam and Louvain-la-Neuve in May and November
1985. It was first published in *Analyzing Marxism* (K. Nielsen and B. Ware
eds.), 15, 1989, 467–95. I am very grateful to Philippe Mongin, Alec Nove,
Roald Ramer, Gérard Roland, Ian Steedman, Robert van der Veen and
Bob Ware, for having helped me out of some of the confusions contained
in earlier versions. Conversations with Hans Achterhuis, Ivan Illich,
Riccardo Cappi and Marc Germain have drawn my attention to neglected
dimensions, which I am sure I have not incorporated to anything like
their satisfaction. I have been greatly exercised by a number of earlier
treatments of these issues, especially by Tartarin, Nove, Phelps and
Roland. It is because these have not left me fully satisfied that I felt I
wanted to have a go at it myself. Without them, however, my job would
have been far tougher, and the end result far rougher.

Envoi: The greening of Marx?

Except for the opening paragraph, this chapter was initially published in
L'Ecologiste (Namur, Belgium) 49, January 1984, 38–40 as an echo to the

celebrations that marked the 100th anniversary of Marx's death. (Dutch version in *Vlaams Marxistisch Tijdschrift* (Gent) 18, 1984, 28–33.) A fuller and more academic formulation of these ideas can be found in my contribution to the Marx conference held in Paris in December 1983 ('Marx, l'écologisme et la transition directe du capitalisme au communisme', in B. Chavance, ed., *Marx en perspective*, Paris: Ecole des Hautes Etudes en Sciences Sociales, 1985, 135–55).

Introduction

The right attitude towards such bulky artefacts as the Marxist tradition is not one of dutiful conservation, but of ruthless recycling. There is nothing wrong, therefore, in chopping up unwieldy chunks, in discarding stultifying mental pollutants, in using the latest intellectual technology to reshape – sometimes beyond recognition – dislocated parts, or in letting the rest rot into oblivion. Only the unashamed adoption of this attitude can keep the Marxist tradition alive as one essential component of the political culture of the Left, that is, of the thought of those individuals and organizations whose action is guided by a paramount concern for the least advantaged, the exploited, the excluded, the oppressed. Only the stubborn, unrelenting enactment of this attitude can make the Marxist tradition suitable for fruitful, relevant, effective thinking in today's world. This is, at any rate, the conviction that permeates all the essays collected in this book.

The recycling of Marxism, to which these essays claim to contribute, is not for me a central, autonomous intellectual project. It has nothing to do with the reconstruction, let alone the rehabilitation, of an authentic Marxism that would be left unscathed by the tragic, sometimes sordid fate of Soviet regimes. It is rather a by-product of an attempt to do for our times – *multis mutandis mutatis* – what someone like Karl Marx (or, for that matter, John Stuart Mill) tried to do for his. For this purpose, Marxism is just one source of inspiration, one compartment in the tool box – just as French socialist thought or classical economics were for Marx's own purposes. And there is no reason to believe that the outcome will be recognizably Marxist. No doubt those who care about dogmatic purity will find the outcome truncated, impoverished, sullied, adulterated by the admixture of countless alien elements. But for the Left in the sense indicated – the only sense in which I care to belong to it – the intellectual

1

tasks ahead are daunting. Steering our complex, heavy societies in a direction which can confidently be expected to make things better, or at least no worse, is a strenuous business. If we are to succeed, no valuable intellectual resource must be wasted. Hence, no time or ingenuity must be wasted on exegetical quibbles. Nor must any patience be spared for the sterile claim that intellectual heritages must be accepted *in toto* or not at all, or for the crazy belief that answers to the vital questions that face us today are to be found in nineteenth-century writings. Never mind purity or orthodoxy. Anything usable must be used, whatever its origins.

For the very same reason, we cannot afford to chuck out the precious concepts and insights that are to be found in the Marxist tradition. Indeed, it takes little effort to discover that the way in which we, the inhabitants of late twentieth-century industrial countries, think about our social world, and in particular about what we find less than satisfactory about it, is permeated by that tradition. Even some of those who see themselves as the fiercest opponents of Marxist regimes cannot help paying tribute to Marxist thought. When identifying exploitation and alienation as two cardinal ills of the capitalist world order, for example, Pope John Paul II is using, vaguely but forcefully, two concepts which have played the most central role in the Marxist critique of capitalism and which owe their current use far beyond Marxist circles to the momentous historical influence of that critique.[1] These concepts are more than handy slogans. They can provide the core of, or at least a fruitful starting point for, meaningful critiques of present conditions and sensible proposals for reforming the latter. In the process of spelling out these critiques and proposals with the help of such concepts, it would be absurd to settle any issue by appealing to some orthodox doctrine. But it would be no less absurd to ignore the rich and insightful critical discussion to which these concepts have been subjected in the Marxist tradition.

If (and only if) it is viewed in this light and mobilized in this way, this tradition is not just alive. It also has a future. But this is not the future of an intact, monolithic, pure, coherent, all-encompassing doctrine. It is the future of an endlessly revised, heterogeneous, motley family of concepts and conjectures, of explanations and justifications, constantly facing challenges from different traditions and mixing with them in a chaotic, heretical and fertile way. Whether in the East or in the West, Marxism does not need to be dumped any more than it deserves to be worshipped. It needs and deserves to be recycled.

Most of the essays that make up this volume were written before the dramatic events of 1989. But these events, I believe, will make it easier for many to share the attitude towards Marxism that I have been advocating. When Marxism no longer scares, one can allow oneself to listen to what it says. When Marxism no longer exalts, one becomes able to listen to what is being said against what it says. Marxist credentials, as a result, cease to provide sufficient ground for either rejecting or endorsing a claim, and room is thereby made for a more relaxed, easy-going, intellectually fruitful attitude. Adopting the latter does not require us to turn a blind eye to the immense amount of unnecessary suffering inflicted by Marxist-inspired regimes. Nor does it oblige us to belittle the bitter disappointment of the many people, East and West, who had put all their hopes of improving their society in the Marxist creed and sometimes spent their whole lifetimes serving a cause they now realize is lost. Very far from being an insult to the victims of Marxist regimes or to those disappointed by their failure, the attitude advocated and displayed in these essays is a key component of what is needed to rekindle their faith in a better future and to refurbish the intellectual equipment required to fight for it.

The essays selected show this attitude at work on a wide range of topics, not all of which bear a direct connection with political concerns.[2] Part I focuses on historical materialism and explains what makes it a very peculiar instance of a potentially fruitful general approach to social change. In the process, it clarifies how the primacy Marxism ascribes to the forces of production is to be understood, indicates how catastrophe models can be used to shed light on a theory of social revolutions and corrects G. A. Cohen's classic thesis about the role played by functional explanations in historical materialism.

Part II looks at what is undoubtedly the most distinctive variant of Marxist crisis theory – the now infamous theory of the falling rate of profit – and provides a rational reconstruction of the degenerative research programme it gave rise to. From this it draws a number of methodological lessons whose implications reach far beyond this particular controversy, especially concerning the place of microfoundations, their role in fighting empiricist fallacies and their compatibility with structural explanations.

Part III articulates the various Marxist notions of exploitation, shows how the most distinctive among them assumes a theory of justice which is formally very close to libertarianism and indicates how another – the game-theoretical notion developed by John Roemer – can be generalized and then used to illuminate both the class structure of welfare capitalism – providing one makes room for job-based exploitation – and the ethical issues raised by the transnational migration of people and capital – providing one allows for citizenship-based exploitation.

Finally, Part IV presents and defends, in a somewhat provocative way, a 'capitalist road to communism': in order to get closer to Marx's 'realm of freedom', there is no need for socialism, but rather for a gradually increasing unconditional basic income or universal grant. A number of objections raised against the desirability, the economic feasibility and the political feasibility of the proposal are systematically discussed. And the family of abundance and scarcity concepts is analysed in order to clarify the sense in which the feasibility of the proposal presupposes abundance.

The collection closes with a short, less academic essay, in which I indicate how I reconcile what I find attractive in the Marxist tradition with what drew me, over a decade ago, into the green movement.

All the essays, except the last one, were written and initially published in English. They are reprinted here with only minor stylistic and biblio-graphical modifications, a couple of abridgements and a number of additional cross references. Written over a ten-year period, they may not be fully consistent. But their purpose, here, is to illustrate an attitude I believe to be scientifically fruitful and politically important, not to set out a systematic theory. A more integrated treatment of some of the issues dealt with can be found in my other books.[3]

Even though some of the essays are older, I doubt that I would ever have written anything resembling this book, had I not joined, in September 1981, what was later to become the 'September Group'. Attending the yearly meetings of this small group of 'analytical Marx-ists and fellow travellers' (Pranab Bardhan, Sam Bowles, Bob Brenner, Jerry Cohen, Jon Elster, Adam Przeworski, John Roemer, Hillel Steiner, Robert van der Veen, Erik Wright) has been – and will probably remain – the most exhilarating experience of my intellectual life. Several of the pieces included have been discussed at one or other of the group's meetings. Two of them have been written jointly with another member of the group (Robert van der Veen, to whom I am particularly grateful both for this fruitful collaboration and for having agreed to the present reprinting of both pieces). And throughout the book, the work of my fellow members is often referred to, discussed, used and criticized. But these many explicit references do not give a full picture of what I owe to the tremendous stimulation of this bunch of kindred spirits, gathered in the flesh once a year, but present throughout the year as a sympathetic though demanding invisible audience. This book is at one and the same time a very imperfect attempt by the group's youngest member to live up to the standards it has instilled in him, a critical introduction to the group's work and a display of the freedom of thought the group has tolerated on the part of one of its 'fellow travellers'.

The book also contains most of my own small contribution to what will have been one of the group's main achievements. Starting a decade before the 1989 events, it has been busy sorting through the Marxist heritage and selecting the insights and lessons worth retrieving before it was too late. While insignificant as long as the vessel's splendour remained intact in many people's eyes, the job is proving invaluable now that the vessel has irreversibly sunk. Invaluable, at any rate, for those people around the world whose confidence and hopes have been shaken, but whose gut feelings are unaltered: this world is too bad to be the best that can be had, let us think and fight towards a better one.

Notes

1 'The Marxist solution has failed, but the world still contains situations of marginalization and exploitation, especially in the Third World, and situations of human alienation, especially in the developed countries' (John Paul II 1991, §42).
2 Not all the articles I have published in English in connection with Marxism have been taken up in this volume. Two pieces on dialectics (Van Parijs, 1982a; 1989) were left out because I find the very project of trying to make sense of 'dialectics' too unpromising to encourage other people to give further (even negative) thought to this question. Two other pieces largely concerned with Marxist-inspired evolutionary explanations (Van Parijs 1982a; 1987) fitted better into the systematic exploration of the deep structure of the social sciences recorded in Van Parijs 1990 (chs 6 and 7). Finally, two pieces in which I assess the resources Marxism provides for the elaboration of a theory of justice (Van Parijs 1983; 1984) fitted better into the critical examination of contemporary theories of justice conducted in Van Parijs 1991 (chs 4 and 6).
3 See Van Parijs (1981; 1990) for the epistemological issues in parts I and II; Van Parijs (1991; and forthcoming) for the ethical issues in parts III and IV.

References

John Paul II. 1991. *Centesimus Annus*, Vatican City.
Van Parijs, Philippe. 1981. *Evolutionary Explanation in the Social Sciences*, Totowa: Rowman and Littlefield; London: Tavistock.
   1982a. 'Functionalist Marxism rehabilitated. A comment on Elster', *Theory and Society* 11, 497–511.
   1982b. 'Perverse effects and social contradictions. Analytical vindication of dialectics?', *British Journal of Sociology* 33, 589–603.

1983. 'Nozick and Marxism: Socialist responses to the libertarian challenge', *Revue Internationale de Philosophie* 146, 337–62.
1984. 'What (if anything) is intrinsically wrong with capitalism?', *Philosophica* 34, 85–102.
1987. 'The evolutionary explanation of beliefs', in W. Callebaut and R. Pinxten, eds., *Evolutionary Epistemology. A Multi-paradigm Approach*, Boston and Dordrecht: Reidel, 1987, 381–401.
1989. 'Dialectic reminders and catastrophe models. A sceptic's note', in F. Vandamme and R. Pinxten, eds., *The Philosophy of Leo Apostel*, Ghent: Communication and Cognition, 495–506.
1990. *Le Modèle économique et ses rivaux*, Geneva: Droz.
1991. *Qu'est-ce qu'une société juste*, Paris: Le Seuil.
Forthcoming. *Real Freedom for all*, Oxford: Oxford University Press.

Part I

A new start for historical materialism?

1. From contradiction to catastrophe

The constitutive *claim* of historical materialism, of the materialist conception of history, consists in giving an explanatory primacy to a social formation's 'material structure', i.e. to its productive forces (over its relationships of production) and to its economic base (over its superstructure). The central *difficulties* of historical materialism consist in reconciling this claim with (1) the idea that 'non-material' structures play a significant role; (2) the idea that history is an (objectively) 'goal-directed' process; and (3) the idea that political action may play a decisive role. These three difficulties I shall call (1) the 'primacy puzzle', (2) the 'paradox of teleology' and (3) the 'riddle of historical determinism'.

Among modern attempts to rephrase or reconstruct historical materialism in such a way that these difficulties can be solved, Althusser's Marxism was, for a long time, the most influential and also, apparently, the most rigorous. Unfortunately, the concepts it used in this attempt – e.g. 'determination in the last instance', 'dominance', 'overdetermination' – are so muddled and confusing, that they seem much more useful for dodging the issue than for shedding light on it.

In this chapter, I should like, with the help of very simple formal tools, to sketch an alternative to the Althusserian attempt to resolve these questions. I shall start with a reformulation of the materialist claim and then, by progressively enriching the basic model, show how the three difficulties mentioned above can be dealt with, without obscurity or *ad-hoc-ness*.[1]

1.1 Attractors and the materialist claim

The two central propositions of historical materialism state that, in spite of possibly considerable time lags, there is a necessary tendency towards *correspondence*, or non-contradiction, on the one hand between the level of development of the productive forces and the nature of the relationships of production, and on the other hand between the economic base and the (legal-political and ideological) superstructure.[2]

What these laws of correspondence mean is, first, that not all combinations of material structures (productive forces, economic base) and non-material structures (relationships of production, superstructure) are possible, or at least viable – i.e. that only some of the logically possible combinations constitute stable equilibrium states, or *attractors*, of the social system.[3] But the laws of correspondence are more than just equilibrium laws, in which the two dimensions (the material one and the non-material one) could play symmetric roles. Also implied in them – and this is what makes them the core of historical *materialism*, of a *materialist* theory of history – is the claim that, whenever there is *contradiction*, i.e. non-correspondence, between the two dimensions, the non-material structure (relationships of production, superstructure) adjusts to the material one (productive forces, economic base), and *not* the other way round. This fundamental asymmetry between the two dimensions we can call the *primacy* of the material structures.

For the sake of convenience, let us now restrict our attention to the first proposition (which asserts the necessary correspondence between productive forces and relationships of production), and even to a particular fraction of the domain to which that proposition applies. Let us concentrate on the assertion that up to a certain level of development of the productive forces, the 'corresponding' relationships of production are *capitalist*, i.e. based on the private ownership of the means of production, whereas beyond that level, the 'corresponding' relationships of production are *socialist*, i.e. based on the collective ownership of the means of production. Let us then assume that the two terms of this correspondence can be considered as *continuous* variables – which is fairly straightforward as far as productive forces are concerned, and also as far as relationships of production are concerned, providing one bears in mind that qualitative variables can always be made quantitative by considering the frequency distribution of their values. This assumption enables us to represent in the diagram in figure 1.1 the instance of the first proposition of historical materialism to which we have restricted our attention.

What historical materialism amounts to claiming, in this particular case, is, first, that the curve in this diagram represents the set of stable equilibrium states (or attractors) of a social formation's mode of production, and, secondly, that the dynamics which leads to this curve is 'vertical'.

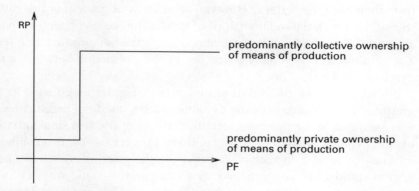

Figure 1.1   Historical materialism without catastrophe

The first point simply means that, if the mode of production happens to be at a point of the surface (which represents all logically possible combinations of *RP* and *PF*) which is not on the curve, it will tend to move towards the latter. The second point means that this movement will occur along vertical lines or, in other words, that from an initial position of contradiction between productive forces and relationships of production (i.e. from a point of the surface which is not on the curve), the mode of production will move towards correspondence by adjusting the level of *RP* (i.e. by an institutional change which privatizes or collectivizes the means of production), not by adjusting the level of *PF* (i.e. by increasing or decreasing the level of development of the productive forces). If the dynamics was 'horizontal' instead of 'vertical', correspondence would be restored by adjusting *PF*, not *RP*, and there would be a primacy of the 'non-material' relationships of production, not of the 'material' productive forces.

1.2 Slow versus fast dynamics and the primacy puzzle

The account of historical materialism proposed so far is obviously over-simplified. In particular, it does not accommodate the important fact that the relationships of production exert a crucial controlling influence on the development of the productive forces. Under given conditions, for instance, the introduction of capitalist relationships of production has the effect of freeing the productive forces from their feudal bonds and thus of dramatically fostering their development. And under different con-ditions, a socialist revolution similarly liberates the forces of production from their capitalist fetters.[4] How can an acknowledgement of this causal role of 'non-material' relationships of production be reconciled with the assertion of an unambiguous primacy of the 'material' productive forces? The solution to this *primacy puzzle* lies in the distinction between a fast dynamics and a slow one.[5]

In order to make this solution understandable, let us go back to the graphical representation of the dynamic system 'mode of production'. It was assumed, in the previous section, that one of the two state variables of this dynamic system (PF) was entirely exogenous, i.e. insensitive to internal influences, in such a way that the (long-term) evolution of the system could only be explained in a comparative-static way, i.e. as a succession of adjustments to exogenous changes. We can now drop this assumption, while keeping the 'primacy' thesis in its full rigidity. All we need to reach this result is to suppose that, while the modification of PF is completely negligible (compared to the modification of RP) for any point of the surface which is not on the curve, it ceases to be so on the curve itself or in its immediate vicinity. In other words, while the mode of production adjusts 'vertically' whenever there is contradiction between productive forces and relationships of production (*fast dynamics*), it will move horizontally (presumably from left to right) as soon as correspondence is restored, i.e. as soon as productive forces are 'unfettered' (*slow dynamics*). Contrasting the vertical and horizontal dynamics as fast and slow just means that, at nearly every point of the surface, the horizontal movement (if any) is negligible, compared to the vertical one.[6]

Clearly, this constitutes a solution to the primacy puzzle, since it allows us to hold at the same time that, in case of contradiction, material structures always have primacy, and that, nevertheless, non-material structures play a crucial role in the evolution of the system. Equally clear is the fact that, depending on how much one wants to soften the primacy claim, one can expand the vicinity of the 'equilibrium' curve in which the horizontal dynamics is allowed to be of some significance. Some form of 'primacy' is maintained as long as this area covers only a small fraction of the total surface. Even with the most rigid form of 'primacy', however, the introduction of this feedback from non-material structures makes it possible to have a dynamic theory (not only, as in the previous section, a comparative-static one) of the (long-run) evolution of a mode of production: changes affecting it need no longer be exogenous, but can be endogenously generated.

1.3 Marx the functionalist and the paradox of teleology

Let us now further admit, as an essential component of historical materialism, that the historical development of Humanity is a goal-directed, teleological process, that it tends towards an 'End'. How can this be asserted without our being driven into 'subjectivism' or 'idealism', without our giving up a materialist perspective? Or how can the *paradox of teleology* be solved? The answer lies, this time, in interpreting the explanation of a society's 'non-material' structures by its 'material' structures as a particular kind of *functional explanation*.

That the basic propositions of historical materialism must be interpreted as functional explanations is precisely the central claim in G. A. Cohen's (1978) masterly reconstruction of Marx's theory of history.[7] One of the ways in which he justifies that claim is by pointing to the fact that his functional interpretation enables him to solve what has been referred to above as the primacy puzzle.[8] Although it is true that this interpretation solves the primacy puzzle, it does not do so by virtue of its functional character, but rather by implicitly assuming, on the lines indicated above, the coexistence of a fast and a slow dynamics. However, by *embedding* the fast and the slow dynamics in such a way that they fulfil the conditions for a functional explanation, it does solve the second difficulty mentioned above, the 'paradox of teleology'. This can be shown as follows.

A *fast* dynamics, as we have seen, is reflected in an equilibrium law, here a law to the effect that, to a given level (pf) of development of the productive forces will correspond to a given type (rp) of relationships of production, or, for short:

$$pf \rightarrow rp \text{ (at equilibrium)}, \tag{a}$$

where the arrow denotes a causal relationship. The *slow* dynamics, on the other hand, consists in the fact that the equilibrium relationships of production promote the development of the productive forces, or for short:

$$rp \rightarrow \Delta PF, \tag{b}$$

where the arrow again denotes a causal relationship. Now, Cohen's 'trick' consists in pointing out that the reason why rp is called forth by pf (at equilibrium) is that it promotes PF. In other words, rp's disposition to promote PF is the intermediate factor between pf and rp, or, for short (in a compact formulation loosely warranted by the transitivity of the relationships):

$$pf \rightarrow (rp \rightarrow \Delta PF) \rightarrow rp \tag{c}$$

where the last two arrows are as above, while the first arrow represents the relationship that exists between a structural and a dispositional property of an object (here a social formation).

The *embedding* of the slow dynamics (b) into the fast dynamics (a) makes the whole formula (c) a particular instance of the paradigmatic structure of *functional explanations*, as illustrated e.g. by:

soot-covered trees →	(black wings → hiding) →	black wings	
('structural' feature	('dispositional' feature	(feature to be	(d)
of the context)	of the context)	explained)	

in the case of a functional explanation of some moths' black wings by the fact that in a soot-covered environment, black wings conceal a moth from its predators far better than lighter wings would. Crucial to any functional explanation is the double occurrence of the feature to be explained: once as the last consequent, and once as the antecedent of the disposition. This makes any functional explanation 'teleological', in the weak sense that a feature is explained by the (dispositional) fact that it has certain consequences.

In the above functional interpretation of historical materialism (c), however, it is not only the case that *rp* occurs at the two expected positions. *PF* too appears twice, albeit under different modalities (*pf* and ΔPF). Clearly, the phrase 'functional explanation of the relationships of production by the productive forces', which can be used to paraphrase (c), has therefore two distinct meanings: 'functional explanation of the relationships of production by the achieved level of development of the productive forces (*pf*)' and 'functional explanation of the relationships of production by the fact that they promote the development of the productive forces (ΔPF)'. Moreover, as a result of the same fact, whereas (d) only allows for (comparative-) static or exogenous explanations of change (c), being an instance of the double dynamics discussed in the previous section, makes dynamic or endogenous explanations possible.

More importantly for our present purposes, a functional interpretation which embeds a slow dynamics into a fast one, in the way (c) does, can be said to be objectively *teleological* in a particularly strong sense. It does not only explain static features by the consequences they have in a given context (as any other functional explanation); it can also be said to explain the movement of history by the end-state towards which it is moving. For what it implies is that a given level of development of the productive

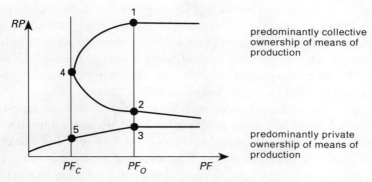

Figure 1.2 Historical materialism with catastrophes

forces calls forth a particular type of relationships of production (fast dynamics), not for any old reason, but precisely because the latter will further promote the development of the productive forces. The whole process of history is thereby given a 'teleological' unity: it is led from stage to stage by a principle of maximization of the productive forces.[9]

1.4 Catastrophe surfaces and the riddle of historical determinism

Even as modified by the previous two sections, the theory of history (locally) expressed in our little model remains a purely 'structural' one: the evolution of a social formation is just the outcome of the interaction of material and non-material structures. It seems vital to historical materialism, however, that it should be able to claim that there is room for voluntaristic intervention, e.g. for the repressive policies of the bourgeois state or for the revolutionary action of the proletarian party. How can such a claim be made part of our model, rather than just added to it as an *ad hoc* qualification? The solution to this problem – the *riddle of historical determinism* – requires the introduction of catastrophe surfaces, the simplest of which is represented in Figure 1.2.[10]

In Figure 1.2, the upper (4–1) and lower (5–3) curves, like the only curve of Figure 1.1, represent stable equilibrium states (for fixed values of PF) or *attractors* of the system, while the middle curve (4–2) represents a set of unstable equilibrium states (for fixed values of PF) or *crest points* of the system. This implies that, for certain values of PF (those greater than PF_C), there is an *attractor conflict*: when the development of the productive forces reaches PF_O, for instance, the system could stabilize at either 1 or 3, depending on whether, initially, it happened to be above or beneath the crest point 2. Behaviour surfaces like this one are called catastrophe surfaces because they are so shaped (here, as a *fold*) that continuous changes in the control variable (here PF) may force the system to jump from one attractor to another non-adjacent one (e.g. from 4 to 5 as PF reaches PF_C from above), and because such abrupt jumps may bear some resemblance to what everyday language calls a 'catastrophe'.

How does the introduction of such oddly shaped surfaces help us to solve the riddle of historical determinism? Let us first remember that attractors are not the only possible states for the system, but merely its (locally) stable equilibrium states. This means that the position of the system may constantly fluctuate around the attractor, due to stochastic noise, i.e. to the interference of other (minor) variables. As long as, for any given level of development of the productive forces, the system has only one attractor (as in Figure 1.1), this fact does not have any important consequence, as it does not affect the position at which the system can be expected to settle. But as soon as there is an attractor conflict, and in particular when the system approaches the crest line (4–2), fluctuations around the attractor (e.g. point 3) may be decisive for carrying the system over the crest point (here 2) into the basin of the other attractor (here 1).[11]

This means that we can stick to a very rigid primacy thesis – i.e. to the idea that, because of an exclusively vertical fast dynamics, the position of the attractors of the system can be determined on the sole basis of the level reached by the productive forces – while at the same time ascribing a decisive causal role to human agency. The key to the conciliation lies in the fact that attractors may be many (for a given value of PF), and one of them so close to the crest line that stochastic noise becomes crucial. In such an 'objectively revolutionary' situation, voluntaristic repression by the ruling class and subversion by its opponents acquire an efficacy of which they are completely deprived in other situations. The question here is not just whether an unavoidable evolution is being slowed down or accelerated, but whether or not the 'catastrophic' jump will ever be made.

Human agency, therefore, can significantly affect the otherwise structurally determined long-term evolution of the mode of production. The riddle of historical determinism has vanished.

1.5 A beginning or an end?

The previous sections have sketched a way in which the materialist claim can be reconciled with the idea that non-material structures play a significant role (primacy puzzle), that history is a goal-directed process (paradox of teleology) and that political action may play a decisive role (riddle of historical determinism). Being a sketch, they have remained both very abstract – hardly any hint has been made as to the nature of the mechanisms which underlie the postulated causal relationships – and very restricted in scope – precapitalist modes of production have been completely ignored, as well as the relationships between base and super-structure. Concretization and generalization are of course possible in principle. But they would require the serious treatment of a number of tricky problems, which here have quietly been swept under the carpet. I mention only a few of them. How can one meaningfully define a concept of 'level of development of the productive forces' that could be both universal and operational? How can the various stages of the super-structure be classified? What exactly is the mechanism that leads from the development of a contradiction to crises, breakdown and transition? Is this mechanism always the same, whatever the mode of production considered?

This should make it obvious that the task of concretizing and generalizing the above sketch is quite formidable – a first good reason for not taking the present analysis beyond the level of a sketch. Another, more serious reason, is that theoretical work, if it is to do more than reformulate existing theories, cannot healthily be carried out without being kept in check by critical discussion on the basis of empirical material. Finally, and more radically, one could argue that taking historical materialism's causal-explanatory ambitions seriously, and trying to sharpen, polish and develop it as a 'formal-empirical' general theory of history, would reflect a 'positivistic' misunderstanding of its real claims: like any philosophy of history, it is just meant to provide a general intuition which can serve as a key to the overall interpretation of the historical process, but which cannot but be dogmatically hardened as soon as one tries to work it out rigorously and systematically. In such a perspective, the sketch proposed above would not be a beginning but an end. Its only claim would be to show, perhaps less obscurely than in the 'orthodox' fashion, that the central intuitions of historical materialism are not self-contradictory. Beyond this, it may help make more manifest the huge difficulties involved in concretizing, generalizing and verifying the theory, when 'causally' interpreted. Rather than a suggestion as to how to carry on, however, this would be an invitation to engage in more promising pursuits.

Notes

1 Chapter 2 deals in more detail with the first of these difficulties.
2 The canonic texts are Marx and Engels (1970: 42–3); and Marx (1970: 20–1).
3 On the concept of attractor, see e.g. Thom (1974: 257–9).
4 Cf. above all Marx (1976: chapter 32).
5 On the notions of slow and fast dynamics, see e.g. Zeeman (1977: 390–1).
6 It may be somewhat counterintuitive (and seem misleading) to refer e.g. to the hesitant process by which capitalist relationships of production established themselves as a 'fast dynamics', while the tumultuous development (under capitalism) of the productive forces belongs to the 'slow dynamics'. It should be clear, however, that there is no way of making sense of the primacy claim unless a given *level* of development of the productive forces is much faster in bringing about the corresponding type of relationships of production, than the latter in bringing about the next *level* of development of the productive forces (to which it will eventually lead). For if relative speeds were the other way round, the 'equilibrium law' would associate *to* a given type of relationships of production the 'corresponding' level of development of the forces of production, and a contradiction (an incompatibility between the two dimensions of the mode of production) would be solved by the latter 'adjusting' to the former, not the former to the latter.
7 Cohen is not the first author to draw attention to the similarity between Marxist and functionalist theories of social change – see e.g. Emmet (1958: 91); Lockwood (1964: 249–52); Sztompka (1974: 168–78) – but he does so in a particularly systematic and illuminating way.
8 See e.g. Cohen (1978: 278).
9 Whether this teleology can be said to be 'purely objective' depends on the nature of the mechanism by which the 'optimal' type of relationships of production is assumed to be selected: cf. the discussion of various possible 'elaborations' in Cohen (1978: 285–96). If it can, however, one may argue that it constitutes an 'as if' teleology. For it is not really the consequence, the end state, the *telos*, which plays a causal role (e.g. through being consciously pursued by human agents), but only the explained feature's disposition to bring it about.
10 A brief and useful critical discussion of catastrophe models is provided by Zahler and Sussmann (1977: 759–63). A more specific discussion of their relevance can be found in Van Parijs (1990: chapter 8)
11 This is a way of making abstractly the 'anti-gradualist' point that a little nationalization – say, 25 companies – cannot be successful in effecting the transition to socialism: it is just a temporary disturbance which will soon be corrected by the dynamics of a society in which the bulk of the means of production is privately controlled. Beyond a certain threshold or 'crest point', however – say, nationalization of the country's top 200 monopolies – the system will irreversibly be carried towards a new equilibrium state in which collective ownership of the means of production is massively predominant.

References

Cohen, G. A. 1978. *Karl Marx's Theory of History. A Defence*, Oxford: Oxford University Press.
Emmet, D. 1958. *Function, Purpose and Powers*, London: Macmillan.
Lockwood, D. 1964. 'Social integration and system intergration', in G. K. Zollschan and W. Hirsch, eds., *Explorations in Social Change*, London: Routledge and Kegan Paul, 244–57.

Marx, K. 1970 [1859]. *A Contribution to the Critique of Political Economy*, Moscow: International Publishers.

1976 [1867]. *Capital*, vol. 1, London: Penguin/NLR.

Marx, K. and F. Engels. 1970 [1846]. *The German Ideology*, London: Lawrence and Wishart.

Sztompka, P. 1974. *System and Function*, New York: Academic Press.

Thom, R. 1974. *Modèles mathématiques de la morphogénèse*, Paris: Union Générale d'Edition.

Van Parijs, P. 1990. *Le Modèle économique et ses rivaux*, Paris and Geneva: Droz.

Zahler, R. S. and H. J. Sussmann. 1977. 'Claims and achievements of applied catastrophe theory', *Nature* 269.

Zeeman, E. C. 1977. *Catastrophe Theory*, Reading, Mass.: Addison-Wesley.

2. Marxism's central puzzle

At first sight, Marxist theories explain in very different ways. The explanation of the real wage level as the outcome of class struggle seems to have little, if anything, in common with the explanation of a society's religious beliefs by reference to its economic structure. And the explanation of the form taken by the capitalist state by reference to the structural imperatives to which it is subjected does not seem to share much, if anything, with the explanation of individuals' voting behaviour by their class position. It is therefore by no means a trivial task to try to work out the nature of *Marxist causation*, that is, to identify whatever features are specific, whether conjunctively or disjunctively, to explanations put forward by Marx and the Marxist tradition.

Presumably a good way to start such an inquiry – and in this discussion I shall go no further than this start – is by looking closely at the central explanatory statements of what many view as Marxism's core: historical materialism. The choice of this starting point is particularly appropriate as G. A. Cohen's widely celebrated *Karl Marx's Theory of History: A Defence* (1978) has decisively clarified the explanatory status of these statements. In particular, Cohen has shown in all clarity how the explanatory framework provided by historical materialism unavoidably raises a (two-fold) problem that I shall call the *primary puzzle* and that can be expressed as follows. First, how is it possible, at the same time, to claim that there is a causal primacy of the productive forces over the relations of production and to recognize that the development of the productive forces causally depends on the form taken by the relations of production? And second, how is it possible to assert the subordination of the superstructure to the economic base, while conceding that the latter is somehow controlled by the former? To this irritating puzzle, which threatens the very core of Marx's social theory, Cohen claims to have found a satisfactory solution,

20

which follows directly from the central thesis of his book. He claims that the primacy puzzle is solved as soon as one realizes that the historical-materialist explanations of production relations by productive forces and of the superstructure by the economic base are *functional explanations*, that is, explanations by a propensity to produce certain consequences.

I shall challenge this claim by focusing on the first component of the primacy puzzle, namely, the relation between productive forces and relations of production. I shall argue that Cohen's solution, however helpful, rests on a fundamental ambiguity in the formula, 'explanation of production relations *by* productive forces'. Once this ambiguity is disclosed, I shall show, the historical-materialist 'primacy thesis' and the closely related 'development thesis' also turn out to be systematically ambiguous, whereas Cohen's claim that his functional interpretation constitutes the only way of solving the primacy puzzle turns out to be either trivial or wrong. What does solve the primacy puzzle (in its most sensible interpretation), and uniquely solves it, is what I shall call the coexistence of a *slow* and a *fast dynamics*. Realizing this is of crucial importance both if one is to vindicate the consistency of historical materialism and if one is to delineate the exact nature of Marxist causation.

2.1 Two ways of explaining relations by forces

There is no question that historical materialism claims to explain the form of the relations of production *by* the development of the productive forces.[1] But this claim can be understood in two distinct ways. One may mean that the relations of production can be explained by reference to *the level currently achieved by* the development of the productive forces. But one may also mean that they can be explained by reference to *their ability to enhance* this development. In symbols:

$$PF \rightarrow RP \tag{a}$$

that is, the level reached by the productive forces (PF) determines ($\rightarrow$) the form taken by the relations of production or economic structure (RP); and

$$(RP \text{ is best for } \Delta PF) \rightarrow RP \tag{b}$$

that is, the form of the relations of production (RP) that is best for the development of the productive forces (ΔPF) determines ($\rightarrow$) the form the relations of production will actually take (RP). The remainder of this chapter will simply consist in following up the consequences of this distinction.

Before doing so, however, let us make the latter more intuitive by imagining situations in which one of the two senses of the explanation of relations by forces is present while the other is not. Suppose, for example, that the level of development achieved by the productive forces determines which relations of production are best for the sake of maintaining *cohesion* in the society under consideration: at a fairly low level of development of the productive forces, it is, say, slavery that secures the smoothest running of society, whereas at a very high level of development only socialism can free society from endless strife. Suppose further that whatever relations are most conducive to cohesion will tend to prevail. In such a hypothetical situation, one can correctly say that the form of the relations is explained by the current level of the forces. But the form of the relations is not explained by its ability to enhance productive development (rather, by its ability to maintain cohesion). The structure of such a situation is expressed by the following (somewhat excessively) compact formula:

$$PF \rightarrow (RP \text{ is best for } SC) \rightarrow RP \tag{c}$$

that is, the level of productive development (*PF*) determines which economic structure (*RP*) is best for social cohesion (*SC*), and this in turn determines the structure that will actually prevail (*RP*). Clearly, by transitivity (a) is satisfied in (c), whereas (b) is not.

Next, let us turn to a scenario that will sound familiar to those acquainted either with Wallerstein's (1974) analysis of the origins of capitalism or with the so-called dependency theory of underdevelopment (e.g. Frank 1979). Let us suppose that it is the position in the world system (say, centre or periphery) that determines which relations of production (say, capitalist or socialist) are best for developing the productive forces, and that whatever relations are best from this angle tend to prevail. In this second hypothetical situation, it is correct to say that the form of the relations is explained by its ability to enhance productive development. But one cannot say that it is explained by the current level of the productive forces (rather, by the society's current position in the world system). The structure of such a situation can be expressed as follows:

$$WS \rightarrow (RP \text{ is best for } \Delta PF) \rightarrow RP \tag{d}$$

that is, the position in the world system (*WS*) determines which economic structure (*RP*) is best for productive development (ΔPF), and this in turn determines which economic structure will actually prevail (*RP*). In this case (b) obviously holds, whereas (a) does not.

What is thus made plain is the possibility of having each of the two senses of 'explanation by the development of the productive forces' without the other. Perhaps the chief (though not fully explicit) achievement of Cohen's book has been to demonstrate that these two senses, however distinct, are not incompatible, indeed that one very plausible interpretation of historical materialism corresponds precisely to the case where they go together. The structure of this case can be depicted as follows:

$$PF \rightarrow (RP \text{ is best for } \Delta PF) \rightarrow RP \tag{e}$$

that is, the level currently achieved by the productive forces (PF) determines which form of the relations of production (RP) is best for productive development (ΔPF), and the best form from this angle tends to prevail (RP).[2] Here, clearly, one explains the form taken by the relations of production both by the current level of the productive forces and by its propensity to enhance the latter's development: (a) and (b) both hold.

Though this will not retain us in the sequel, note that a somewhat more complicated structure preserves the truth of (a) and (b), while providing a more convincing interpretation of both historical materialism and the relevant historical evidence. The level achieved by the forces, rather than the form of relations that is optimal for productive development, may well determine which forms of relations are currently possible. What happens at the end of the Middle Ages or under late capitalism, in this account, is not that capitalism or socialism, which had been possible all along, becomes more productive than feudalism and capitalism, respectively. What happens is rather that capitalism or socialism, which would at any time have performed better than feudalism and capitalism, then becomes possible. In short:

$$PF \rightarrow \left. \begin{array}{l} (RP \text{ is possible}) \\ (RP \text{ is best for } \Delta PF \\ \text{among possible forms}) \end{array} \right\} \rightarrow RP \tag{f}$$

that is, the level of productive development (PF) determines which forms of relations (RP) are possible, and whatever form of relations is both possible and optimal for productive development (ΔPF) will tend to prevail (RP). In such a situation, the form of the relations can still be said to be explained by the level of the forces (a) and by its propensity to develop them (b), though in both cases only partly.

2.2 The primacy thesis

Bearing in mind this distinction between two senses of the 'explanation of the relations by the forces', and the ways in which they can be combined, we can now examine what the primacy thesis is supposed to assert. Cohen, I shall argue, uses this notion in two different senses, which correspond to the two senses in which an explanation of relations by forces can be understood. In a first sense: 'The primacy thesis is that the nature of a set of production relations is explained by the level of development of the productive forces embraced by it (to a far greater extent than vice versa)' (Cohen 1978: 134). A shorter formulation is also sometimes used: 'The nature of the production relations of a society is explained by the level of development of its productive forces' (ibid.). In short:

$$PF \rightarrow RP \qquad \text{(PT0)}$$

which exactly amounts to the claim that the forces determine the relations in sense (a). However, Cohen warns us in a footnote that the qualifying phrase appearing in parentheses in the first of the two sentences just quoted 'is always to be understood whenever the primacy thesis is asserted' (Cohen 1978: 134 n1). This first sense of the primacy thesis can then roughly be pictured as follows:

$$PF \rightarrow RP \text{ to a far greater extent than } RP \rightarrow PF \qquad \text{(PT1)}$$

If there remains any doubt as to the sense of the 'explanation of relations by forces' involved here, the following clarification removes it completely: 'The primacy thesis implies that changes in productive forces bring about changes in production relations' or, more precisely, that 'for any set of production relations, there is an extent of further development of the productive forces they embrace which suffices for a change in those relations' (Cohen 1978: 135). Clearly, the explanation involved is an explanation by the level achieved by the forces (a), not an explanation by the propensity to favour productive development (b).

Cohen, however, does not stick to this interpretation of the primacy thesis. Unambiguous evidence is provided by the following conclusion he draws from the 'somewhat naive story' with which he illustrates 'the nature of the primacy of the forces':

One may now say that the relations have changed (in a way required to ensure an efficient operation of the newly invented treadmills) because otherwise the forces would not have progressed, and that the forces do progress because the relations have changed. But it is clear, despite the second part of the last sentence, that the change in the forces is more basic than the change in relations: the relations change *because* the new relations facilitate productive progress. The story illustrates the type of primacy the forces have in the Marxian theory of history. (1978: 162)

Primacy, here, makes no reference to an explanation of the relations by the current level of the forces (a). Rather, it is closely linked to the claim that relations are explained by their propensity to further the development of the forces (b). Indeed, in this second sense, the primacy thesis reduces to this claim and can therefore by symbolized as follows:

$$(RP \text{ is best for } \Delta PF) \rightarrow RP \qquad \qquad \text{(PT2)}$$

In words: The reason why the prevailing relations do prevail is that they facilitate the development of the productive forces.[3]

2.3 The development thesis

Before discussing where this distinction of two senses of the primacy thesis leaves the formulation of the primacy puzzle, we need to clarify the closely associated *development thesis*: 'The productive forces tend to develop throughout history' (Cohen 1978: 134). According to Cohen (1978: 158), the development thesis is what needs to be added to the purely symmetrical 'facts of constraint' (the fact that not every combination of forces and relations is possible or stable) in order to get the primacy thesis.[4] However, two very different interpretations of the development thesis can be given, which are connected, again, to the two senses in which one can speak of an explanation of relations by forces.

The first interpretation is strongly suggested by the following passage: 'Given the constraints, with sufficient development of the forces, the old relations are no longer compatible with them. Either they will have changed without lag along with productive development, or – the theoretically prescribed alternative – there will now be "contradiction" between forces and relations. But if contradiction obtains, it will be resolved by alteration of the production relations' (Cohen 1978: 158). What the development thesis asserts, this suggests, is that

There is an autonomous tendency for the forces to develop   (DT1)

Such an assertion gives a causal direction to the 'facts of constraint' between forces and relations, thereby generating PT0, that is, the claim that the form taken by the relations is determined by the current level of the productive forces. This interpretation of the development thesis is clearly embraced by the bulk of Levine and Wright's review article, whose very structure is strongly influenced by the passage just quoted.[5] Drawing on the way in which Cohen (1978: 150–7) argues his case for the development thesis, they construe the latter as asserting that rational adaptive practices tend to develop the productive forces, whatever the form taken by the relations of production. All the latter can do is brake or accelerate, but not alter the basic trend.[6]

When interpreted in this way, however, the development thesis seems to contradict Cohen's (1978: 278) emphatic claim that 'production relations profoundly affect productive forces'. If one takes this claim seriously, that is, if one assumes that the development of the productive forces is genuinely controlled by the relations of production, there is still another way of construing the development thesis, which can be phrased as follows:

> There is a tendency for those relations to prevail which are best for (or facilitate) the development of the forces.   (DT2)

Whereas DT1 assumes some search-and-selection process that operates directly on the productive forces, DT2 assumes one that operates on the relations of production, which in turn then control the search and selection of productive forces. In both cases, it is possible to say that there is a tendency for the productive forces to develop. But only in the second case is it also possible to say that whether the productive forces develop fully depends on the nature of the production relations. In this second interpretation, the development thesis (DT2) is obviously very close to the second interpretation of the primacy thesis (PT2). Indeed, the only significant difference between the two theses is that the latter makes fully explicit the causal claim that is only hinted at in the former. Whereas both PT1 and DT1 are directly relevant to the explanation of relations by the current level of forces, both PT2 and DT2 are directly concerned with the explanation of relations by their propensity to further productive development.

2.4 Two primacy puzzles

Perhaps the most original feature of Cohen's reconstruction of Marx's theory of history, and certainly the feature that has attracted the most critical attention, is his *functional* interpretation of the central propositions of historical materialism: These propositions explain the forms taken by the production relations and the superstructure in terms of their func-

tions of facilitating productive development and stabilizing the production relations, respectively. The most interesting argument Cohen
puts forward in favour of this functional interpretation is that it enables
him to solve what can be called the *primacy puzzle*: 'Construing [Marx's]
explanations as functional makes for compatibility between the causal
power of the explained phenomena and their secondary status in the
order of explanation' (Cohen 1978: 278). Or, as he puts it even more
explicitly elsewhere, 'No other treatment (but a functional one) preserves
consistency between the explanatory primacy of the productive forces
over the economic structure and the massive control of the latter over the
former, or between the explanatory primacy of the economic structure
over the superstructure and the latter's regulation of the former' (Cohen
1980: 129–30). However, since the primacy puzzle, thus phrased, is
nothing but the problem of reconciling the primacy of the productive
forces (and the economic structure) over the production relations (and
the superstructure) with the recognition that the latter also control the
former, what the primacy puzzle means will depend on which interpretation the primacy thesis receives.

As far as the explanation of relations by forces is concerned, we have
seen that the primacy thesis, as formulated and illustrated by Cohen, can
mean two different things. Let us take the second sense first. The primacy
of the forces then consists in the fact that the reason why the prevailing
relations do prevail is that they facilitate the development of the forces
(PT2). How is this primacy to be reconciled with the fact that the relations
control the forces? Clearly, there is no problem whatsoever about such a
reconciliation, as the primacy thesis, in this sense, *presupposes* that the
forces are controlled by the relations: if the relations did not determine
the evolution of the forces, they could not be selected in such a way that
they facilitate their development. Consequently, as primacy is here
understood, there is no primacy *puzzle* for which a functional interpretation could provide a solution. Moreover, as the primacy of the forces
consists, *by definition*, in the relations being functionally explained by
reference to them, the claim that a functional explanation is necessarily
involved becomes plainly trivial.

We may be able to make better sense of Cohen's justification of his
functional interpretation of historical materialism if we turn to the other
sense of the primacy thesis. The latter then asserts that the form of the
relations is explained by the level of the forces embraced by it to a far
greater extent than *vice versa* (PT1). Strictly speaking, it is here again
possible to argue that there is no primacy *puzzle*, no paradox to dissolve,

as the primacy thesis (thus formulated) presupposes some sort of causation from the relations to the forces. But this is sophistry. Though
inaccurately formulated, the underlying problem is clear: granted the
assumption of two-way causation, what sense can be made, if any, of the
primacy of the forces (or the subordination of the relations), as caught by
the expression 'to a far greater extent'?

One possible, though farfetched, interpretation of this expression takes
us straight back to the second interpretation of the primacy thesis (PT2).
The 'greater extent' could reflect the fact that although the relations
control the development of the forces, they are in turn explained by the
forces *twice over*: by reference to the level achieved by the forces (PT0) *and*
by reference to their ability to facilitate the latter's development (PT2). I
have mentioned that is does not make much sense to ask how the control
of the forces by the relations can be reconciled with the primacy of the
forces as expressed in PT2, which presupposes such control. But it does
make sense to ask how this primacy (and its presuppositions) can be
reconciled with the logically independent claim that the level reached by
the forces explains the form of the relations (PT0). What enables us to
perform such a reconciliation, Cohen's answer would be, is our recourse
to a functional interpretation of the core of historical materialism. Clearly,
not any functional interpretation would do. The 'social cohesion' (c) and
'Wallersteinian' (d) scenarios both involve a functional explanation.[7] But
whereas the former fulfils PT0, not PT2 (relations are explained by their
ability to maintain social cohesion, not by their ability to facilitate productive development), the latter fulfils PT2, not PT0 (relations are explained
by the society's current position in the world system, not by its current
level of productive development), and neither therefore performs the
required reconciliation of PT0 and PT2. What we need, obviously, is a
scenario of the kind actually put forward by Cohen (e), which also
involves a functional explanation, but of a particular form. The functional
nature of the interpretation proposed, therefore, is not sufficient for the
required reconciliation. All Cohen claims, however, is that it is necessary.
But as pointed out earlier, the latter claim is plainly trivial, since PT2 on its
own *already* asserts that the relations are functionally explained by reference to the forces.

2.5 The genuine primacy puzzle and its solution

Is there any way of saving Cohen's claim from triviality? At the beginning
of the previous paragraph, I warned that the interpretation I there chose

for the expression 'to a far greater extent' was farfetched. I believe that a different interpretation, though nowhere discussed by Cohen, has the two-fold advantage of being closer to the sense in which historical materialists grant primacy to the forces (when they do so) and of saving from triviality Cohen's claim that only a functional interpretation can solve the primacy puzzle. The primacy of the forces, according to this interpretation, is fully contained in the fact that when there is a *contradiction* between the level currently achieved by the forces and the form taken by the relations, the latter adjusts to the former, and *not* the former to the latter. When used in this way, the notion of contradiction clearly presupposes the existence of *laws of correspondence* between various levels of development of the forces and various forms of production relations.[8] What the primacy thesis does is specify the causal direction of the adjustments that make it possible for these laws of correspondence to hold at equilibrium, that is, when the adjustment mechanisms have had time to operate. And it thereby enables historical materialism to provide a comparative-static theory of changes in the relations of production by reference to changes in the levels achieved by the productive forces. Put differently, each of these levels defines an *attractor* in the space of possible forms of production relations, a position in which the latter will eventually settle until the forces move on to a different level.

But here comes the genuine primacy puzzle. Does not the primacy of the forces, understood in this way, prevent the forces from being explained to *any* extent by the relations? Does not the claim that in case of contradiction, the relations always adjust to the forces and never the other way around undermine the very possibility of two-way causation? This is not the case. For a recourse to (equilibrium) laws of correspondence is not only legitimate when one of the two variables is exogenously determined. It is also legitimate when there is, in most possible combinations of their values, a significant difference in the *speeds* at which the two variables affect each other's level, here between the (higher) speed at which the relations adjust to the current level of the forces and the (lower) speed at which they carry the forces from one level to another. Somewhat more specifically, the situation envisioned can be depicted as follows. For most possible combinations of levels of forces and forms of relations (those of 'non-correspondence'), there is hardly any movement in the level of the forces compared to the much faster change (towards 'correspondence') in the form of the relations. In a small area (of correspondence), however, there is no tendency for the relations to change, and the speed of the change in the forces (whose development is facilitated by 'corresponding' relations) ceases to be insignificant in comparison. In other words, whenever the form of the relations 'contradicts' the current level of the forces, the latter can be viewed as (nearly) fixed and as exerting on that form a (nearly) exogenous pressure towards change. But as soon as correspondence is restored the forces lose their (near-) fixity and start progressing, while the relations could now be viewed as exogenously fixed. To the extent that most possible combinations of levels of forces and forms of relations are contradictory, the adjustment of the relations to the forces can be referred to as the *fast* dynamics (though it slows down at or near the correspondence point), whereas the furthering of the development of the forces by the relations can be labelled the *slow* dynamics (though its speed ceases to be negligible at or near a situation of correspondence).[9]

When this fast and this slow dynamics coexist, it thus turns out, it is possible for the relations of production both to invariably adjust to the level of the forces in case of contradiction and to determine whether the forces will develop or stagnate. Such coexistence, in other words, solves the genuine primacy puzzle, the problem of reconciling the primacy of the forces, as interpreted here, and their control by the relations of production.

2.6 Is a functional explanation necessarily involved?

In this light, we can return to Cohen's claim that his functional interpretation of the core of historical materialism, as captured in (e) or (f), enables him to solve the primacy puzzle. Note, first of all, that his functional interpretation implies the coexistence of a fast and a slow dynamics. His functional explanation is an explanation of the presence of some item *at equilibrium*, assuming all relevant parameters (here the level of development of the forces) are fixed.[10] And being a functional explanation by the ability to facilitate productive development, it also assumes a relaxation of this fixity when the relations take on their equilibrium form. However, it is not by virtue of its involving a functional explanation alone that Cohen's interpretation of historical materialism combines a fast and a slow dynamics. Take scenario (c), where the forces determine the form of the relations (at equilibrium) by picking out the form most conducive to social cohesion. There is a functional explanation of the relations (by their ability to preserve social cohesion), and a fast dynamics from the forces to the relations is clearly implied. However, though not ruled out (the relations may well affect *both* social cohesion and productive development in a situation in which only the former influence is relevant to the explanation of the form they take), a slow dynamics from the relations to the forces is not necessarily involved. Or take scenario (d), where a society's position in the world system determines the form of the productive relations (at equilibrium) by picking out the form that is best for productive development. Here again, there is a functional explanation of the relations, and this time a slow dynamics from the relations to the forces is clearly implied. But unless the position in the world system is in turn ('quickly') determined by the level of development of the forces, no fast dynamics from the forces to the relations is involved.

Consequently, the functional nature of the explanation does not suffice to guarantee that a fast and a slow dynamics are combined or, therefore, that the primacy puzzle is solved. Cohen's claim, one might reply, is not that the functional nature of the interpretation is sufficient, but that it is necessary for the primacy puzzle to be solved. But this is wrong too. Suppose, in the usual way, that the form taken by the relations of production determines whether the forces develop or stagnate (slow dynamics from the relations to the forces) and also that the level reached by the forces determines which form the relations will take at equilibrium (fast dynamics from the forces to the relations). By no means does this imply that the form that prevails at equilibrium has been chosen because it facilitates productive development. Indeed, the determination of the relations by the forces may proceed without involving any functional selection. As Veblen suggests, for example, the use of certain instruments of production may shape the producers' minds in such a way that their relations to one another are profoundly altered (1899: 208, 215–16). Given this scenario, it may be the case that the relations which prevail at equilibrium further the development of the productive forces, but this fact has no role here in explaining why those relations prevail. What the Veblenian scenario shows is that one can have primacy and two-way causation with no recourse to a functional explanation. All a functional account does is *embed* the slow dynamics in the fast one, as in (c), by stipulating that the reason why a particular level of the forces picks out a particular form of the relations involves the effect of these relations on the development of the forces. But this embedding is in no way required for primacy to be reconciled with two-way causation.[11]

2.7 Cohen's dilemma

I began by pointing out that there are two senses in which one commonly speaks of the explanation of the relations of production by reference to the productive forces. Corresponding to these two senses, there are also two senses, both explicitly used or strongly suggested by Cohen, in which one can understand what he calls the primacy thesis and the associated development thesis. In one sense, the primacy thesis asserts that the form taken by the relations is explained by its ability to further the development of the forces (PT2), and the primacy puzzle, understood as the problem of reconciling the primacy thesis and the control of the forces by the relations, then fails to make any sense, since the primacy thesis in itself presupposes such a control. In the other sense, the primacy thesis asserts that the level of the forces explains the form of the relations to a far greater extent than the other way around (PT1), and the primacy puzzle then becomes the problem of reconciling this 'greater extent' with a (full) control of the development of the forces by the relations. When construed in this way, the primacy puzzle makes much more intuitive sense and is clearly central to historical materialism. Cohen's interesting claim is that this puzzle can be solved only if the core of historical materialism is interpreted as a set of functional explanations.

Much hinges, we have seen, on how we interpret 'to a far greater extent'. What is meant might simply be that the relations are explained by reference to the forces in the two ways mentioned (PT0 and PT2). But as one of these ways (PT2) essentially involves a functional explanation, the claim that only a functional interpretation of historical materialism can solve the primacy puzzle becomes altogether trivial. More plausibly, the primacy of the forces may consist in the fact that in case of contradiction, the relations adjust to the forces and not the other way around. There is a general way in which such a primacy can be reconciled with the control of the forces by the relations. It is by building a dynamic model in which a fast and a slow dynamics can be distinguished. Cohen's functional interpretation presupposes such a model. It corresponds to the special case in which the slow dynamics is *embedded* in the fast one. But precisely because it is but a special case of a more general solution, Cohen's claim that it provides the only way of solving the primacy puzzle (in the most plausible interpretation of the latter) is plainly false.

Thus emerges Cohen's dilemma. His functional interpretation of historical materialism is certainly exciting and possibly correct. But the justification he gives for it by arguing that it provides the only way of solving Marxism's central puzzle is, depending on how the latter is construed, either trivial or false. My claim is that the more general model somewhat abstractly sketched here not only helps in displaying the structure of a remarkable pattern of 'Marxist causation'. It also covers all

possible solutions of the primacy puzzle in its most relevant interpretation. This claim, I venture, is neither trivial nor false – and is the only way
out of Cohen's dilemma.

Notes

1 For a precise definition of the 'productive forces' and the 'relations of production', I refer
to Cohen's (1978: chs. 2, 3) excellent discussions. Note that it will be assumed throughout
here that both forces and relations admit of a classification into a discrete set of 'levels' or
'forms'.

2 Here are some of Cohen's most synthetic formulations: 'The favoured explanations take
this form: the production relations are of kind R at the time t [RP] because relations of
kind R are suitable to the use and development of the productive forces at t [RP is best
for Δ PF], given the level of development of the latter at t [PF]' (1978: 160); 'forces [PF]
select structure [RP] according to their capacity to promote development [RP is best for
Δ PF]' (1978: 162); or 'the character of what is explained [RP] is determined by its effect
[RP is best for Δ PF] on what explains it [PF]' (1978: 278).

3 Some critics of Cohen have adopted the first interpretation of the primacy thesis. Levine
and Wright (1980: 52) insist, for example, that the 'compatibility thesis' (to the effect that
a given level of development of the productive forces is compatible with only a limited
range of relations of production) 'is plainly essential for the Primacy Thesis', which
makes sense only if the latter is taken in the first sense. Others have adopted the second
interpretation. According to Elster, for example, 'Cohen explains and defends the thesis
that the productive forces have primacy over the production relations ... in the sense
that the latter are what they are because of the kind of influence they exert on the
former' (1980: 123: see also 1981: 639 and 1983: ch. 6).

4 Note, incidentally, that the 'facts of constraint', as specified by what Levine and Wright
call the compatibility thesis, i.e. the claim that 'a given level of productive power is
compatible only with a certain type, or certain types, of economic structure' (Cohen
1978: 158), are *not* symmetrical in the sense that the reciprocal of this claim (a given type
of economic structure is compatible only with a certain level, or certain levels, of
productive power) automatically follows, contrary to what Levine and Wright take for
granted. This is easily shown by the following counter-example. Suppose we have two
levels of forces 1 and 2 and three forms of relations *A*, *B*, and *C*, with *A* or *B* 'corresponding to' 1 and *B* or *C* 'corresponding to' 2. In this case, it is true that any level of forces is
compatible with only certain forms of relations, but it is false that any form of relations is
compatible with only certain levels of forces, since *B* is compatible with both 1 and 2. And
it is therefore false to say that the compatibility thesis, as stated, 'involves' both claims
(Levine and Wright 1980: 60). (It would do so if the initial 'a given' were to be understood
as 'some given' rather than as 'any given', but I am sure this weakening of the claim
would be endorsed by neither Cohen nor Levine and Wright as an interpretation of
what historical materialism asserts.) The symmetrical character of the facts of constraint,
consequently, must lie elsewhere, namely, in their failure to specify the direction of
causation.

5 What they call the contradiction thesis and the transformation thesis are just meant to
spell out the path that unavoidably leads from the facts of constraint (compatibility
thesis) and the assumption of an autonomous tendency for the productive forces to
grow (development thesis) to (the initial segment of) the primacy thesis: $FP \rightarrow RP$. See
Levine and Wright (1980: 51–6).

6 Levine and Wright's conception of the role played by the development thesis is neatly
depicted in their diagram (1980: 54), where 'rational adaptive practices' are shown to
determine the forces 'from outside', independently of the relations of production.

7 A *functional* explanation is the explanation of the presence of an item by the fact that it has some differential consequences (compared to its absence or the presence of some alternative item). This fact, which is a dispositional feature of the context in which the item appears, is sometimes in turn explicitly accounted for by reference to some structural (or non-dispositional) feature of the context. Hence the general structure of a functional explanation, which can be (loosely) represented as follows: $S \rightarrow (i \rightarrow C) \rightarrow i$, and is illustrated by (c) and (d) as well as by (e). See Cohen (1978: ch. 9) and Van Parijs (1981: ch. 2) for a general analysis of the logic of functional explanations.

8 As illustrated by Cohen's Table 4 (1978: 198):

Level of productive development	Form of economic structure
No surplus	Pre-class society
Some surplus, but less than	Pre-capitalist class society
Moderately high surplus, but less than	Capitalist society
Massive surplus	Post-class society

9 For illustrative diagrams and further discussion, see sections 1.1 and 1.2 above.

10 I argue elsewhere that functional explanations are necessarily static in this sense (see Van Parijs 1981: 40–4).

11 This embedding may be required, however, for primacy to be reconciled with two-way causation *and* other views Marx or Marxists hold. But (1) these other views would have to be specified, which Cohen does not do, and (2) my guess is that, once these views are stated explicitly, the alleged solution once again will become tautological.

References

Cohen, G. A. 1978. *Karl Marx's Theory of History: A Defence*, Oxford: Oxford University Press.
    1980. 'Functional explanation: reply to Elster', *Political Studies* 28, 129–35.
Elster, Jon. 1980. 'Cohen on Marx's Theory of History', *Political Studies* 28, 121–8.
    1981. 'Clearing the decks', *Ethics* 91, 634–44.
    1983. *Explaining Technical Change: A Case Study in the Philosophy of Science*, Cambridge: Cambridge University Press.
Frank, Andre G. 1979. *Dependent Accumulation and Underdevelopment*, New York: Monthly Review Press.
Levine, Andrew, and Erik O. Wright. 1980. 'Rationality and class struggle', *New Left Review* 123, 47–68.
Van Parijs, Philippe. 1981. *Evolutionary Explanation in the Social Sciences: An Emerging Paradigm*, Totowa, NJ: Rowman and Littlefield.
Veblen, Thorstein, 1899. *The Theory of the Leisure Class*, London: Allen and Unwin, 1970.
Wallerstein, Immanuel. 1974. *The Modern World-System. Capitalist Agriculture and the Origins of the European World Economy in the 16th Century*, New York: Academic Press.

Part II

Crisis theory shattered

3. A rational reconstruction by way of obituary

For the purposes of this chapter, the *falling-rate-of-profit theory of crises* (or for short, the FRP theory) is defined as the theory which attempts to predict and explain the occurrence of economic crises under capitalism with the help of the following three propositions:

(i) The capitalist mode of production is such that the organic composition of capital (OCK) necessarily rises.
(ii) A rise in the OCK necessarily leads to a fall in the (general) rate of profit.
(iii) A fall in the (general) rate of profit necessarily leads to crises.

From the conjunction of these three propositions it obviously follows that

(iv) The capitalist mode of production is such that crises necessarily occur.

However familiar such a theory may now sound to those acquainted with Marxian economics and however uncontroversial its presence in Marx's writings from the *Grundrisse* to volume 3 of *Capital*, it is not until the 1930s that it came to constitute the core of the Marxist interpretation of crises. Earlier Marxist approaches rather tended to locate the origin of crises either in disproportionality or in underconsumption, and it is only with Grossmann's (1929: ch. 2) and Dobb's (1937: ch. 4) influential presentations, that a prominent place was given, in the explanation of crises, to the theory of the falling rate of profit. At about the same time, however, severely critical treatments of the theory by Moszkowska (1935: ch. 4), Sweezy (1942: ch. 6) and Robinson (1942: ch. 5) opened the modern debate, which, as a result of a general revival of interest in Marxist economics, attracted many contributions and aroused much passion throughout the 1970s.

Some recent discussion, especially the one arising from Shaikh's (1978b) cunning vindication of the theory, suggests that the time has now come to look back on the whole debate and write the theory's obituary. In this chapter, I shall try to do so by providing a *rational reconstruction* of the debate, i.e. by reconstructing it in such a way that unnecessary assumptions, irrelevant remarks, terminological inconsistencies, confusions and misunderstandings are, as far as possible, removed from the arguments actually put forward.

The justification for reconstructing the debate, rather than subjecting the issues it deals with to a straightforward discussion, is three-fold. First of all, a rational reconstruction is likely to be more effective in convincing those who object to the conclusion to which it leads, that their arguments have been taken fully into account and that, nevertheless, the conclusion is what it is. Secondly, by providing a systematic survey of the literature, it may help some students (and teachers) to find their way in this frequently confusing area of Marxist theory. Thirdly, and perhaps most importantly, it will give some hints as to the way in which 'bad news' (most spectacularly, as we shall see, the implications of Okishio's theorem) progressively spreads and is resisted in a scientific community which is more exposed than many others to the pressure of 'extra-scientific' considerations.

3.1 The simplest suitable capitalist world

In order to keep the discussion as clear as possible, we shall assume the simplest possible universe in which the fundamental issues raised by the theory can be addressed. We shall be considering a society in which there are two classes: the capitalists, who own the means of production, and the workers, who own their labour-power. While the workers consume their means of subsistence, the capitalists do not consume anything. There is only one kind of means of production (commodity I), one kind of means of subsistence (commodity II) and one kind of labour-power (commodity LP).[1] The economy, therefore, has only two industries, one with a daily production of Y_I units of commodity I and one with a daily production of Y_{II} units of commodity II. And it uses daily, for the sake of this production, k units of commodity I and NT units of labour-power (i.e. NT labour hours of average intensity), with N the number of workers and T the length of the working day. Commodity I is assumed to consist of fixed capital, which means that the rate of turnover of the means of production (t_c) is smaller than 1, or that the stock (K) of good I is larger than its daily flow:[2]

$$K = k/t_c > k \tag{A1}$$

Workers, on the other hand, are assumed to be paid at the beginning of each day, which can be taken to mean that the rate of turnover of labour-power (t_v) is 1, or that the stock (L) of labour-power is equal to its daily flow:

$$L = NT/t_v = NT \tag{A2}$$

Further, it would be very convenient if we were able to formulate the equilibrium (or general) rate of profit, with whose behaviour the theory is concerned, in simple value terms. Therefore, we shall boldly assume that the *law of value* holds in its simplest form,[3] i.e. that

$$p_I^*, p_{II}^* \text{ and } w^* \text{ are proportional to } \lambda_I, \lambda_{II} \text{ and } \lambda_{LP} \tag{A3}$$

where p_I^* and p_{II}^* are the competitive equilibrium unit prices of commodities I and II, where w^* is the competitive equilibrium hourly money wage, where λ_I and λ_{II} are the unit values of commodities I and II (i.e. the amounts of labour time directly or indirectly required to produce one unit of each) and where λ_{LP} is the (hourly) value of labour-power, equal to the value of the daily subsistence bundle (B) divided by the length of the working day:

$$\lambda_{LP} = \lambda_{II} B/T \tag{D4}$$

Now, the (daily) rate of profit can be defined as

$$\pi = (\text{daily receipts} - \text{daily costs})/\text{capital advanced} \tag{D5}$$

If the law of value holds, the competitive equilibrium rate of profit is then given by the familiar expression:

$$\pi^* = s/(C + V) \tag{from 3, 5) (T6}$$

where

$$s = y - (c + v) \tag{D7}$$

i.e. the daily flow of *surplus-value* is given by the value of the daily gross product $(y = \lambda_I Y_I + \lambda_{II} Y_{II})$ minus the value of the means of production and labour-power used up $(c + v)$;

$$c = \lambda_I k \tag{D8}$$

i.e. the (daily) flow of *constant capital* is given by the value of the (daily) flow of means of production used up;

$$C = \lambda_I K = c/t_c \tag{D9}$$

i.e. the *stock* of constant capital is given by the value of the stock of means of production, itself equal to the corresponding flow divided by the rate of turnover t_c (see A1 above), and

$$V = v = \lambda_{LP} NT \tag{D10}$$

i.e. the (daily) flow or stock of *variable capital* is given by the value of the amount of labour-power used daily, itself equal to the amount of labour-power in stock (see A2 above).

Within the framework of this elementary capitalist economy, I shall now try to review, as briefly and systematically as possible, the major arguments in favour of and against the FRP theory as stated above. In the next three sections, I consider what I shall call the *traditional* arguments. They basically concern the question of whether the tendencies asserted by the theory in its first two propositions are really *necessary* or just *contingent*. In the last two sections, I turn to the fatal issues which have recently gained prominence in the debate and which throw into irrelevance most of the traditional arguments. Roughly, these fatal issues are about the very *possibility* of technical change generating a fall in the rate of profit and of such a fall in the rate of profit (if it did occur) generating crises.

3.2 The rise in the organic composition of capital

Both proposition (i) and proposition (ii) of the theory make reference to the organic composition of capital. The OCK can be understood in at least two ways.[4] On the one hand, it can be understood as identical to the *value composition of capital* (VCK), defined as the ratio of the stock of constant capital to the stock of variable capital:

$$VCK = C/V \tag{D11}$$

On the other hand, it can be understood as identical to the *ratio of dead to living labour* (RDL), defined as the ratio of the stock of constant capital to the flow (or the stock) of labour-power:

$$RDL = C/NT \tag{D12}$$

I shall call *textbook variant* of the FRP-theory the variant which adopts the first interpretation (OCK = VCK). And I shall call *modern variant* the one which adopts the second interpretation (OCK = RDL).[5]

Proposition (i) of the theory states that, under capitalism, the OCK necessarily rises. Whichever variant of the theory is adopted, it is crucial, in order to establish proposition (i), that one should be able to assert the necessity of a rise in the *technical composition of capital* (TCK), defined as the ratio of the stock of means of production to the flow (or stock) of labour-power:

$$TCK = K/NT \qquad (D13)$$

Now, *if* we can make it plausible that, under capitalism, technical progress necessarily tends to be *labour-saving*, i.e. that the mass of means of production necessarily grows faster (or falls less) than the amount of labour employed, or[6]

$$\dot{K} > \dot{N} + \dot{T} \qquad (A14)$$

then it directly follows that, under capitalism, the TCK must rise:

The TCK rises   (from 13, 14) (T15)

However, why should individual profit-maximizing capitalists necessarily prefer to save labour rather than to save 'capital'? The standard argument in support of this view is that, if the economy grows substantially faster than the potential labour force – a plausible assumption to make under capitalism – then labour-saving technology must be an intrinsic feature of the system (if it is to keep growing), whereas capital-saving technology is not.[7] However, it is a logical fallacy to infer from the fact that some feature x is necessary while another feature y is not, to the necessity of having more of x than of y. While there are good reasons why the capitalists should try to economize on labour, there are no good reasons (once K has ceased to be negligible) why they should economize on labour more than on (constant) capital. In the course of capitalist development, the balance of labour-saving and capital-saving innovations may be such that A14 holds and the TCK therefore rises. But this would be a contingent fact, not one stemming from the nature of the capitalist mode of production.[8]

Suppose, however, for the sake of the argument, that under capitalism the TCK necessarily rises. This still does not mean that the OCK must rise. For the *textbook variant*, which interprets OCK as VCK, two additional steps are needed, as is clear from the following relationship between the VCK and the TCK:

$$VCK = (\lambda_I/\lambda_{II}) (T/B) \, TCK \qquad \text{(from 11, 13, 9, 10, 4) (T16)}$$

The necessity of a rise in VCK could be safely inferred from the necessity of a rise in TCK[9] if one could assume that, necessarily,

λ_I/λ_{II} is constant or rises   (A17)

i.e. that productivity (as measured by $1/\lambda_I$ and $1/\lambda_{II}$) must increase at least as fast in industry II as in industry I, and also that, necessarily,

B/T is constant or falls   (A18)

i.e. that the subsistence bundle per hour of labour does not increase, or, since under the law of value

$w^*/p^*_{II} = B/T$ (from 2, 4) (T19)

that the equilibrium wage (w^*/p^*_{II}), does not rise. If these two assumptions are warranted, it is easy to conclude

The VCK rises   (from 16, 17, 18) (T20)

But it seems exceedingly hard to find any compelling argument which would rule out as impossible, under capitalist conditions, the two kinds of development which such a reasoning needs to exclude: technical change which substantially reduces the value of the means of production compared to that of the means of subsistence[10] and 'cultural' change which substantially increases the amount of means of subsistence deemed 'necessary' for the performance of one day's work.[11] Neither A17 nor A18, therefore, are given the solid foundation they need and T20 remains contingent even if the necessity of a rise in the TCK is taken for granted (T15).

The step which the *modern variant* must take (beyond T15) is very different. As it interprets the OCK as RDI, the relevant connection between OCK and TCK is now given by:

RDL = λ_I TCK   (from 12, 13, 9) (T21)

Whether or nor a rising TCK implies a rising OCK now depends on the trend in the unit value of the means of production, i.e. on the productivity trend in industry I.[12] If we can suppose that the level of productivity in industry I (represented by $1/\lambda_I$) is an increasing function of the TCK, i.e. that:

$1/\lambda_I = f(\text{TCK})$, with $df/d\text{TCK} > 0$ (A22)

and if we can further suppose that the impact of the TCK on productivity decreases as both increase, i.e. that:

$df/d\text{TCK} < f/\text{TCK}$ (A23)

then it is correct to infer that the development of productivity in industry I cannot offset the rise in TCK, i.e.

$(1/\lambda_1) < \dot{\text{TCK}}$ (from 22, 23) (T24)

which is clearly equivalent to

The RDL rises[13] (from 21, 24) (T25)

Here again, however, and even more than in the case of the rise in TCK, the problem is to show the (capitalist) necessity of the assumptions. No argument can make the postulated technological fact (that the 'marginal productivity' of TCK-increasing technical progress tends to fall) more than a contingent fact of capitalism – if it is a fact at all.

For the sake of pursuing the argument, however, let us suppose that in addition to the necessity of a rising TCK (T15), we can take for granted the necessity of equal productivity increases in both industries and of a constant hourly real wage (textbook variant), as well as the necessity of a falling 'marginal productivity' of TCK-increasing technical progress (modern variant). Let us suppose, in other words, that proposition (i) is established under both interpretations, i.e. that the capitalist mode of production is such that both the VCK and the RDL necessarily rise. If this is so, and even in the absence of any other downward pressure, proposition (ii) then claims, the equilibrium rate of profit will fall.

3.3 The fall in the equilibrium rate of profit

In order to examine critically this second proposition, we must start by ruling out the possibility of alternative downward pressures. This requires our reformulating beforehand, in a more explicit way, the value rate of profit (T6). Given that the value of the (daily) net product (value of the gross product minus constant capital used up) is equal to the number of man-hours per day, i.e.

$y - c = NT$ (from the definition of value) (T26)

the (daily) flow of surplus-value can be reformulated as

$s = NT - N\lambda_{\text{II}}B$ (from 7, 26, 10, 4) (T27)

and the equilibrium rate of profit, therefore, as

$\pi^* = (T - \lambda_{\text{II}}B)/(\lambda_{\text{I}}K/N + \lambda_{\text{II}}B)$ (from 6, 27, 9, 10) (T28)

In order to make the influence of the OCK (in its two interpretations) more explicit, this expression can in turn be transformed into

$$\pi^* = (T - \lambda_{II}B)/[\lambda_{II}B(VCK + 1)] \qquad \text{(from 28, 11) (T29)}$$

$$\pi^* = (T - \lambda_{II}B)/(RDL.T + \lambda_{II}B) \qquad \text{(from 28, 12) (T30)}$$

These two formulas make it clear that apart from a rise in the OCK, there are three potential sources of downward pressure on the equilibrium rate of profit: a fall in the length of the working day (T), a rise in the real wage (B) and a rise in the unit value of the means of subsistence (λ_{II}).

The first two of these factors are typically stressed in a *profit-squeeze* approach to the falling rate of profit.[14] We want to discard them here because what the FRP-theory asserts, in its proposition (ii), is that *even* if the length (as well as the intensity) of the working day is not pushed down nor the real wage pushed up by working-class resistance, the rate of profit will still fall as a reflection of a rising organic composition of capital. We must therefore assume, for the sake of the argument:

T is constant   (A31)
B is constant   (A32)

The third factor (rising λ_{II}) is the one picked out in the Ricardian account of a falling rate of profit in terms of declining productivity for agricultural products.[15] Marx emphatically rejected this account on the grounds that, under capitalism, productivity keeps rising. His claim – the claim of proposition (ii) – is that, *although* productivity keeps increasing (i.e. values keep falling), the rate of profit must fall when the organic composition of capital rises. We can therefore suppose that:

λ_I and λ_{II} fall   (A33)

i.e. that productivity rises in both industries, as a reasonable assumption about what is bound to happen under capitalism.

After having thus ruled out all alternative sources of downward pressure on the equilibrium rate of profit, we can now turn to a critical examination of proposition (ii), i.e. to the question: why should a rise in the organic composition of capital necessarily lead to a fall in the equilibrium rate of profit? As in the case of proposition (i), let us take first the textbook variant and then the modern one.

The textbook variant can most conveniently be formulated in terms of the concept of *rate of exploitation* (e), defined by

$$e = s/v \qquad\qquad\qquad\qquad\qquad\qquad\qquad\qquad \text{(D34)}$$

The equilibrium rate of profit can easily be formulated in terms of this rate and the VCK:

$$\pi^* = e/(\text{VCK} + 1) \qquad\qquad\qquad\qquad \text{(from 6, 11, 34) (T35)}$$

Bearing in mind that the discussion of proposition (i), in its textbook variant, is supposed to have established that the VCK must rise (T20), it is obviously sufficient to assume that:

e is constant $\qquad\qquad\qquad\qquad\qquad\qquad\qquad\qquad\qquad$ (A36)

in order to be able to assert that the equilibrium rate of profit must fall:

π^* falls $\qquad\qquad\qquad\qquad\qquad\qquad$ (from 35, 36, 20) (T37)

Unfortunately, this additional assumption directly contradicts the three previous assumptions we have just made (A31–33), which jointly imply that the rate of exploitation must rise:

e rises $\qquad\qquad\qquad\qquad$ (from 34, 27, 10, 4, 31, 32, 33) (T38)

Therefore, if we want to show that a rising VCK leads to a falling rate of profit even if T and B are constant and productivity rises – which is the claim of proposition (ii) – then we cannot assume a constant rate of exploitation.[16]

This is not the end of the story for the textbook variant, for instead of A36 we can make a weaker assumption which would still enable us to derive a fall in the equilibrium rate of profit. We can assume that the ratio of the increase in the rate of exploitation (Δe) to the increase in the VCK (Δ VCK) is bound by an upper limit $e/(\text{VCK} + 1)$:

$$\Delta e/\Delta\text{VCK} < e/(\text{VCK} + 1) \qquad\qquad\qquad\qquad\qquad \text{(A39)}$$

which is equivalent to

$$\dot{e} < (\text{VCK} \dot{+} 1) \qquad\qquad\qquad\qquad\qquad\qquad \text{(from 39) (T40)}$$

and hence directly implies:

π^* falls $\qquad\qquad\qquad\qquad\qquad\qquad$ (from 40, 35) (T41)

The new assumption (A39), unlike the old one (A36), is compatible with a rising rate of exploitation (T38). But this is not enough to make it plausible.

The most defensible attempt to establish the plausibility of assumption

A39 runs along the following lines.[17] Given our assumption on the rate of turnover of variable capital (A2), the only difference between e ($= s/v$) and VCK ($= C/V$) lies in their numerators (s and C). Now, whereas e's numerator has a finite upper limit – the daily flow of surplus value (s) cannot exceed the daily flow of value ($v + s = NT$ by T7 and T26) –, VCK's numerator (C) can grow without limits. Clearly, this should tell us something about the (eventual) inability of increases in e to offset the negative influence of increases in VCK on the rate of profit. The trouble is that, however much VCK increases, it is always possible, in principle, for e to increase by an even larger amount: it may be true that s cannot tend towards infinity, but v can tend towards 0, and e ($= s/v$), therefore, can increase indefinitely. This crucial fact cannot but undermine any attempt to provide the weaker assumption A39, indispensable to establish the link between a rising VCK and a falling rate of profit, with more than a very shaky foundation.[18] What the previous argument was trying to get at, however, is a valid and important point. It is precisely the failure of the textbook variant to capture that point adequately, which led to the elaboration of the modern variant of the theory.

The modern variant of the theory tries to derive, from a rise in the ratio of dead to living labour (T25), the necessity of a fall in the equilibrium rate of profit. We shall see that it does not quite succeed in doing so. But it comes as close to it as possible, by taking full account of the following trivial mathematical fact:[19]

$$s/(C + V) \leqslant (v + s)/C \qquad \text{(tautology) (T42)}$$

i.e. whatever the (non-negative) values taken by C, V, s and v, the ratio obtained by adding v to the numerator of s/C cannot possibly be smaller than the ratio obtained by adding V to its denominator. Using previous results, this tautology can immediately be transformed into the following inequality:

$$\pi^* \leqslant 1/\text{RDL} \qquad \text{(from 42, 6, 12, 26, 7) (T43)}$$

i.e. the equilibrium rate of profit cannot possibly be larger than the ratio of living to dead labour, or the reciprocal of the RDL. Therefore, we can define the *maximum rate of profit* as

$$\pi_{\text{Max}} = 1/\text{RDL} \qquad \text{(D44)}$$

And it could not be more obvious that, if the RDL rises, the maximum rate of profit must fall:

$$\pi_{\text{Max}} \text{ falls} \qquad \text{(from 44, 25) (T45)}$$

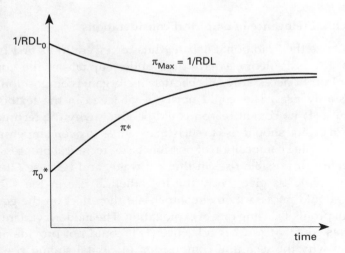

Figure 3.1   Rate of profit and ratio of dead to living labour

However, the maximum rate of profit is not the equilibrium rate of profit, and a fall in the former does not have any straightforward implication as far as the latter is concerned. A fall in the maximum rate of profit does not even imply an eventual fall in the equilibrium rate:[20] the former can fall forever, while the latter keeps rising, as in Figure 3.1. What we need is the stronger assumption that, necessarily,

the RDL rises sufficiently   (A46)

i.e. that at some future time x, the maximum rate of profit (1/RDL) will be lower than the current equilibrium rate (π_0^*).[21] Only then can we validly derive

π^* will eventually fall   (from 43, 46) (T47)

In other words, the modern variant of the FRP-theory can only vindicate its proposition (ii) – which asserts that if the RDL rises the equilibrium rate of profit must fall – providing the latter's antecedent is strengthened (from a rise to a sufficient rise of the RDL) and its consequent weakened (from an actual to an eventual fall in the equilibrium rate of profit).[22] This means that even more is required from component (i) of the theory than what it has already proved unable to provide (the necessity of a rising RDL) and that component (iii) is provided with even less than what, as we shall soon see, is in any case insufficient to enable it to do its job (i.e. to prove the necessity of an actual fall in π^*).

3.4 The potential relevance of empirical considerations

Let us summarize the 'traditional debate' thus reviewed. In its first two propositions, the FRP-theory asserts that, under capitalism, the equilibrium rate of profit necessarily falls because the organic composition of capital necessarily rises. This could not be established in the textbook variant because (1) no cogent reason could be given why the technical composition of capital should rise to such an extent as to overcompensate the effect on the value composition of possibly faster technical progress in industry I and/or of possible rises in the real wage, and because (2) no cogent reason could be given why the hypothetical rise in the value composition should necessarily overcompensate the effect on the equilibrium rate of profit of a rising rate of exploitation. The modern variant of the theory was equally unsuccessful, since (1) it could not provide any cogent reason why the technical composition of capital should rise to such an extent as to overcompensate the effect, on the ratio of dead to living labour, of a fall in the value of the means of production, and since (2) it could not provide any cogent reason why the hypothetical rise in the ratio of dead to living labour should be such as to make its reciprocal (the maximum rate of profit) smaller than the current equilibrium rate.

If no compelling theoretical foundation can be given to the first two propositions of the theory, one may be tempted to turn to the facts. If it turns out that in all capitalist economies the organic composition of capital consistently rises and the equilibrium rate of profit consistently falls, it seems that this would constitute good evidence for the theory, even if it must be admitted that what happens *always* does not necessarily happen *out of necessity*. Since, on the other hand, what happens out of necessity must necessarily happen always, one must not overlook that turning to the facts also involves a serious risk for the theory. But it is at least worth a try, since coming up with favourable evidence, although it would not dispense us from looking for theoretical grounds, would give some credibility to the attempt to do so.

As is well known, however, the organic composition of capital, in capitalist economies, does not consistently rise, and the equilibrium rate of profit does not consistently fall.[23] Should this mean that the first two propositions of the theory are definitively refuted? This would be far too simple. If in a given (capitalist) economy, at a given time, the organic composition fails to rise and/or the rate of profit fails to fall, it may first be possible to claim that these facts are irrelevant to the theory as it is intended. If, as is the case here, the theory is intended to provide an explanation of *crises* (by showing their necessity under capitalist conditions), one need not be committed to the existence of secular trends in the organic composition and in the rate of profit. All one needs to claim is that in a period leading to a crisis, the organic composition rises and the rate of profit falls, however much these trends are offset by what happens during the crisis. On the other hand, if the theory is intended to provide a prediction of the *breakdown* of capitalism (by showing its eventual necessity), then there is no need to claim anything about the actual behaviour of the rate of profit: a consistent rise in the organic composition will bring about its eventual fall, however long the period during which it keeps rising.

Suppose, however, that – as is actually the case – the available evidence shows that the organic composition does sometimes fail to rise and the rate of profit to fall in intercrisis periods and that the organic composition, at least in some capitalist economies, does not display a consistent upward secular trend. Does this mean that the theory, in the appropriate sense (i.e. either as a theory of crises or as a theory of breakdown), is refuted? Not yet, for at this stage various types of defensive strategies can be used.

First of all, it may be possible to claim that the embarrassing evidence does not really prove that (at a particular place, at a particular time) the organic composition actually falls or that the equilibrium rate of profit actually rises. This may be simply because of defects in the collection of the data, or because no distinction was made between a 'productive' sector (the only one which must come into consideration for the estimation of constant and variable capital) and an 'unproductive' sector (the public sector, and, perhaps, the financial sector or the services, all of which 'live off' surplus-value), or else because prices and wages can temporarily fall below or rise above their equilibrium positions.[24]

Secondly, it may be possible to concede that (at a given place, at a given time) the organic composition is actually shown to fall and/or the equilibrium rate of profit shown to rise, while claiming that the economies considered are not purely capitalist. The embarrassing behaviour of the organic composition and/or of the equilibrium rate of profit could then be attributed to 'precapitalist' or, possibly, to 'socialist' elements in the economy.[25]

Finally, it may perhaps even be possible to accept both that the organic composition falls and/or that the equilibrium rate of profit rises, and that the economy in which this happens is purely capitalist, while still maintaining that rising organic composition and falling equilibrium rate of profit are necessary, intrinsic, fundamental features of the capitalist mode of production. The fact that these features do not reach the 'level of appearances', not even in intercrisis periods nor in the long run, need not bother us too much. This can easily be explained by pointing out that the capitalist system can 'make efforts', 'mobilize countertendencies' (presumably of a more contingent, extrinsic, superficial nature) in order to prevent the 'deeper' features from coming into the open.[26]

If one rejects this third type of strategy as empirically vacuous – there is no way, not even in principle, of testing its claims – one may well have to face the existence of genuine counterinstances, i.e. of adverse evidence which cannot be disposed of by a defensive strategy of the first ('not really falling/rising') or of the second ('not really capitalist') type. Even among Marxist authors, the prevailing opinion now seems to be that such genuine counterinstances do exist. There may well have been periods, in the history of capitalist economies, in which consistent rises in the organic composition coincided with consistent falls in the rate of profit. But there were also periods in which this was not the case. Neither the rise in the organic composition nor the fall in the rate of profit, therefore, can be said to be fundamental, intrinsic, necessary features of the capitalist mode of production, though they may be fairly typical of certain periods in its development.[27]

What are the implications of this defeatist attitude, which seems to be the natural outcome both of the traditional theoretical debate and of a critical discussion of the empirical evidence? In so far as the theory is meant to provide a 'scientifically grounded' prediction of *breakdown*, there is no way in which its ambition can be reconciled with such a defeatist attitude: if capitalism is doomed to collapse, this cannot be because a necessary rise in the organic composition necessarily leads to a necessary fall in the rate of profit, since these features have been shown to be contingent features of capitalism.

The theory's ambition to explain capitalist *crises*, on the other hand, is not completely destroyed by the adoption of a defeatist attitude. After all, one may argue, a rise in the organic composition of capital need not be 'intrinsic to capitalism' in order to bring about a fall in the rate of profit, which in turn need not be 'intrinsic to capitalism' in order to generate crises. Even those who adopt a defeatist position in the traditional debate (about necessity versus contingency), therefore, usually leave open the possibility that the so-called falling-rate-of-profit approach may play a very significant role in the explanation of crises.

In the remaining two sections of this chapter, I shall reconstruct other less 'traditional' aspects of the debate which show that the assumption on which such an open-minded attitude rests is doubly wrong. Firstly, it will be argued that, however much the rate of profit falls as a result of a rising organic composition, such a fall cannot, as such, generate capitalist crises. Secondly and more radically it will be argued that, under capitalist conditions, a rise in the organic composition is, in any case, incapable of causing a fall in the general rate of profit. Open-mindedness, in other words, is not on: it is *impossible* (not just contingent) for the rate of profit to fall as a result of a rising organic composition, and *impossible* (not just contingent) for crises to be generated by such a fall. The theory of the falling rate of profit is not only unable to show that crises are a necessary feature of capitalism (the defeatist position): it is completely irrelevant to the explanation of them.

3.5 The generation of crises

The preceding sections have been discussing the merits of the first two propositions of our theory. Let us now turn to its proposition (iii), which asserts that a fall in the equilibrium rate of profit induced by a rise in the organic composition of capital necessarily leads to crises. In conformity with standard usage, I shall take 'crisis' to refer to a crisis of overproduction, i.e. to a situation in which production, employment and capacity utilization fall as a result of commodities being unable to find buyers at the going prices. And the question we must ask is: what makes the occurrence of such a crisis necessary when the rate of profit falls for the reasons mentioned in propositions (i) – (ii)?

A first, rather devious, reply to this question is in terms of functional necessity. Roughly, the argument runs as follows.[28] By powerfully counteracting the tendency for the equilibrium rate of profit to fall, crises of overproduction perform a vital curative function for the capitalist mode of production. The way in which they do so, basically, is by decreasing the value of the means of production and/or of labour-power, i.e. by increasing productivity in industries I and/or II. And this is achieved both through the elimination of the least efficient capitalists and through the pressure exerted on the remaining ones to introduce (labour- and capital-saving) technical innovations as well as to reorganize, concentrate and rationalize the production process.[29]

However, showing that crises have the 'beneficial' effect of keeping in check the falling tendency of the equilibrium rate of profit does *not* amount to showing that crises are made necessary by such a tendency. Firstly, one may want to argue that crises, though possibly sufficient, are not necessary to prevent the equilibrium rate of profit from falling (i.e. that there are 'functional equivalents', alternative ways of achieving the same result) and, furthermore, that such a fall is perfectly compatible with the survival of the capitalist system (i.e. that keeping it in check, is not a 'functional prerequisite', an 'essential need' of the system). Secondly and more radically, *functional necessity* (for the survival of a system) should not be confused with *causal necessity* (within the structure of that system). Even if we discard the previous objection and take it for granted that crises of overproduction are functionally necessary to the survival of capitalism, this does not imply that they will necessarily occur, unless some omniscient, omnipotent agent makes whatever the system 'needs' (i.e. whatever is functionally necessary to it) unavoidable (i.e. causally necessary). If such an assumption is implausible – as it certainly is – considerations of 'functional necessity' cannot help us to show that a fall in the rate of profit makes the occurrence of crises (causally) necessary.

A second kind of argument, the one most frequently used, does not confuse functional and causal necessity. It first proceeds to show that a fall in the equilibrium rate of profit implies a fall in the *rate of accumulation*, defined as the rate of increase of the capital advanced:

$$a = (C \overset{\cdot}{+} V) \tag{D48}$$

The second step in the argument must then try to show that a fall in the rate of accumulation must lead to crises of overproduction.

First, then, why should the rate of accumulation fall when the equilibrium rate of profit falls? Since, by definition, surplus-value consists in what is left of the value of the gross product when one has taken away the amounts of value $(c + v)$ required for the reproduction of the stock of capital $(C + V)$, it also constitutes the upper limit to the amount by which the stock of capital can be increased (rather than just reproduced):

$$\Delta C + \Delta V \leqslant s \tag{from 7, 9, 10 (T49)}$$

This obviously implies that:

$$a \leqslant \pi^* \tag{from 48, 49, 6 (T50)}$$

i.e. that the equilibrium rate of profit is the upper limit of the rate of accumulation.

Of course, a fall in the maximum rate of accumulation (i.e. in the equilibrium rate of profit) need not mean a fall in the actual rate if it is compensated by an increase in the proportion of surplus-value which is accumulated. But we have already assumed above (section 3.1) that capitalists do not consume. If *we* further assume – also in agreement with Marx's ideal-typical image of the capitalist – that:

whatever is not consumed is accumulated (A51)

then it immediately follows that all the surplus-value produced is accumulated and, therefore, that the rate of accumulation is equal to its maximum value:

$$a = \pi^*$$ (from 50, 51 and section 3.1) (T52)

If the equilibrium rate of profit falls, then, clearly, the rate of accumulation must fall:

a falls (from 52, 41) (T53)

So far so good. But how do we get from such a fall in the rate of accumulation to the emergence of 'realization problems', i.e. of crises of overproduction? The standard view seems to be that at some point – the 'definite point' at which the law of the falling rate of profit becomes a 'barrier' to the capitalist mode of production – the amount of surplus-value produced becomes insufficient to purchase (for the sake of accumulation) all the commodities produced which are not consumed.[30] Exactly where this point lies is usually left vague. There are some suggestions, however, that it will be reached – crises of overproduction will break out – as soon as the amount of surplus-value begins to decline, not only in relation to capital advanced, but also in absolute terms.[31] The trouble is that, under the very assumptions of the theory: (1) such a point *cannot* possibly be reached, and (2) even if it were reached, this would not trigger off a crisis. Let us examine why this is so.

First, a rise in the amount of surplus-value produced is not only compatible with the theory of the falling rate of profit, as is often acknowledged. It is also implied by the very assumptions we have had to introduce in order to discard alternative sources of downward pressure on the equilibrium rate of profit. Providing we assume that, previous to the crisis, there is no fall in the overall level of employment, i.e.

N does not fall (A54)

it follows from the assumption of a constant real wage, of a constant working day and of a rising productivity, that:

s rises (from 27, 31, 32, 33, 54) (T55)

In spite of a falling rate of profit (due to a rising organic composition), therefore, each period of production does not only make a positive amount of value available for accumulation (on top of what is required for simple reproduction), but the amount thus made available is larger than during the previous period.

In any case, whether the amount (s) available for accumulation increases or does not is irrelevant to the question of whether overproduction crises must appear. Apart from interindustrial disproportionalities, assumed to be swiftly corrected under the law of value, overproduction can only arise from a lack of effective aggregate demand. But we have assumed (A51) that all the net value produced ($v + s$) which does not enter the workers' consumption (v) is accumulated by the capitalists. There is no discrepancy, therefore, between savings and investment, between the output produced and the (consumption and accumulation) demand for it. Say's law holds. There is no room for a lack of aggregate demand, no room for a crisis of overproduction.[32]

The failure of this second, more frequent argument does not mean that there is no way in which a fall in the equilibrium rate of profit (induced by a rise in the organic composition) can be understood as potentially relevant to the explanation of crises of overproduction. It only means that there is no way in which it can be so understood by appealing to its influence on the amount of surplus-value *available* for accumulation – notwithstanding the frequent claims that this constitutes a decisive advantage of the FRP-theory.[33] The only way in which such a fall in the equilibrium rate of profit can be conceived to enter the process by which crises are generated is by affecting the capitalists' subjective expectation of profitability and, thereby, their subjective propensity to invest. Within this 'Keynesian', rather than 'Marxian' perspective, it is at least possible to imagine that the rate of profit may become so low that capitalists lose any incentive to accumulate and, thereby, generate a lack of demand for means of production as well as (via a fall in the level of employment) for means of subsistence.

However, there remains a major difficulty. Technical change takes time. A rise in the organic composition of capital, therefore must be a slow, long-run phenomenon. And so must be the resulting fall in the equilibrium rate of profit. In the long run, however, capitalists have plenty of time to adjust their level of expectation, i.e. their definition of what constitutes a reasonable rate of profit. If the fall in the rate of profit under consideration were a short-run one, it would be conceivable to explain the interruption of investment by the reaching of some threshold value – e.g. the rate of interest on bonds or the rate of profit abroad. But in a long-run perspective, such an interruption would only be part of the short-run adjustments which contribute to the formation of the equilibrium rate of profit. Showing that there is a long-run tendency for the equilibrium rate of profit to fall (as a result of rising organic composition), therefore, is of no relevance to the explanation of crises of overproduction, even if one allows for the operation of a 'Keynesian' mechanism.[34]

Let us sum up. It has been argued in this section that proposition (iii) of the theory is false, i.e. that a fall in the rate of profit induced by a rise in the organic composition does not make crises of overproduction necessary. This is so, firstly, because, even if we can show that it makes them *functionally necessary to* capitalism, this does not show them to be *causally necessary under* capitalism. This is so, secondly, because even if we admit that a fall in the equilibrium rate of profit depresses the rate of accumulation, there is no way in which this can lead to realization problems unless the capitalists' propensity to invest is brought in. And this is so, finally, because a fall in the equilibrium rate of profit induced by a rising organic composition can only be a long-run phenomenon – in such a way that it will not generate an abrupt interruption of the accumulation process, even if the role of the propensity to invest is acknowledged.

This shows that it is impossible for a fall in the equilibrium rate of profit (due to a rise in the organic composition) to generate crises. But it still assumes that it is possible (though not necessary, as argued above) for a rise in the organic composition to generate a fall in the equilibrium rate of profit. The next section turns to an argument which shows that this too is impossible.

3.6 The fatal theorem

The so-called choice of technique argument is the most serious of all objections formulated against the theory of the falling rate of profit. It is so devastating that it deprives all the arguments (pro and contra) presented in the preceding sections of their relevance. It applies whether the theory is meant as a theory of crises or as a theory of breakdown, whether it is formulated in terms of value composition (textbook variant) or in terms of the ratio of dead to living labour (modern variant) and whether the equilibrium rate of profit can be expressed simply in value terms or not. Although the argument first appeared – albeit in a sketchy formulation – only a few years after the publication of volume 3 of *Capital*, it was not until the 1970s that it really entered the Marxist discussion.[35]

The central claim of the argument, sometimes referred to as Okishio's theorem, can be briefly formulated as follows. Under competitive capitalism, a profit-maximizing individual capitalist will only adopt a new technique of production (whether it increases the organic composition of capital or not) if it reduces the production cost per unit or, equivalently, increases profits per unit at going prices. A technical innovation which satisfies this condition – what we can call a *viable* innovation – enables the capitalist to get (temporarily) a transitional rate of profit higher than the initial general rate of the economy. Clearly, this does not, as such, say anything about the new *general*, 'socially imposed' rate of profit, i.e. the rate that will prevail once the generalization of the technique within the industry and capital movements between industries will have equalized the rates of profit throughout the economy.[36] The point of Okishio's theorem is precisely to assert that viable innovations necessarily increase the general rate of profit, if they affect it at all. Very roughly, this is due to the fact that the process by which prices are equalized must involve a cheapening of the products of the innovating industry, and if the real wage remains constant, this can only *increase* the rate of profit in other industries – unless the innovation has taken place in a luxury-good industry (in which case capitalist consumers are the beneficiaries). Consequently, it is completely impossible for the general rate of profit to fall as a result of a viable technical innovation if real wages are kept constant.[37]

A shrewd attempt at refuting this powerful objection has been made by Anwar Shaikh (1978). Okishio's version of the argument, he correctly points out, assumes the absence of fixed capital and, therefore, the identity of the rate of profit (π) and the profit margin (μ), defined respectively by

$$\pi = \frac{\text{price per unit} - \text{cost per unit}}{\text{investment per unit}} \tag{D56}$$

$$= \frac{\text{total profits (per period)}}{\text{total investment (at a given time)}}$$

$$\mu = \frac{\text{price per unit} - \text{cost per unit}}{\text{cost per unit}} \tag{D57}$$

$$= \frac{\text{total profits (per period)}}{\text{total costs (per period)}}$$

As soon as fixed capital is allowed, however, the rate of profit and the profit margin are no longer identical, and they need not vary in the same direction as a result of technical change. Furthermore, the criterion of

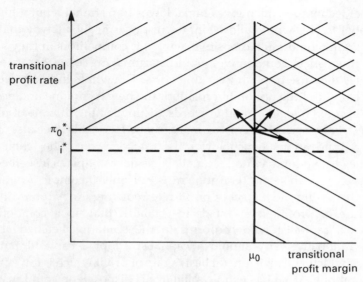

Figure 3.2   Moves from the initial position (μ_0, π_0^*) into the Northern area (above π_0^*) represent profit-rate-increasing technical changes. Moves into the Eastern area (to the right of μ_0) represent profit-margin-increasing technical changes. The success of Shaikh's rescue operation requires some moves into the South-eastern area to be viable.

viability becomes ambiguous. If capitalists care about their profit margins, Okishio's theorem can still be used to conclude that the (average) profit margin in the economy cannot fall if real wages are constant. If instead they care about their rates of profit, a generalization of Okishio's theorem to the case of fixed capital shows that the (general) rate of profit in the economy can only rise, if it changes at all. However, if capitalists are *forced* (by competition) to care about their profit *margins* rather than their rates of profit, no Okishio theorem can prevent the general *rate* of profit from falling, as the result of a (capital-using, labour-saving) innovation.[38] The crucial question, therefore, is whether viable innovations, in a competitive capitalist economy with fixed capital, can be represented as moves into the northern area (above the initial general rate of profit π_0^*) or into the eastern area (to the right of the initial profit margin μ_0) of the diagram in Figure 3.2, the two dimensions of which were merged on Okishio's version of the argument.

In order to support the view that profit margins are the crucial factor, Shaikh (1978b: 245–6) proposes a scenario of the following kind. Suppose that one capitalist attempts to increase his sales by introducing a (capital-intensive) technique which gives him a lower transitional π but a higher transitional μ. This would allow him to cut prices in such a way that his profit margin would remain positive, while his competitors (if they want to keep their prices competitive) would start making losses because the techniques they use imply higher unit costs. The whole industry would then be left with little option but to adopt the new technique and accept the rate of profit it yields. In other words, distinguishing the rate of profit from the profit margin seems to make room for viable (because cost-reducing) innovations which lower the rate of profit. The 'choice of technique' argument may not, after all, be as devastating as it seemed.

However, Shaikh's counterargument is not only incomplete (it stops short of discussing the impact of profit-rate-reducing innovations on the *general* rate of profit). It also fails to establish that, in a competitive economy, a capitalist who conforms to the scenario sketched above behaves rationally. Why should a capitalist adopt a capital-intensive technique which will give him (at best) a rate of profit which is lower than the general rate? If he has extra capital at his disposal, he could instead expand his production with the old technique, or invest elsewhere in the economy at the general rate of profit, or at least buy safe financial assets which will give him the equilibrium rate of interest. If he has to borrow the capital he invests, it even becomes a matter of life and death (and not just a matter of opportunity cost) to avoid a transitional rate of profit which is lower than the interest rate. Admittedly, the equilibrium rate of interest (i^*) will tend to be smaller than the general rate of profit (as in Figure 3.2), and this leaves a narrow area (to the southeast of the starting point) in which profit-margin-increasing profit-rate-decreasing innovations could take place without carrying the innovating capitalist below the interest rate and so inflicting (unacceptable) real or opportunity losses on him. At 'equilibrium', however, the gap between i^* and π^* is precisely what is needed to induce capitalists to take the risk of investing productively. Consequently, under competitive capitalism, profit-maximizing capitalists are condemned to technical innovations which yield a transitional rate of profit superior to the initial general rate. Okishio's (generalized) argument allows no exception. Shaikh's rescue operation has failed.

3.7 Away from perfect competition and profit maximization

This is not quite true, however, if one is willing to shift from competitive to oligopolistic capitalism. Fair enough, one must then drop the notion of a general rate of profit (in terms of which the whole FRP discussion has been conducted). But room can then be made for a fall in the (equilibrium) average rate of profit. This can be seen as follows. First of all, introducing a profit-margin-increasing profit-rate-decreasing innovation may here be preferable to expanding production with the current technique, because oligopolists have to face the constraint of a limited demand, and increasing their output may 'spoil the market'.[39] Secondly, one can also see that such technical change may be better than investing elsewhere in the economy, if one thinks of an oligopolistic economy as a hierarchy of industries with entrance barriers of different 'heights' and, correspondingly, with different 'equilibrium' rates of profit deviating upward from the equilibrium interest rate. In such a situation, a particular oligopolist may well be prevented (by the 'barriers') from investing in an industry with a higher rate of profit. And the rate of profit which he can get by investing at a lower transitional rate (but a higher profit margin) in his own industry, may well be higher than the rate of return available in less well-protected industries or on financial markets, since the gap between the interest rate and the initial rate of profit in the industry is generally much wider here than in the competitive case (Figure 3.2). In the oligopolistic case, therefore, a cost-reducing innovation which leads to a lower transitional rate of profit in one industry may well be viable. Furthermore, since the oligopolistic scenario does not require prices to be lowered in the innovating industry, a lower rate of profit in one industry will often unambiguously mean a lower average rate of profit. The shift to oligopoly not only makes Shaikh's argument more plausible; it also makes it complete. Thus if one is prepared to move sufficiently far away from the ideal competitive world which is generally taken for granted in the discussion, some room can be made for the possibility (*just* the possibility) of a fall in the average (*not* the general) rate of profit, with a constant real wage and profit-maximization as the only criterion in the choice of techniques.

In addition, one may want to argue, the capitalist choice of techniques need not be profit-maximizing, and this opens up further possibilities for a fall in the (general or average) rate of profit, compatible with a constant real wage. Firstly and most obviously, the capitalist choice of techniques may fail to be profit-maximizing because of the capitalists' mistakes. They adopt a new technique because they think it will enable them to make bigger profits, but for some reason it does not. If such mistakes are to be more than random events, there must be reasons why they should occur systematically. One such reason could be the acceleration of technical progress, which may shorten the economic life of new investment in a way which was not expected when the investment was decided upon. It seems unlikely, however, that capitalists would remain unable, for more than a short period, to anticipate the rate of technical progress and so to prevent such systematic mistakes.[40]

Secondly, one can imagine a competitive 'capitalist' system in which profit-maximization governs the formation of prices and the allocation of factors, but not the choice of techniques, which is performed by some central authority according to a principle of productivity-maximization. Now, whereas all profit-increasing innovations are productivity-increasing, the reverse is not true: if the real wage is low, there may be productivity-increasing or labour-time-reducing, innovations (of a capital-using, labour-saving kind) which are not profit-increasing, because the reduced *cost* of living labour they involve cannot compensate for the increased *cost* in dead labour (on which a rate of profit has to be paid). In such a 'Lange-type' or 'market-socialist' economy, therefore, technical change may clearly lead to a fall in the transitional and in the general rate of profit.[41]

Thirdly, and most importantly, capitalists may knowingly (unlike case 1) and freely (unlike case 2) introduce a technology which lowers their profits at current prices, if they believe that such a technology makes them more immune to the threat of workers' resistance. A highly capital-intensive technology, which considerably reduces the level of skill required on the part of the labour involved, for instance, may well be introduced, even if, at current wages and prices, it yields lower profits. The promise that the heavy weight of the reserve army of the unemployed will secure the compliance and moderate the wage claims of unskilled workers, may seem worth the sacrifice of higher profits in the short terms.[42]

These three qualifications, like the previous remark about oligopoly, are meant to stress the dependence of Okishio-type objections on two of their crucial premises: profit maximization and perfect competition. When either of these assumptions is relaxed, a fall in the (general or average) rate of profit, without a rise in the real wage, can no longer be excluded on *a priori* grounds. But the claim that there is anything like a *systematic* tendency for such a fall to occur gains no support from this fact.

3.8 Three concluding remarks

Let me conclude this sketchy rational reconstruction of a long debate, with three brief remarks. First of all, the discussion on the '*law* of the falling rate of profit' – our propositions (i) and (ii) – can very roughly be divided into three stages. What one could perhaps call the Grossmann stage of the discussion takes it for granted that a fall in the general rate of profit due to a rise in the organic composition is both possible and actually taking place, and focuses on the question of whether it constitutes a necessary feature of capitalism. What one could perhaps call the Mandel stage of the discussion admits that there may be no good grounds for asserting the necessity of a fall in the rate of profit due to a rising organic composition. However, it still takes the possibility of this fall for granted, and focuses on whether or not it has actually taken place. Finally, what one could call the Shaikh stage of the discussion admits that there may be no good grounds for asserting either the necessity or the reality of a fall in the rate of profit caused by a rise in the organic composition, and it concentrates on the question of whether or not such a fall is possible. This shift in the focus of the discussion is clearly of a degenerative kind. By using the latter expression, I do not mean that the quality of the discussion has fallen: on the contrary, arguments have rather tended to become increasingly subtle, rigorous and sophisticated. What makes the shift 'degenerative' is rather that the discussion starts with a powerful claim (the capitalist necessity of a tendency for the rate of profit to fall because of a rising organic composition), which is potentially useful for explanatory, predictive and even practical purposes. But it ends up with a much weaker claim (the capitalist possibility of such a tendency), which, even if it can be successfully established, is of very little (and purely negative) interest in an attempt to explain or to predict, to shape or to smash, capitalist realities.

My second concluding remark concerns the importance of theoretical debate in forging the spectacles through which empirical reality is perceived. At the Grossmann stage of the discussion, it was the critics of the theory who came up with empirical data about profit rates and capital coefficients, while the proponents of the theory dismissed them as illusory appearances which could not shake their confidence in a theoretically grounded *necessity*. At the Shaikh stage of the discussion, the tables have turned. It is now the proponents of (whatever is left of) the theory who have to plead that empirical data are relevant, while its critics dismiss them as mere appearances which could not affect their confidence in a theoretically grounded impossibility. If profit-maximization and perfect competition can be safely assumed, then, they say, whatever the empirical evidence at the aggregate level, one can be certain that a fall in the equilibrium rate of profit must be attributed to a rise in the real wage.[43]

Even if the equilibrium rate of profit falls regularly as the organic composition rises, for instance, while the rate of exploitation remains constant, one can be *sure* (under the microeconomic conditions mentioned) that the fall in the rate of profit is due to a rise in the real wage (which is reflected in the fact that the rate of exploitation failed to rise) and that it occurred *in spite of* the technical changes which took place (and whose impact is reflected in the rise of the organic composition and in the fact that the rate of exploitation failed to fall). However, in so far as the qualifications about oligopoly and non-profit-maximizing choice of technique are relevant, a somewhat more lenient look at the data is required.

Finally, the persistent favour which the falling-rate-of-profit theory of crises (and breakdown) has enjoyed in the Marxist scientific community also has 'extrascientific' reasons: by asserting that crises (and breakdown) are objectively bound to occur even in the absence of any increase in the real wage, the theory unambiguously clears the working class of the responsibility for generating the 'fundamental problems' of the capitalist system. Therefore, as 'bad news' accumulates about the soundness of the theory, the conflict, between what one ought to believe and what one would like to believe, between 'scientific' and 'extrascientific' considerations, may become increasingly acute. The more vulnerable the community feels, the more likely 'extrascientific' considerations are to prevail. The more self-confident it feels, on the other hand, the more able it becomes to give way to 'scientific' considerations – and to stomach the truth. If contemporary Marxist economics is in the latter position, rather than in the former, then calling this rational reconstruction an *obituary* should turn out to be more than just wishful thinking.

Notes

1 The point of these oversimplifying assumptions is that they enable us to speak in scalar terms rather than in terms of vectors and matrices. The disadvantage is that we shall be forced to conceive of technological changes as just variations in the proportions of one kind of means of production and one kind of labour-power needed for the production of the same commodities I and II. But the reasoning can easily be extended to more realistic situations.

2 In order to facilitate further reference, crucial propositions will be isolated and numbered. The letter which precedes the number indicates whether the proposition is a definition (D), an assumption (A) or a theorem (T). No proofs will be given for the theorems, but only the numbers of the propositions from which they follow.

3 For a discussion of the conditions under which the concept of value makes sense, see e.g. Morishima (1973: chapter 14), Steedman (1977: chapters 6–8, 10–13), Armstrong et al (1978). And for a discussion of the conditions under which the (simplest) law of value holds, see e.g. Morishima (1973: chapter 6). The behaviour of the equilibrium rate of

profit under less restrictive conditions is discussed e.g. by Armstrong (1975: 8–10) and Steedman (1977: 129–32).

4 Marx's (1867: 641) tricky definition of the OCK is familiar enough. For a recent discussion, see e.g. Fine and Harris (1979: 59–61). The VCK-interpretation is the textbook one (with sometimes a $V/(C + V)$ variant): see e.g. Sweezy (1942: 46), Mandel (1964: 49). The RDL interpretation (with sometimes a C/N or $C/(NT)$ variant), already used by Moszkowska (1935: 52) or Okishio (1961: 87) has subsequently become increasingly popular: see e.g. Okishio (1972: 3–4), Cogoy (1973: 56–8), Hodgson (1974: 80–1), Wright (1975: 13), Shaikh (1978a: 233), Robinson (1978: 6).

5 The *textbook variant* is the one Marx clearly uses in his most explicit formulation of the theory (1894: 221–4). In various formulations, it also appears e.g. in Sweezy (1942: 96–7), Robinson (1942: 35–6), Meek (1960: 129–30), Mandel (1962: I, 210–15), Salama and Valier (1973: 108–13), Bullock and Yaffe (1975: 19–20), Gamble and Walton (1976: 129–30), Gouverneur (1978: 168–70), etc. That Marx had the *modern variant* of the theory in mind is defended e.g. by Rosdolsky (1956: 209–15) and Bader et al. (1975: 398–99). Passages particularly favourable to this interpretation are Marx (1858: 635–6, 643, 653) and Marx (1894: 223, 226). The underlying reasoning is present in Rosdolsky (1956), Dickinson (1957), Meek (1960), Okishio (1961). It received its definitive, most elegant formulation from Okishio (1972) and has since tended to become standard: see e.g. Glyn (1972: 100–1), Purdy (1973: 17–20), Hodgson (1974: 80–2), Himmelweit (1974: 2), Holländer (1974: 113–14), Itoh (1975: 6), Wright (1975: 13–16), Bader et al. (1975: 401–5), Shaikh (1978a: 233; 1978b: 239), etc.

6 Dotted variables are here used to represent rates of growth (*not* derivatives): for example, $\dot{K}$ is short for $(dk/dt)/K$, not for dK/dt. Remember that the growth rate of a product is the sum of the growth rates of its factors: for example $(\dot{N T}) = \dot{N} + \dot{T}$.

7 This kind of argument is most explicitly defended by Yaffe (1972: 21). See also Sensat (1979: 143–4).

8 A similar view is adopted e.g. by Lange (1973: 157), Sweezy (1973: 45–6, 49), Hodgson (1974: 60–2), Wright (1975: 17–18), etc.

9 However, there have been attempts at short-circuiting the argument by skipping the TCK intermediary and dealing straight away with the necessity of a rising VCK. For instance, Bullock and Yaffe (1975: 18–19) and, in a more sophisticated way, Bader et al. (1975: 420–59) claim to derive the rise in the VCK from the concept of capital itself, defined as self-expanding value. Their argument runs roughly as follows: first, with a given labour force (N) and a given length of the working day (T), the amount of living labour employed is necessarily limited. As a consequence, with a fixed rate of turnover of variable capital (t_v), the value of the stock of variable capital can only decrease, as productivity improves and depresses its unit value (λ_{LP}). This implies that, if (constant plus variable) capital is to grow in value terms, there is only one way in which it can do so: through an increase in constant capital (dead labour) which more than offsets the fall in variable capital (the value of living labour). Hence the logical necessity of a rising VCK. This provides a good example of how heavy assumptions can be quietly smuggled in, in the guise of innocent-looking definitions.

10 This assumption is discussed e.g. by Glyn (1972: 95), Morishima (1973: 34–5), Shaikh (1978b: 250–1). It may gain some plausibility from the fact that any reduction in the value of the means of production also reduces the value of the means of subsistence (by reducing the amount of dead labour their production requires), not the other way round.

11 The possibility of such changes was clearly allowed for by Marx (1867: 185, 534–6).

12 This is the old 'cheapening of the elements of constant capital' countertendency, mentioned by Marx (1867: 651–2; 1894: 245–6) and discussed e.g. by Mandel (1962: I, 213–14), Hodgson (1974: 64–5), Hussain (1977: 447–9), Shaikh (1978a: 234).

13 The above formulation is indirectly suggested by Lebowitz (1976: 252–3). Arguments of a

similar type are presented by Glyn (1972: 95–8) and Stamatis (1976a: 80; 1976b: 106–7). Alternatively but (nearly) equivalently, the necessity of a rise in the RDL (or, as we shall see, of a fall in the maximum rate of profit) can also be derived from the necessity of mechanization, defined as technical progress which increases the amount of machinery per unit of output (not only per man) without decreasing the amount of other material inputs per unit (see e.g. Purdy 1973: 19; Shaikh 1978b: 239–40). Mechanization, which corresponds to a TCK growing faster than average productivity, is a slightly stronger condition than T24.

14 See e.g. Glyn and Sutcliffe (1972), Boddy and Crotty (1975) or Roemer (1978). The primary emphasis, both in a secular and in a cyclical perspective, is usually on the increase in the real wage, interpreted either as an increase in the 'historical subsistence level' or as deviation from it due to the growth of working-class power. Occasionally, the role of a decrease in the intensity of labour is also stressed: see e.g. Crotty and Rapping (1978: 463–4), Weisskopf (1978: 248).

15 See Ricardo (1817: 71–4). This type of account is occasionally revived, for instance with an emphasis on the growing cost of distribution and advertising (Shibata 1939: 55) or on the exhaustion of the world's natural resources (Steedman 1977: 129).

16 Put differently, a constant rate of exploitation can only be assumed if hourly real wages (B/T) *grow* at the same rate as productivity $(1/\lambda_{II})$. (See e.g. Sweezy 1942: 100–2, Robinson 1942: 36, Samuelson 1957: 892.)

17 Variants of this assumption are discussed by Sweezy (1942: 102) and by Stamatis (1976a: 106–7; 1976b: 109–10).

18 This 'most defensible' line of argument is repeatedly used (not always very clearly) by Marx himself (see e.g. 1858: 335–6, 340, 389; 1867: 444–5; 1894: 257–8). Attempts at rephrasing it more satisfactorily can be found e.g. in Meek (1960: 133–5), Mandel (1962: I, 212–13; 1964: 49–50), Mattick (1969: 62–3), Bader et al. (1975: 400–1), Bullock and Yaffe (1975: 20), Lebowitz (1976: 242–3). The decisive objection (that e can anyway rise without limits) is clearly stated e.g. by Robinson (1942: 38–40), Glyn (1972: 100) and Hodgson (1974: 60–1). It is quite true, as is sometimes retorted (e.g. by Mandel 1964: 50 or Mattick 1969: 63), that the necessary labour time (v) will never be equal to 0 (nor, therefore, e equal to infinity). But will the value stock of constant capital (C) (and therefore VCK) ever be equal to infinity?

19 The central role of this tautology (in the modern variant) is clearly emphasized, e.g. by Okishio (1961: 89, 1972: 5), Glyn (1972: 100–1), Himmelweit (1974: 2), etc.

20 Contrary to what is often implicitly assumed (e.g. by Okishio 1961: 89; Hodgson 1974: 82, Itoh 1975: 6; Shaikh 1978a: 233, 1978b: 240). This point (that an actual fall in the maximum rate of profit does not imply an eventual fall in the equilibrium rate) is also made, e.g. by Holländer (1974: 114), Stamatis (1976a: 107–9; 1976b: 113), Steedman (1977: 126–7), etc.

21 A particular specification of this condition corresponds to the assumption that, as time tends towards infinity, the RDL tends towards infinity. Under this stronger assumption, suggested e.g. by Steedman (1977: 127) or Sensat (1979: 130) and claimed by Armstrong et al. (1978: 25) to be generally assumed in the discussion, the eventual fall in the equilibrium rate of profit (T47) can be derived *whatever* the initial rate of profit. One serious difficulty with such an assumption is that it can be shown (e.g. Stamatis 1976a: 127–9) that, with NT constant, π_{Max} can only tend towards 0 if productivity in industry I $(1/\lambda_I)$ stops growing. Otherwise, it has a strictly positive lower limit equal to $-\dot{\lambda}_I$.

22 Dissatisfaction is sometimes expressed with this reformulation, on the grounds that Marx meant more than an eventual fall (see e.g. Stamatis 1976b: 113; 1977: 8–9) and that claiming an eventual fall is empirically vacuous, as it is compatible with an actual rise for any finite length of time, however long (see e.g. Stamatis 1976a: 108–10). The answer, I suppose, is that it is better to be revisionist and vacuous than wrong.

23 A sophisticated discussion of empirical data is provided by Weisskopf (1979).

24 Yaffe (1973: 50, 57) and Fine and Harris (1976a: 101) provide typical examples of this kind of strategy.

25 It may be argued, for instance, that the rate of profit is prevented from falling by the spreading of capitalism into non-capitalist areas or by an increase in state intervention.

26 See, typically, Mattick (1969: 61), Cogoy (1972: 407–8; 1973: 54–5, 61–2), Kay (1976: 73–4), Holloway and Picciotto (1977: 91). Since it is unanimously recognized that the 'countertendencies' cannot just be dismissed as exogenous with respect to the capitalist system (see e.g. Rosdolsky 1956: 209–13; 1968: 467–72; Cogoy 1973: 56–9), it is hard to see how this third kind of strategy can avoid the following dilemma. Either a symmetric reasoning applies to the countertendencies, and then one ends up with a 'law of the tendency for the rate of profit to fall and the tendency for counteracting influences to operate' (see e.g. Fine and Harris 1976a: 162–3; 1979: 63–4) – the remaining difference from the defeatist position being purely verbal. Or one is left with a stiff and strong but empirically vacuous claim about what is 'fundamental' in capitalism – a nice example of how political economy can degenerate into full-time theory immunization.

27 This defeatist position has had a growing number of supporters since Moszkowska (1929: 71–2, 83–4, 118) and Sweezy (1942: 102). An 'epistemological' rationalization for it – the 'law of tendency' is 'just one possibility in the Discourse of Capital' – has recently been offered by Cutler et al. (1977: 160–5). Attempts at periodizing capitalism in terms of whether the 'tendency' is operative or not (e.g. Wright 1975: 5–6; Stamatis 1976a: 129–35 and 1977: 287–90) must presuppose a similar position.

28 See e.g. Marx (1894: 268) and, more explicitly, Cogoy (1973: 60), Fine and Harris (1976b: 94, 110–11). A critique of this 'functionalist' type of argument is given by Itoh (1975: 10, 1978: 3).

29 See e.g. Mattick (1969: 70–1), Yaffe (1972: 30), Bullock and Yaffe (1975: 22), who also mention other ways in which crises perform a 'curative function'. But, as convincingly argued by Glyn (1972: 101–2), only those which will affect productivity are relevant to the fall in the equilibrium rate of profit.

30 This kind of argument seems to be put forward by Marx (1894: 251–2, 268) and also by Mattick (1969: 66–8, 75–9), Cogoy (1973: 64), Gamble and Walton (1976: 131–2), Shaikh (1978a: 231).

31 For instance, Shaikh (1978a: 237).

32 The point is clearly made e.g. by Robinson (1942: 85) and Berger (1979: 8).

33 It is often said that an emphasis on available (rather than expected) profits is the mark of a Marxian (rather than Keynesian) approach. See e.g. Robinson (1942: 29, 50–1, etc.), Mattick (1969: 21, 54–5), Yaffe (1972: 42), Itoh (1975: 10), Shaikh (1978a: 230), etc.

34 The connection between the theory of the falling rate of profit and crisis theory is challenged e.g. by Robinson (1948: 114), Itoh (1978: 13) and, with a specific reference to the long-run character of the former, by Sweezy (1942: 148), Sowell (1967: 64), Sherman (1967: 492), Berger (1979: 8).

35 The first formulation of the argument (in the particular case in which there is only one kind of product) is due to Tugan-Baranowsky (1901: 212–15). A more general formulation is given by Bortkiewicz (1907: 454–70). The argument then sporadically reappears but is hardly noticed: see e.g. Moszkowska (1929: 77–80, 105–7; 1935: 46–9), Shibata (1934: 65–71; 1939: 50–2, 56–61), Samuelson (1957: 892–5; 1972: 54–6), Okishio (1961: 91–9). But it is only in the mid-seventies that it really entered the Marxist discussion. See e.g. Glyn (1973: 104–7), Holländer (1974: 123–4), Himmelweit (1974: 2–5), Nutzinger and Wolfstetter (1974: 171–2), etc. The most comprehensive and rigorous formulation of the essential mathematical results is Roemer (1977). See also Roemer (1979) for a further generalization.

36 This valid point is what misled many Marxists into believing that Okishio-type argu-

ments were of no relevance to Marx's theory of the falling rate of profit. See especially Sweezy (1942: 104–5n).
37 Formal proofs of this proposition can be found e.g. in Okishio (1961: 98–9), Glyn (1973: 106–7), Roemer (1977: 417–18).
38 See Shaikh (1978b: 242–5). Generalizations of Okishio's theorem to the case of fixed capital and joint production are presented and proved by Roemer (1979: 11–22).
39 See Armstrong and Glyn (1979).
40 See Persky and Alberro (1978), discussed in Roemer (1979).
41 See e.g. Shibata (1939: 58–60), Roemer (1977: 411–14).
42 See e.g. Roemer (1978: 162–5), Sensat (1979: 152–3).
43 Similar formulation can be found, not always with the necessary emphasis on the 'if', in Bortkiewicz (1907: 469), Shibata (1934: 71–4; 1939: 60–1), Okishio (1961: 96), Himmelweit (1974: 6), Nutzinger and Wolfstetter (1974: 171–2), Roemer (1977: 415), etc.

References

Armstrong, Philip. 1975. 'Accumulation of capital, the rate of profit, and crisis', *CSE Bulletin* 11, 1–17.
Armstrong, Philip, and Andrew Glyn. 1979. 'The law of the falling rate of profit and oligopoly – a comment on Shaikh', *Cambridge Journal of Economics* 4, 69–70.
Armstrong, Philip, Andrew Glyn and John Harrison. 1978. 'In defence of value', *Capital and Class* 5, 1–31.
Bader, Veit-Michael, Johannes Berger, Heiner et al. 1975. *Krise un Kapitalismus bei Marx*, 2 vols. Frankfurt: EVA.
Berger, Johannes. 1979. 'Der Grundgedanke der Marxschen Krisen theorie', *Das Argument* 35.
Boddy, Raford and James Crotty. 1975. 'Class conflict and macro-policy: the political business cycle', *Review of Radical Political Economics* 7, 1–19.
Bortkiewicz, Ladislaus von. 1907. 'Wertrechnung und Preisrechnung im Marxschen System', *Archiv fur Sozialwissenschaft und Sozialpolitik* 235, 445–88.
Bullock, Paul and David Yaffe. 1975. 'Inflation, the crisis and the post-war boom', *Revolutionary Communist* 3–4, 5–45.
Cogoy, Mario. 1972. 'Les Théories néo-marxistes. Marx et l'accumulation du capital', *Les Temps Modernes* 9, 396–427.
Cogoy, Mario. 1973. 'The fall of the rate of profit and the theory of accumulation', *CSE Bulletin* 8, 52–67.
Crotty, James and L. A. Rapping. 1978. 'Class struggle, macropolicy and the business cycle', in R. C. Edwards, M. Reich and T. E. Weisskopf, eds., *The Capitalist System*, Englewood Cliffs: Prentice-Hall, 461–9.
Cutler, Antony, Barry Hindess, Paul Hirst and Athar Hussain. 1977. *Marx's Capital and Capitalism Today*, vol. 1, London: Routledge.
Dickinson, H. D. 1957. 'The falling rate of profit in Marxian economics', *Review of Economic Studies* 24, 120–30.
Dobb, Maurice. 1937. *Political Economy and Capitalism*, London: Routledge, 1973.
  1973. *Theories of Value and Distribution*, Cambridge: Cambridge University Press.
Fine, Ben and Lawrence Harris. 1976a. 'State expenditure in advanced capitalism. A reply', *New Left Review* 98, 97–112.

1976b. 'Controversial issues in Marxist economic theory', in R. Miliband and P. Saville eds., *Socialist Register*, London: Merlin Press, 141–78.

1979. *Rereading Capital*, London: Macmillan.

Gamble, Andrew and Paul Walton. 1977. *Capitalism in Crisis*, Atlantic Highlands: Humanities Press.

Glyn, Andrew. 1972. 'Capitalist crisis and organic composition', *CSE Bulletin* 4, 93–103.

1973. 'Productivity, organic composition and the falling rate of profit', *CSE Bulletin* 6, 103–7.

Glyn, Andrew and Bob Sutcliffe. 1972. *Capitalism in Crisis*, New York: Pantheon Books.

Gouverneur, Jacques. 1978. *Eléments d'économie politique marxiste*, Brussels: Contradictions.

Grossmann, Henryk (1929). *Das Akkumulations- und Zusammenbruchsgesetz des kapitalistischen Systems*, Frankfurt, 1970.

Himmelweit, Susan. 1974. 'The continuing saga of the falling rate of profit. A reply to Mario Cogoy', *CSE Bulletin* 9, 1–6.

Hodgson, Geoffrey. 1974. 'The theory of the falling rate of profit', *New Left Review* 85, 55–82.

Holländer, Heinz. 1974. 'Das Gesetz des tendenziellen Falls der Profitrate. Marxens Begründung und ihre Implikationen', *Mehrwert* 6, 105–31.

Holloway, John and Sol Piccioto. 1977. 'Capital, crisis and the state', *Capital and Class* 2, 76–101.

Hussain, Athar. 1977. 'Crises and tendencies of capitalism', *Economy and Society* 6, 436–60.

Itoh, Makato. 1975. 'The formation of Marx's Theory of Crisis', *CSE Bulletin* 10, 1–19.

1978. 'The inflational crisis of world capitalism', *Capital and Class* 4, 1–10.

Kay, Geoffrey. 1976. 'The falling rate of profit, unemployment and crisis', *Critique* 6, 55–75.

Lange, Oscar. 1935. 'Marxian economics and modern economic theory', in D. Horowitz, ed., *Marx and Modern Economics*, New York: Monthly Review Press, 1968, 68–87.

Lebowitz, Michael A. 1976. 'Marx's falling rate of profit: a dialectical view', *Canadian Journal of Economics* 9, 232–54.

Mandel, Ernest. 1962. *Traité d'économie marxiste*, 4 vols., Paris: UGE

1964. *An Introduction to Marxist Economic Theory*, New York: Pathfinder Press.

Marx, Karl. 1858. *Grundrisse der Kritik der politischen Oekonomie*, Berlin: Dietz, 1954.

1867. *Das Kapital*, vol. 1, Berlin: Dietz, 1962.

1894. *Das Kapital*, vol. 3, Berlin: Dietz, 1964.

Mattick, Paul. 1969. *Marx and Keynes*, Boston: Porter Sargent.

Meek, Ronald L. 1960. 'The falling rate of profit', in *Economics and Ideology and other Essays*, London: Chapman and Hall, 1967, 129–42.

Morishima, Michio. 1973. *Marx's Economics*, Cambridge: Cambridge University Press.

Moszkowska, Nathalie. 1929. *Das Marxsche System. Ein Beitrag zu dessen Ausbau*, Berlin: Englemann.

68   Crisis theory shattered

1935. *Zur Kritik moderner Krisentheorien*, Prague: Kacha.
Nutzinger, H. G. and E. Wolfstetter (eds.). 1974. *Die Marxsche Theorie und ihre Kritik*, 2 vols., Frankfurt and New York.
Okishio, Nobuo. 1961. 'Technical change and the rate of profit', *Kobe University Economic Review* 7, 85–99.
1972. 'A formal proof of Marx's two theorems', *Kobe University Economic Review* 18, 1–6.
Persky, Joseph and J. Alberro. 1978. 'Technical innovation and the dynamics of the profit rate', Chicago: University of Illinois.
Purdy, David. 1973. 'The theory of the permanent arms economy – a critique and an alternative', *CSE Bulletin* 5, 12–33.
Ricardo, David. 1817. *On the Principles of Political Economy and Taxation*, London: Dent and Sons, 1977.
Robinson, Joan. 1942. *An Essay on Marxian Economics*, New York: St Martin's Press, 1976.
1948. 'Marx and Keynes', in D. Horowitz, ed., *Marx and Modern Economics*, New York: Monthly Review Press, 1968, 103–16.
1978. 'The organic composition of capital', *Kyklos* 31, 5–20.
Roemer, John E. 1977. 'Technical change and the tendency of the rate of profit to fall', *Journal of Economic Theory* 16, 403–24.
1978. 'The effect of technological change on the real wage and Marx's falling rate of profit', *Australian Economic Papers*, 152–66.
1979. 'Continuing controversy on the falling rate of profit: fixed capital and other issues', *Cambridge Journal of Economics* 3, 379–98.
Rosdolsky, Roman. 1956. 'Zur neueren Kritik des Marxschen Gesetzes der fallenden Profitrate', *Kyklos* 9, 208–26.
1968. *Zur Entstehungsgeschichte des Marxschen 'Kapital'*. Frankfurt: EVA.
Salama, Pierre and Jacques Valier. 1973. *Une introduction à l'économie politique*, Paris: Maspero.
Samuelson, Paul A. 1957. 'Wages and interests: a modern dissection of Marxian economic models', *American Economic Review* 47, 884–912.
1972. 'The economics of Marx: an ecumenical reply', *Journal of Economic Literature* 10, 51–7.
Sensat, Julius. 1979. *Habermas and Marxism*. Beverley Hills (Cal.): Sage Publications.
Shaikh, Anwar. 1978a. 'An introduction to the history of crisis theories', *U.S. Capitalism in Crisis*, New York: URPE, 219–41.
1978b. 'Political economy and capitalism: notes on Dobb's theory of crises', *Cambridge Journal of Economics* 2, 233–51.
Sherman, Howard J. 1967. 'Marx and the business cycle', *Science and Society* 31, 486–504.
Shibata, Kei. 1934. 'On the law of decline in the rate of profit', *Kyoto University Economic Review* 9 (1), 61–75.
1939. 'On the general profit rate', *Kyoto University Economic Review* 14 (1), 31–66.
Sowell, Thomas. 1967. 'Marx's Capital after one hundred years', *Canadian Journal of Economics* 33, 50–74.
Stamatis, Georgios. 1976a. 'Zum Marxschen Gesetz vom tendenziellen Fall der allgemeinen Profitrate', *Mehrwert* 10, 70–138.

68   Crisis theory shattered

1976b. 'Zum Beweis der Konsistenz des Marxschen Gesetzes vom tendenziellen Fall der allgemeinen Profitrate', *Prokla* 25, 105–16.

1977. *Die spezifisch kapitalistischen Produktionsmethoden und der tendenzielle Fall der allgemeinen Profitrate bei Karl Marx*, Berlin: Mehrwert.

Steedman, Ian. 1977. *Marx after Sraffa*, London: New Left Books.

Sweezy, Paul M. 1942. *The Theory of Capitalist Development*, New York: Monthly Review Press, 1970.

1973. 'Some problems in the theory of capital accumulation', *Monthly Review* 26 (5), 38–56.

Tugan-Baranowsky, Michael. 1901. *Theorie und Geschichte der Handelskrisen in England*, Jena: Fischer.

Weisskopf, Thomas E. 1978. 'Marxist perspectives on cyclical crises', in *U.S. Capitalism in Crisis*, New York: URPE, 241–60.

1979. 'Marxist crisis theory and the rate of profit in the postwar U.S. economy', *Cambridge Journal of Economics* 3, 341–78.

Wright, Erik O. 1975. 'Alternative perspectives in Marxist theory of accumulation and crisis', *Insurgent Sociologist* 6 (1), 5–39.

Yaffe, David S. 1972. 'The Marxian theory of crisis. Capital and the state', *CSE Bulletin* 4, 5–58.

1973. 'The crisis of profitability: a critique of the Glyn-Sutcliffe Thesis', *New Left Review* 80, 45–62.

4. Why Marxist economics needs microfoundations

In the previous chapter, I attempted a rational reconstruction of the falling-rate-of-profit controversy which convincingly led, I thought, to the following conclusions. Under the assumptions usually made by those who took part in the controversy: (1) there is no necessity for the organic composition of capital to rise; (2) it is not possible, let alone necessary, that the rate of profit should fall as a result of a rise in the organic composition of capital; and (3) it is not possible, let alone necessary, for such a fall (if it were possible) to generate economic crises. These conclusions were challenged in a vigorous critical comment by Patrick Clawson (1983), not on the grounds that they do not follow from the assumptions, but rather on the grounds that the assumptions were not the right ones to make. More specifically, Clawson argued, I was wrong in assuming perfect competition, in abstracting from class struggle within the labour process and in taking the real wage rate to be constant. Moreover, he argued, this wrong choice of assumptions ultimately derives from a mistaken methodological stance which he labels *neoclassical Marxism*.

In the present chapter, I shall briefly reply to these charges. But my purpose is broader. I want to take this opportunity to review some additional literature which subsequently came to my attention and to tackle explicitly some general methodological issues whose relevance for contemporary Marxism reaches far beyond the falling-rate-of-profit controversy. Readers who are by now convinced that the latter is a dead horse may want to move right away to the third or even the fourth section of this chapter.

4.1 Perfect competition and prisoners' dilemmas

The assumptions I make, according to Clawson, 'correspond neither to Marx's theory nor to contemporary capitalist reality'. And so what? To start with, my purpose was neither to interpret Marx nor to describe contemporary capitalism, but merely to reconstruct a debate which has been taking place among Marxists for the last fifty years or so. And can anyone deny that the bulk of that debate has been conducted on those assumptions? Moreover, it can be argued I believe, that those who made these assumptions were right in doing so. For what justified this choice was in the main neither exegetical accuracy nor empirical relevance, but rather the fact that it enabled us to formulate the following strong and interesting 'even if' claim: *even without* monopolies (perfect competition) and *even without* class struggle within the labour process (no concern with intra-firm control) or about the wage level (constant real wage) the rate of profit is bound to fall and its fall is bound to generate crises.[1]

True, if this strong claim needs to be abandoned, it is worth examining what happens if one or more of the assumptions are relaxed. The most obvious candidate for relaxation – both given the degree to which it affects the strength of our claim and given Marx's 'law of concentration and centralization' – is the assumption of *perfect competition*. Giving it up means giving up the notion of a tendency towards equal profit rates in all sectors and hence the notion of a 'general rate of profit', in terms of which most of the discussion, from Marx onwards, has been conducted. But if this is the price to be paid for salvaging the theory, why not? Following Armstrong and Glyn (1980), I showed how dropping this assumption makes it invalid to say that a rise in the organic composition of capital cannot possibly lead to a fall in the (average) rate of profit.[2] But Clawson goes much further.

To start with, he claims that giving up perfect competition also invalidates my second impossibility claim, i.e. the claim that it is impossible for a fall in the rate of profit (due to a rise in the organic composition of capital) to generate crises. He seems to be arguing that crises may consist in overinvestment (and idle capacity) rather than in overproduction (and unsold inventories) and that the former (though not the latter) is made possible by dropping perfect competition, because the idling of capacity brought about by one firm going bust may then no longer be negligible. This argument is flawed. Both overproduction and overinvestment (even on a massive scale) can happen with, as well as without, perfect competition (as defined by atomicity, free entry and perfect information). The argument is also irrelevant. What is at issue is not the possibility of crises *tout court*, but the possibility of crises generated by a fall in the rate of profit which itself derives from a rise in the organic composition of capital. I presented and rejected three standard ways of conceiving the possibility (and necessity) of *such* crises (see section 3.5). Clawson makes no attempt to vindicate one of them nor to provide an alternative scenario.[3]

Dropping perfect competition, according to Clawson, also enables us to prove that the organic composition necessarily rises. His (sketch of an) argument involves two steps: (1) 'in a world of cut-throat competition among large firms' (as opposed to 'perfect competition'), each firm 'must accumulate in the hopes of beating the others with a better product or lower cost', and (2) 'rapid accumulation necessarily eventually leads to a rising organic composition of capital'. As far as the first step is concerned, it is easy enough to reply that the urge to accumulate and innovate (on pain of elimination) should be, if anything, much stronger in the case of ('cut-throat') perfect competition between small capitals than in situations which depart from this extreme case. As far as the second step is concerned I must begin by referring briefly to Jon Elster's (1982a) illuminating game-theoretical analysis of technical change in a situation of labour shortage. Contrary to Clawson's suggestion, the structure of such a situation, Elster argues, is not that of prisoners' dilemma, but what game theorists call a 'chicken' structure.[4] Consequently, what each capitalist is going to do is rather indeterminate. He may introduce a labour-saving bias in his technical innovations in the expectation that wages will rise. But if all act likewise, wages will not rise. If each of them realizes this, none of them will find it rational to introduce a labour-saving bias and all will refrain from it; and so on.[5] Of course, Elster's analysis is premised on the assumption that a single firm's demand has no significant impact on the going wage rate, in such a way that a labour-saving bias cannot be motivated by the hope of preventing wages from rising, but only by the expectation that they will rise. Although getting rid of perfect competition does not guarantee the falsity of this premise, there are certainly cases of 'less-than-perfect' competition (with little geographical and sectoral labour mobility) where it does not hold. It thus turns out that the 'law of concentration and centralization' does affect the argument, but in strengthening the link between accumulation and labour-saving bias, not (as Clawson suggests) in increasing the pressure towards accumulation. Even in the most favourable hypothesis (about the structure of the labour market and the rate of growth of the working population), however, what can be shown is only the necessity of a rise in the technical composition, not the necessity of a rise in the organic composition, let alone the necessity of a rise in the organic composition which is sufficient to bring down the rate of profit.

4.2 Profit-rate-maximization and Shaikh's scenario

Since dropping the assumption of perfect competition is not sufficient to establish such a necessity, let us now examine what follows when we relax the assumption that technical change is entirely governed by the capitalists' concern with their profit rates. In particular, it is worth conjecturing with Clawson that 'the rising use of machines is a key element in the class struggle waged by capitalists against workers'.[6] True, *in so far as* technical change is governed by such considerations, it is hard to deny that the technical composition of capital will tend to rise.[7] But from this nothing can be concluded, at least under perfect competition, as to the overall direction of changes in the technical composition. Further, whether under perfect competition or not, no necessary rise in the organic composition or fall in the rate of profit can be inferred either. All we can say, as I pointed out above (section 3.7), is that the influence of such considerations makes it *possible*, even under perfect competition and with a constant real wage, for the rate of profit to fall as a result of technical change.[8] Neither dropping perfect competition, nor giving up profit-rate maximization, therefore, can carry the argument beyond mere possibility.

Before turning to the third assumption, that of a constant real wage, I shall briefly reconsider Anwar Shaikh's (1980) related argument to the effect that taking Marx's conception of competition seriously makes it possible to envision a fall in the rate of profit as a result of a rise in the organic composition of capital (even with a constant real wage). Whatever may be suggested by his title and his terminology, the assumption which Shaikh drops is not that of perfect competition (as defined by the conditions on size, information and entry which are required for profit rates to converge across sectors), since he keeps using the concept of a general rate of profit. What he does challenge is the assumption that technical change is governed by profit-rate maximization. In his reply to some of the comments aroused by his earlier paper, he stresses the distinction between the maximization of the rate of profit (or the minimization of the 'cost of production'), which he calls the *optimality criterion*, and the maximization of the profit margin (or the minimization of the 'cost price'), which he calls the *competitive criterion*. He accuses his critics of being misled by neoclassical habits of thought into assuming that the choice of techniques is governed by the optimality criterion, not the (Marxian) competitive criterion. And while the optimality criterion does indeed prevent technical change from inducing a fall in the rate of profit (with a constant real wage), the competitive criterion does not.[9]

There are two major difficulties with this scenario, neither of which is disposed of by Shaikh's reply. Firstly, given his explicit acknowledgement that interest costs (and opportunity costs) need to be taken into account by the competitive criterion (Shaikh 1980: 78), the room it makes for admissible profit-rate-decreasing technical changes is very small indeed. The technique to be introduced must at the same time be profitable enough to lower the cost (including the interest cost), but not so profitable as to increase the innovator's transitional rate of profit. It must be capital-intensive enough to lower the latter, but not in such a way that it also raises the (inclusive) cost per unit. Even when there is a sizeable difference between the rate of interest and the general rate of profit, only a small proportion of potential capital-using labour-saving innovations will fulfil this condition.

Secondly, even when such innovations happen to be technically possible, it is by no means certain that capitalists will implement them. The point of introducing such techniques, Shaikh argues, is that it would enable the innovating capitalist to drive out his competitors (unless they follow suit) by dropping his prices in such a way that he will still be making profits (though at a rate which is lower than his transitional rate at current prices, itself lower than the initial general rate), while his competitors, due to a higher (inclusive) cost, will soon be making losses. However, even if fully successful, why should any capitalist be attracted by this type of innovation? In the short run, he will be producing and selling at a rate of profit dangerously close to the rate of interest. And in the longer run, after an exodus of capital out of his sector will have allowed him to raise prices in such a way as to earn again the general rate of profit,[10] the latter will be lower than it was (*ceteris paribus*) before the innovation. Why should any capitalist engage in such an unpromising course of action? The only suggestion Shaikh (1980: 81) comes up with is: because he fears that his competitors will do so before him. But since prospects are equally poor for each of the competitors, such a fear is hardly warranted nor therefore, I should think, likely.[11]

4.3 Constant real wages and the meaning of causal terms

A very different and, I believe, more puzzling set of issues comes up when, instead of challenging perfect competition or profit maximization, we challenge the assumption of a constant real wage rate. If we cannot establish the necessity of a fall in the rate of profit under the assumption that real wages are constant, perhaps we can still make the weaker claim that the rate of profit is bound to fall (as a result of technical change) under the assumption that real wages grow at the same pace as productivity, i.e. that the value of labour-power is constant. Note, first of all, that since we want to assert a theoretical necessity, empirical evidence on which assumption 'is more in tune with the history of capitalism' is not sufficient to justify the assumption we make on the evolution of real wages. Foundations for the constancy assumption could be found in the standard proposition that the reserve army of the unemployed exercises sufficient pressure to keep wages at the subsistence level. How could one justify the necessity of a rise in the real wage roughly parallel to the growth of productivity? One possibility is to claim that the 'historical and moral element' involved in the definition of a subsistence level has evolved in such a way as to prevent the *value* of labour power from falling, despite considerable decreases in the value of wage goods.[12] Alternatively, it is also possible to point out that, without a corresponding rise in the real wage, the productivity gains generated by technical changes could not be *realized*. The swelling of the flow of surplus value would be pointless, as the additional goods produced at an unchanged total cost would (in general) find no buyers.[13] However, while the first strategy is purely *ad hoc*, the second strategy merely points to a functional necessity, whose transformation into causal necessity requires further argument about the underlying mechanism (see below). In any case, even if it could be shown that real wages are bound to rise along with productivity, and hence that the rate of exploitation is bound to remain (roughly) constant, the necessity of a fall in the rate of profit would still be contingent upon the necessity of a rise in the organic composition of capital. And we have seen above that there is no conclusive argument for the latter necessity.

The interesting (and puzzling) question, however, is not whether assuming a rising real wage makes it necessary, but whether it makes it *possible* for the rate of profit to fall *because of* a rise in the organic composition. Chapter 3 presents an argument to the effect that, given perfect competition and profit maximization, this is *not* the case. True, the organic composition may rise while the rate of exploitation remains constant (due to an increase in the real wage), and this *entails*, under the usual conditions, that the rate of profit falls. But from Okishio's theorem and its generalizations we know that, under those conditions and whatever happens to the organic composition, *without* a rise in the real wage, the rate of profit cannot fall. And it seems therefore correct to say, in the situation envisioned, that the rate of profit falls *because* the real wage rises, not because the organic composition does so (see section 3.6 above). In other words, while it is perfectly accurate to say that, given a constant rate of exploitation, a rising organic composition *entails* a falling rate of profit (using a logical expression), it is incorrect to say that it can, let alone that it must, *lead to* such a fall (using a causal expression).

I can think of three objections to this conclusion. First of all, one may argue that it is perfectly legitimate to use such terms as 'because', 'influence', 'accounts for', etc. in a purely logical or arithmetical sense. One can say, for example, that given a constant rate of exploitation, the rate of profit fell *because* the organic composition rose *just in the sense that,* had the organic composition not risen, the rate of profit would not have fallen.[14] However, one must realize that it is then equally legitimate to say, given a constant rate of exploitation, that the organic composition rose *because* the rate of profit fell. If the latter statement does not sound acceptable, we can conclude that the 'because' we have in mind is truly causal, and it is therefore misleading to use it in order to refer to purely logical or arithmetical relations.

Secondly, even when it is clear that we are talking about causal relations – between the introduction of new technology and the evolution of the rate of profit in a subsequent period – we may still want to say that the rate of profit fell (with a constant rate of exploitation) *because* the organic composition of capital rose, even though we admit that the technical change to which this rise corresponds had a positive impact on the rate of profit. For we may only mean that, had another, less capital-intensive, innovation been introduced instead of the organic-composition-increasing one which was actually introduced, the rate of profit would not have fallen. This too, however, is a misleading formulation. Clearly, when assessing the causal influence of some (organic-composition-increasing) technical change, one must ask what would have happened if it had not taken place, and not what would have happened if some other, hypothetical, change had taken place instead.

Finally, even when there is no ambiguity about the causal nature of the claim nor about the baseline for counterfactual comparison, there may still be grounds for questioning the above conclusion. For if, under the constant-rate-of-exploitation assumption, technical change were viewed as a reaction to prior increases in the real wage, it would be perfectly clear that the rise in the organic composition (if there is one) is not the cause of the fall in the rate of profit, but rather a 'countertendency'. But it generally makes more empirical sense to suppose that the increase in real wages which enables the rate of exploitation to remain constant is rather the outcome of wage bargaining aiming at reaping from the capitalist part of the gains from a prior productivity rise.[15] Should one not say, in this case, that an organic-composition-increasing technical change can *cause*, through its impact on real wages, a fall in the rate of profit? If it were possible to establish that there is a causal necessity for the rate of exploitation to remain constant, in such a way that real wages 'automatically' rise when productivity increases, then it would indeed be correct to say that the rate of profit has fallen because of the technical change.[16] But if – as is far more plausible – a roughly constant rate of exploitation is rather the contingent outcome of the interaction of various factors, then the rise in the real wage must be viewed as having a dynamic of its own. It does not only depend on productivity, but also much more broadly, on the state of the struggle between social classes. Consequently, even if in the absence of the organic-composition-increasing technical change the rate of profit would not have fallen, it is misleading to say that the *cause* of this fall is the technical change, rather than the class struggle which followed it.

Given these three important qualifications, which I did not make explicit in chapter 3, it is possible to maintain the strong claim presented there: granted perfect competition and profit maximization, if we observe that the equilibrium rate of profit falls while the organic composition rises and the rate of exploitation remains constant, not only are we not allowed to infer that the equilibrium rate of profit falls *because* the organic composition rises, but we can be *sure* that its fall is *not* due to this rise but to a higher real wage (or, conceivably, to a shorter working day). Put differently (and somewhat more accurately), the locus of the events which have brought about this fall in the equilibrium rate of profit is not the process of implementation of technical change, but the process of bargaining over wages (and working hours).

Of course, in real-life situations, it is not possible to cling to the assumptions of perfect competition and exclusive concern with profits, and the strong claim which has just been recalled must be abandoned. Empirical evidence then becomes crucial again in order to tell whether a fall in the equilibrium rate of profit must be explained by organic-composition-increasing technical change or real-wage-rising class struggle. But the kind of macroeconomic evidence which is generally collected for this purpose is of precious little use in this context, even if it were perfectly reliable. Of course, if such evidence shows that the organic composition or the real wage has not risen over a particular period, it becomes impossible to claim that the fall in the equilibrium rate of profit (if any) is due to a rise in the organic composition or in the real wage, respectively. But in the (quite common) case in which the organic composition and the real wage both rise, no amount of macroeconomic data processing will tell us whether the fall in the equilibrium rate of profit is due to organic-composition-increasing technical changes, to real-wage-rising class struggle or to both. The capital-using-labour-saving technical change which shows in a rising organic composition may have been implemented despite a (consciously) lower transitional rate of profit, for example in order to endow capitalists with a better control of the labour process. But it may equally well have been introduced in order to (successfully) raise the transitional rate of profit in the face of actual or (rightly) expected rises in the real wage. Only microeconomic evidence on the process of technical change, in this case, can tell us which theory is correct.[17]

4.4 'Neoclassical Marxism' and the need for microfoundations

Having shown that giving up, whether jointly or separately, the three assumptions challenged by Clawson would not confer theoretical validity to the orthodox position he defends, it is still worth examining what he takes to be my most fundamental mistake, i.e., my commitment to what he calls 'neoclassical Marxism'. Some passages in his paper suggest a first and uninteresting interpretation of this general criticism, one which identifies (quite plausibly) 'neoclassical' and the assumption of perfect competition. He mentions, for example, that my approach is 'permeated with the perfect competition theory of the relation among capitalists' and accuses me of 'follow(ing) the neoclassicals in ignoring the law of concentration and centralization'. I think I have made clear above the reasons which justified the central role played by perfect competition in my argument. In no way do they imply that I, nor indeed any of the participants in the debate, am committed to the claim that contemporary capitalism is anything like perfectly competitive. If nothing else, my brief discussion of oligopolistic competition should have made this clear. This is not to deny that some members of the 'School' to which Clawson wants me to belong sometimes indulge in 'neoclassical Marxism' in this sense, nor indeed to deny the usefulness of such exercises for the sake of conceptual clarification.[18] But I do not rank them among the chief tasks ahead. And certainly I cannot see what, in my argument, would commit me to restricting to them the whole of Marxist economics.

However, the last paragraph of Clawson's paper suggests a different interpretation of his general criticism, which points to a genuine and important issue between us. 'Neoclassical Marxism' is then any (Marxist) approach 'which begins its analysis from the utility-maximizing individual rather than from the self-expansion of value.' The 'methodological foundation of this school', as proclaimed in his quote from Roemer, consists in 'deducing aggregate economic effects from the behavior of individual economic units'.[19] Note, first of all, that this sense of 'neoclassical' is much broader than the first one mentioned. It does not only cover perfect-competition general equilibrium theory but also, for example, Elster's and Clawson's own game-theoretical suggestions briefly discussed in section 4.1 above. And even Shaikh's attempt to vindicate the theory of the falling rate of profit, however vociferous against neoclassical Marxism in the narrow sense, must be viewed as a variety of neoclassical Marxism in this broader sense. Indeed, the most fascinating feature of Shaikh's attempt was precisely that the alternative foundation he proposed for the alleged tendency rested entirely on the rational behaviour of individual capitalists.

These remarks may suggest that 'neoclassical Marxism', in this second sense, is so broad that it is hard to imagine anything that would fall outside its scope. A clue as to what it leaves out is given by the contrast frequently made between *rational-man* (or individualistic) and *structural* (or systemic) explanations. This distinction needs to be made carefully, however, as it is by no means obvious that the two types of explanation are exclusive of each other.[20] By 'structural explanation', one may simply mean an explanation which refers to *structural constraints*, i.e. to social institutions, class relationships and other objective states of affairs which are imposed by past history as an inflexible framework for the actions of the agents involved. Structural explanations in this sense may well be rational-man explanations, as the agents' rational actions, for example the capitalists' efforts to maximize profits or avoid bankruptcy, can provide the mechanism through which economic phenomena are affected or generated by structural constraints. By 'structural explanation', on the other hand, one may also mean an explanation which refers to a *structural imperative*, i.e. to a 'demand' which stems 'from the system itself', say from the structure of the mode of production, and whose causal impact does not reduce to the aggregation of individual actions. It is this kind of structural explanation which Clawson seems to have in mind when he contrasts an analysis which starts 'from the self-expansion of value' with one which starts from the utility-maximizing individual.[21] And this kind of explanation, it must be conceded, is unambiguously rejected by 'neoclassical Marxism' in the second sense.

In order to discuss the latter (and thereby the rejection of such structural explanations), it is useful to see that the methodological principle which underlies it and which can be called *methodological rationalism* entails another, weaker principle, which can be expressed as follows. No explanation of B by A is acceptable unless one specifies the *mechanism* through which A generates B. Or, equivalently, no explanatory theory is acceptable unless it is provided with *microfoundations*. The discussion of 'neoclassical Marxism' can then conveniently be broken down into two steps. Firstly, does Marxist economics need microfoundations? Secondly, what kind of microfoundations (if any) does it need?

To a large extent, the first question has already been implicitly answered in my discussion of Clawson's specific criticisms.[22] To start with, an obvious *ad hominem* argument emerges from the first two sections above. In the process of fighting the no-necessity claims contained in my initial argument, Clawson soon and, I believe unavoidably, gets trapped in the business of providing alternative microfoundations (in terms of monopolistic competition and intrafirm conflict) for the (alleged) tendency for the rate of profit to fall, rather than calling into question the need for any kind of microfoundations. Much more powerful is the argument that emerges from the previous section. Only the explication of underlying mechanisms could provide us with the spectacles required to sort out the relevant causal structure, to identify the exact nature of the empirical evidence needed to test the theory and to avoid the empiricist fallacy of conflating arithmetic and causal relations. Put more generally, in any non-experimental discipline, the specification of the mechanisms through which variables may affect each other plays an essential role in selecting those relations which can be explanatory from those which cannot. Finally, the specification of microfoundations offers the only promising path towards theoretical integration. It is only by explicating the nature of the mechanisms which they presuppose that we can hope to fit a wide array of disconnected explanations and theories into a common framework.[23]

Even if, for one or more of the reasons sketched in the previous paragraph, we accept that Marxism needs microfoundations, we may still challenge the claim that these microfoundations need to be built around the rationality assumption, i.e. that Marxism needs to conform to methodological rationalism. Indeed, I believe that there are scores of Marxist explanations – for example of ideologies or state policies, of the forms taken by production relations or educational systems – which unambiguously transgress methodological rationalism. Though often problematic, such explanations can certainly not be written off on the ground that they are methodologically unsound.[24] None of them, however, belongs to the field usually ascribed to Marxist *economics*. And while I do not think that methodological rationalism is defensible in the case of Marxism as a whole, I believe it is in the case of Marxist economics, providing of course rationality is not restricted to perfect and objective rationality. This is not to deny that someone may think up non-rationalistic foundations. Perhaps one possibility is the natural-selection model developed by Alchian and others.[25] But my (empirical) claim is that only rationalistic microfoundations will be found suitable for a Marxist theory of capitalist (and socialist) economies. If people who accept the need for microfoundations challenge this claim, it is up to them to work out an alternative. I do not take much of a risk by predicting that they will have a hard time.

Clearly, if this two-step argument carries any weight, Marxist economics can only be sound if it accepts to be 'neoclassical' in the second (and rather misleading) sense in which Clawson uses the term. Contrary to what he asserts in the last sentence of his comment, however, its being 'neoclassical' (in this sense) does not lead Marxism to '"prove" that capitalism has no inherent tendency towards crisis'. And I would be very sorry if I had misled any other reader of chapter 3 into believing this. On the contrary, being 'neoclassical' in the sense of working out rationalistic microfoundations – along with Elster, Roemer and Steedman, but also Rowthorn, Glyn and even Shaikh – is an essential precondition if one is ever to provide a proof of any such a tendency, instead of comfortably begging the question.

Notes

1 In order to ward off objections on the part of the critics of 'unicausalism', it is important to emphasize that the main point of such a claim is *not* explanatory. When trying to *explain* some empirical phenomenon, e.g. the current economic crisis, it is obviously total nonsense to disregard what is assumed away in this claim. But when trying to *demonstrate the necessity* of a tendency, the more one can assume away, the better. However important the class struggle in explaining a particular fall in the rate of profit, for example, only a theory which does not rely on its uncertainties can hope to prove the *necessity* of a tendency for the rate of profit to fall.

2 While sticking to the other standard assumptions (see chapter 3, section 3.6). In a situation in which two production techniques, one of which is joint, are operated simultaneously, Salvadori (1981) has shown that one need not even give up perfect competition to make room for such a possibility. Even more than Shaikh's (1980), Salvadori's argument illustrates the Lakatosian notion of a degenerative research pro-

gramme: remarkably ingenious and sophisticated thinking in the service of a smaller and smaller point (from a necessity under very general conditions to a possibility under very special ones).

3 See chapter 3, section 3.5. A more genuine loophole in this impossibility claim has been pointed out to me by Alain Lipietz. As the rate of profit gradually falls (conceivably due to organic-composition-raising technical change) the capitalists (typically with the government's help) may suddenly decide that the time has come to cut into the workers' real wage in order to restore an acceptable level of profitability. The gap thus created between the supply and the demand of consumption goods is very likely to turn into a full-scale crisis of overproduction (see Lipietz 1980: 15–18, 22; 1981: 19). Of course, this scenario is excluded by the assumption that the real wage is constant at the subsistence level (and this is why I left it out). But whereas such an assumption makes sense as an 'even if' clause for the purpose of discussing the necessity or the possibility of a fall in the rate of profit, it can hardly be justified for the purpose of discussing the necessity or the possibility of crises. Notice also that what this scenario makes room for is a possibility (or a likelihood), not a necessity, and that the mechanism is of a 'Keynesian' kind (in the sense of section 3.5).

4 If one writes D for defection (here, no labour-saving bias) and C for cooperation (here, labour-saving bias) the difference between the prisoner's dilemma structure and the 'chicken' structure is brought out by the difference between the following two preference orderings (the first member of each pair represents the strategy chosen by the individual whose preference ordering is being considered and the second one, that chosen by all other individuals involved):

(1) (D,C) (C,C) (D,D) (C,D),
(2) (D,C) (C,C) (C,D) (D,D).

5 Elster (1978: 113–14). See also Elster (1982a: chapter 6).

6 Clawson (1983: 109). See also Lipietz (1980) and Elster (1982a: chapter 6) for forceful statements of the importance of this element.

7 Bleaney (1980: 71) mentions that such considerations do not invariably weigh in favour of mechanization, as the latter makes capitalists more vulnerable to absenteeism. But this is hardly more than a minor 'counter-tendency'.

8 More generally, as pointed out by Reati (1980: 512), as soon as a firm's choices are no longer determined by narrow profit-maximization, but rather by its managers' complex utility function (which is only possible, arguably, under less-than-perfect competition), a similar possibility exists.

9 See Shaikh's (1980: 77, 81–2) reply to Roemer (1979), Armstrong and Glyn (1980), Steedman (1980) and Nakatani (1980).

10 Nakatani (1980: 68) shows that, when profit rates are equal again, the innovating sector's prices will be higher than before the innovation took place.

11 If it can be salvaged at all, Shaikh's scenario must then become a variant of the systematic-mistake argument (see chapter 3, section 3.7). A more plausible variant of that argument has recently been suggested by Makoto Itoh (1980: 171). Technical change is typically introduced in a recession, when the cost of the means of production is more depressed than the cost of labour-power. This may lead capitalists to (irreversibly) introduce capital-using, labour-saving techniques which increase their transitional rates of profit at current prices but not at equilibrium prices.

12 See, for example, Mandel (1962: 180–4).

13 See Lipietz (1980: 15–16; 1981: 8). One might want to argue, along with Tugan-Baranowski, that 'underconsumption' (i.e. the lack of demand for wage goods) is never a sufficient condition for more than a disproportionality crisis. It is in principle always possible to shift demand from wage-goods sectors to capital-goods sectors in such a way

that over-production is avoided. The trouble is that, by and large, the demand for wage goods is much more stable than the demand for capital goods (see Kalecki 1967). Reducing the workers' purchasing power, therefore, may not inevitably create a gap between supply and demand. But apart from creating immediate adjustment problems, it will increase the system's overall instability.

14 Chung (1981: 72–80) made me aware of this possible non-causal use of causal terms.

15 See, for example, Roemer's (1987a) scenario.

16 But why would such a profit-rate-decreasing technical change be implemented? Being automatic, the resulting increases in the real wage can be fully anticipated by the capitalists, who will therefore refrain from such organic-composition-increasing innovations. Unless they are counting on substantial time lags? Or unless they dread spillover wage increases?

17 Of course, if we discover that techniques are often selected according to criteria which do not reduce (for whichever of the reasons recalled above) to cost minimization at equilibrium prices, it does not follow that the equilibrium rate of profit falls, let alone that it falls for this reason. The influence exerted on the rate of profit by technical changes selected in this way can easily be offset by the opposite influence of standard profit-rate-increasing technical changes. But if the rate of profit does fall, then it can be said that part of the fall is not due to the rise in the real wage, but to the occurrence of organic-composition-increasing technical change. Empirical evidence *is* relevant, but it is not of the kind usually envisioned. Important consequences follow from this conclusion as to the validity of empirical contributions to the falling-rate-of-profit controversy. For example, in order to vindicate the relevance of macroeconomic data for testing the 'hypothesis that (the organic composition) rises while (the rate of exploitation) remains constant, thereby *causing* the rate of profit to fall' (my emphasis), it will not do to point out, as Weisskopf (1979: 343) does, that contrary to a key assumption in Okishio's and Roemer's theorems the real wage rises (unless of course a misleadingly weak sense of 'causation' is meant). Similarly, the assumption that a fall in the (equilibrium) rate of profit can be attributed to a squeeze of profits by wages if the rate of exploitation falls, and to a rise in the organic composition if it does not (as stated by Reati (1980: 512) as a basis for his test of the theory) rests on too simple a view of the matter.

18 A prominent example is Roemer (1981: chapters 2 and 3).

19 Clawson (1983: 109). This definition may be accused of being so broad (see below) as to be very misleading. I won't quarrel with it on these grounds, however, as variants of the feature it focuses on are often mentioned as a key difference between neoclassicism and Marxism, including by Rowthorn (1980: 14–15) and by Roemer himself (1978b: 150–3) in an earlier (and somewhat dissonant) article.

20 For example, a few lines down from the passage quoted by Clawson, Roemer (1979: 379) writes: 'That Marx determined individual behaviour as a consequence of the social context and imperatives, while the neoclassical school postulated a hegemonic, ahistorical position for the individual, in no way weakens the claim that Marx's theory possesses a microeconomic foundation.'

21 Clawson (1983: 107). A similar position is defended by Lipietz (1980: n.7) in terms of a rather fuzzy distinction between *lois immanentes* and *lois coercitives*. He argues that the latter, which include the laws of competition and consciously motivate the individual agents, must be seen to derive from the former, which include for example the law of the tendency for the rate of profit to fall, and not the former from the latter, as methodological rationalists would have it. See also Lipietz (1981: n.12).

22 Hence the title of this chapter.

23 See Van Parijs (1981a: chapter 1), Roemer (1981: Introduction and chapter 5) and Elster (1982b) for further discussion of these issues.

24 As I have argued in detail elsewhere. See esp. Van Parijs (1981a: chapter 6; 1981b; 1982; and 1990: chapters 5–7).
25 See, for example, Alchian's (1950) model and its subsequent developments by Winter, Nelson, etc. Notice that microfoundations constructed along these lines would not only violate methodological rationalism, but also the weaker principle of methodological individualism, as the mechanism they focus on operates *on* (rather than within) firms.

References

Alchian, Armen A. 1950. 'Uncertainty, evolution, and economic theory', *Journal of Political Economy* 58, 211–22.
Armstrong, Philip and Glyn, Andrew. 1980. 'The law of the falling rate of profit and oligopoly', *Cambridge Journal of Economics* 4, 69–70.
Attali, Jacques. 1981. *Les Trois Mondes. Pour une théorie de l'après-crise*. Paris: Fayard.
Bleaney, Michael. 1980. 'Maurice Dobb's theory of crisis: a comment', *Cambridge Journal of Economics* 4, 71–3.
Chung, Joseph W. 1981. *La théorie de la baisse tendancielle du taux de profit. Analyse théorique et application empirique au développement du capitalisme américain*, Louvain-la-Neuve: Institut des Sciences Economiques.
Clawson, Patrick. 1983. 'A comment on Van Parijs' obituary', *Review of Radical Political Economics* 15(2), 107–10.
Elster, Jon. 1978. *Logic and Society*, New York: Wiley.
    1982a. *Explaining Technical Change*, Cambridge: Cambridge University Press.
    1982b. 'Marxism, functionalism and game theory', *Theory and Society* 11, 453–82.
Itoh, Makoto. 1980. *Value and Crisis*, New York: Monthly Review.
Kalecki, Michal. 1967. 'The problem of effective demand with Tugan-Baranowski and Rosa Luxemburg', in, *Selected Essays on the Dynamics of the Capitalist Economy*. Cambridge: Cambridge University Press, 1971, 146–55.
Lipietz, Alain. 1980. 'Conflicts de répartition et changements techniques dans la théorie marxiste', *Economie Appliquée* 33, 511–37.
    1981. 'Derrière la crise: la tendance à la baisse du taux de profit', Paris: CEPRE-MAP, Working Paper No. 8115.
Mandel, Ernest. 1962. *Traité d'economie marxiste*, vol. 2, Paris: UGE.
Nakatani, Takeshi. 1980. 'The law of falling rate of profit and the competitive battle', *Cambridge Journal of Economics* 4, 65–8.
Reati, Angelo. 1980. 'A propos de la baisse tendancielle du taux de profit: analyse désagrégée de l'industrie italienne', *Cahiers Economiques de Bruxelles* 88, 507–45.
Roemer, John E. 1978a. 'The effect of technological change on the real wage and Marx's falling rate of profit', *Australian Economic Papers* 17, 152–66.
    1978b. 'Neoclassicism, Marxism and collective action', *Journal of Economic Issues* 12, 147–61.
    1979. 'Continuing controversy on the falling rate of profit: fixed capital and other issues', *Cambridge Journal of Economics* 3, 379–98.
    1981. *Analytical Foundations of Marxian Economic Theory*, Cambridge: Cambridge University Press.
Rowthorn, Bob. 1980. 'Neo-classicism, neo-Ricardianism and Marxism', in, *Capitalism, Conflict and Inflation*, London: Lawrence and Wishart, 14–47.

Salvadori, Neri. 1981. 'Falling rate of profit with a constant real wage', *Cambridge Journal of Economics* 5, 59–66.

Shaikh, Anwar. 1980. 'Marxian competition versus perfect competition: further comments on the so-called choice of techniques', *Cambridge Journal of Economics* 4, 75–83.

Steedman, Ian. 1980. 'A note on the "Choice of Technique" under capitalism', *Cambridge Journal of Economics* 4, 62–4.

Van Parijs, Philippe. 1981a. *Evolutionary Explanation in the Social Sciences.* Totowa, New Jersey: Rowman and Littlefield; London: Tavistock.

1981b. 'Sociology as general economics', *European Journal of Sociology* 22, 299–324.

1982. 'Functionalist Marxism rehabilitated', *Theory and Society* 11, 497–511.

1990. *Le Modèle économique et ses rivaux*, Geneva and Paris: Droz.

Weisskopf, Thomas E. 1979. 'Marxist crisis theory and the rate of profit in the postwar US economy', *Cambridge Journal of Economics* 3, 341–78.

Part III

Exploitation rejuvenated

5. Exploitation and the libertarian challenge

5.1 Facing the libertarian challenge

'Freedom for all', libertarians say, 'there lies capitalism's deepest justi-fication.' 'Rubbish!', is one standard Left reply: 'Who cares about the formal freedom libertarians are obsessed with if it is not matched by a corresponding real freedom? What is the point of granting someone the right to do things which he does not have the power to do?' With these rhetorical questions the debate usually comes to an end, each party remaining convinced that freedom, in the sense that really matters, is on its side. But imagine a variety of capitalism which taxes market incomes in order to give every individual an absolutely unconditional income at the highest level sustainable, given the technical possibilities and individual preferences. Such capitalism is not just concerned with formal freedom: it gives everyone as much real freedom as it can.

Faced with this challenge, advocates of socialism need to offer more than just a distinction between formal and real freedom. Two main strategies are open to them. One of them, on which nothing will be said in this chapter, consists in arguing that a higher level of unconditional income is sustainable under socialism – defined by the collective owner-ship of the means of production in a sense to be clarified below – than under capitalism – defined by the private ownership of the means of production and the 'freedom' of labour-power. On this view, the some-what greater formal freedom enjoyed under capitalism (the right to hire and sell labour-power) is more than offset by the much greater real freedom which can be granted to all under socialism.[1]

The other strategy consists in conceding that there is no freedom-based case in favour of socialism, while arguing that freedom is not all that matters and that socialism is to be preferred to capitalism because it has a decisive advantage in some other respect. Historically the most important variant of this second strategy focuses on *exploitation*, which Friedrich Engels (1893: 214) once referred to as 'the basic evil which the socialist revolution wants to abolish by abolishing the capitalist mode of production'. Just as appealing to freedom provides the simplest and most common ethical argument in favour of capitalism, denouncing exploitation provides the handiest and most widespread ethical argument for condemning it.

Whether Marx himself used the notion in order morally to condemn capitalism, and indeed whether he indulged in any sort of ethical argument at all, are controversial issues.[2] Some argue that the concept of exploitation serves no other purpose, in Marx, than to help formulate the basic 'laws of motion' of various modes of production. Along with the rate of profit and the organic composition of capital, for example, Marx uses the rate of exploitation to analyse the dynamics of the capitalist mode of production.[3] To ask whether he thought exploitation to be right or wrong is, according to this interpretation, totally irrelevant. This is, however, an exegetical issue in which I have no desire and no need to get involved. The problem with which I am concerned is whether the concept of exploitation can serve to characterize a decisive ethical advantage of socialism over capitalism, regardless of whether or not Marx himself said and/or thought it could.

In this chapter, to put the matter more precisely, I shall investigate whether it is possible to provide a rigorous definition of exploitation which

  (i) matches at least roughly the *common use* of the term;

 (ii) makes exploitation *intrinsic to capitalism*, in the sense that no capitalist society can be conceived of without it; and

(iii) does *not* make exploitation *intrinsic to socialism*, in the sense that it is at least possible to conceive of a socialist society without it.

If conditions (ii) and (iii) are met, socialism potentially has an ethical advantage over capitalism. If, in addition, condition (i) is met, this advantage has something to do with what we usually call exploitation – rather than, say, with pollution or democracy. But to turn such a potential advantage into an actual one, one further needs to argue that the chosen definition

(iv) makes exploitation *ethically wrong*.

5.2 Work, benefit and power

As it is commonly understood, the statement 'person A exploits person B' cannot be true without each of the following three conditions being fulfilled:

(a) B works;
(b) A derives a benefit from B; and
(c) A exercises power over B.

I am not claiming that these necessary conditions make up a set of sufficient conditions, nor that the term 'exploitation' (of one person or group of people by another) is never used when at least one of these conditions does not apply. My claim is only that the hard core of intuitively unproblematic uses of the term lies within the boundaries drawn by the conjunction (a)–(c). I shall not vindicate this claim in detail here, but only make a few remarks to clarify the meaning of the three key notions of work, benefit and power.

That B works means that B performs some activity prompted by an external incentive. Being photographed in the street (without having to pose), worrying about one's children (without thereby being driven to do anything for them), or letting one's husband live off one's dowry do not constitute activities, nor (therefore) work, and hence cannot give rise to exploitation. Moreover, spontaneous activities and activities which are performed for their own sake do not constitute work either. If I thoroughly enjoy playing around with your computer the way you tell me to, I do not work, and you do not exploit me even if you make pretty profits from my activity. What turns an activity into work, according to this conception, is not that the activity is paid, but that it would not be performed if it were not paid or, more generally, if it did not fetch an external reward.

The other two conditions indicate that there must be a twofold causal relationship between A and B, and what the nature of this relation must be. That A derives a *benefit* from B means that A would be worse off without B and the opportunities B offers A. Since A's welfare at a certain time could not be affected by B's activity at a later time (due to the temporal nature of causation), it follows from this condition that we cannot exploit future generations, but not that we cannot exploit past generations. Further, benefit need not mean consumption. I may exploit you even if I do not consume any part of the profits I make from your work and invest them instead. What matters is that A's welfare, or A's

income in a broad sense, should be positively affected, and not necessarily A's consumption.

Finally, that A exercises *power* over B means that A controls access to
some resource which is precious to B and uses it to make B do something
which otherwise B would not have done. This notion of power covers the
case of coercion, which involves (the threat of) withdrawing something B
currently possesses (life, freedom, etc.), as well as other situations, in
which A owes her power over B to her wealth, labour-power, skills,
knowledge, or even to B's tender feelings towards her. It covers the case
in which B is forced to do what she does, in the sense that she has no
tolerable alternative (think of the proletarian who would starve if she did
not put up with the capitalist's conditions), as well as the case in which
doing what she does is just in her best interest (think of the same
proletarian in a society in which she could fall back on an adequate basic
income). And it applies whether or not A intentionally uses the power
she objectively has (think of tenants paying you rent even though you
would never dream of expelling them if they did not). Power, as it is
understood here, can be exercised unwittingly.

Nonetheless, this notion of power is not so broad as to exclude nothing.
If B makes A a genuine gift, i.e. a transfer free from any instrumental
consideration, A does not owe the benefit she derives to the power she
exerts, and hence does not exploit B. Furthermore, A may derive a benefit
from B without either power or altruism playing any role, due to some
positive externality. If my wife's standards of tidiness at home are much
lower than mine, I may end up doing (in my own interest) all the tidying
up, before her threshold of tolerance is reached. She will derive some
benefit from my activity, but not because of any resource she controls.
Hence, no power and no exploitation. Finally, for A to exert power over
B, A and B need to be contemporaries. For if A is to make B do something,
A must be there both before B does it (otherwise A could not cause B's
behaviour in any sense) and after B does it (otherwise A could not
implement the threats involved in any exercise of power). Hence, it is not
just future generations, but also past generations, that we cannot exploit.

5.3 The initial dilemma

If only for the sake of this chapter's argument, let us take it for granted
that conditions (a)–(c) must be fulfilled if one is to assert that A exploits B.
Hence, for a response to the libertarian challenge to be 'exploitation-
based', it needs to rest on a concept which involves at least the three

components captured by (a)–(c). Might it do simply to *define* exploitation by the conjunction of these components, i.e. to turn conditions (a)–(c) into a set of sufficient conditions for the exploitation of *B* by *A*? Remember that the concept we are after must not only be in keeping with common usage (requirement (i)); it must also make exploitation intrinsic to capitalism (requirement (ii)) but not to socialism (requirement (iii)). To see that exploitation, as defined by (a)–(c), is unavoidably present under capitalism, it is sufficient to realize that the capitalists' profits are benefits the capitalists derive from the workers by virtue of the wealth-based power they exercise over the workers.

But is exploitation thus defined conceivably absent from socialism? Let us tackle this question indirectly by considering first the case of a market economy consisting of two independent, equally wealthy, equally productive peasants, who exchange with one another part of their respective outputs (say, beans for carrots). Each of them works, each derives a benefit from the other (thanks to the advantages flowing from the division of labour) and each exerts power over the other (in the sense that each controls access to a resource to which the other attaches some value, and uses this fact to make the other do something – give up some of the beans or carrots she has produced – which she would not have done otherwise). Hence, in such a situation, there is exploitation in sense (a)–(c), even though it is mutual exploitation.

If, instead, cooperation between self-interested workers takes the form of joint work in a single production unit (rather than that of trade between separate production units), the power over other workers which each worker owes to her labour-power is no longer materialized in an identifiable product. But conditions (a)–(c) are no less clearly met. As such cooperation lies at the core of any socialist society in which altruism is anything less than perfect (not all labour contributions are genuine gifts) and in which work has not been fully abolished (not all productive activities are performed for their own sake), it can be safely concluded that adopting (a)–(c) as a definition of exploitation *would make the latter just as intrinsic to socialism as to capitalism.*

Since the whole point of the exercise is to enable us to discriminate between capitalism and socialism, we obviously need to strengthen our set of conditions. One straightforward suggestion is to add the mirror image of condition (a):

A does not work   (d)

To see what the implications are, let us start by considering what could be called a *dichotomic* society, i.e. a society whose members can be neatly partitioned into two categories: some get all their income by way of payment for the labour they perform, while the others owe all their income to the power they exert over the former thanks to their control over the means of production or of coercion. In such a society, Marx's own definition of exploitation can safely be phrased as the appropriation by non-workers (the second category) of at least part of the net product, i.e. of whatever is left of the total product once all the material means of production used up have been replaced.[4] And this definition is exactly equivalent to one in terms of (a)–(d).

Strengthening our conditions in this way obviously enables us to solve the difficulty which turned out to be fatal to the weaker definition (a)–(c), since 'mutual exploitation' by workers now ceases to count as exploitation. This time, however, the definition has become too strong. Our notion of work, as explicated in the previous section, is very broad – as it needs to be if we want to apply the concept of exploitation in a precapitalist or a household context as well as under capitalism. Consequently, condition (a) is not very demanding. But condition (d), for the same reason, is very restrictive. In all capitalist societies, all capitalists are very likely to work, however little – for example, by being involved in the management of their firm, by occasionally clipping some coupons or by getting a spoon from the kitchen in order to eat their pudding. And in the absence of non-workers, there can be no exploitation in sense (a)–(d). It thus turns out that adopting (a)–(d) as a definition of exploitation *would fail to make the latter any more intrinsic to capitalism than to socialism.*

Without condition (d), we are not happy because exploitation sticks to socialism. With condition (d), we are equally miserable because exploitation vanishes from capitalism. How can we get out of this dilemma?

5.4 The orthodox solution: net value appropriation

One avenue which seems well worth exploring consists in making exploitation a matter of imbalance between the labour one contributes and the share of the product one appropriates. Working a tiny amount would then no longer make a capitalist immune to the charge of exploitation, and the difficulty we have just met would be solved. At first sight, there are many ways of defining such an imbalance between contribution and income. On closer scrutiny, however, it appears that there is only one simple way of doing so which is consistent with our conditions (a)–(c), and that it coincides with the orthodox Marxian definition, as applied beyond the simple case of a dichotomic economy considered above.

To start with, the requirement (a) that only workers can be exploited dictates that contributions should be measured in terms of labour, or at least in terms of a variable on which one could not score higher than zero without doing any work (work effort, sweat secreted while working, etc.). If some other standard of measurement were chosen, someone who does not work at all could conceivably have an excess balance, and hence be exploited. This suggests the following general formulation: individual *A* is an exploiter if *A*'s labour contribution (somehow measured) is less than proportional to *A*'s income (somehow measured), while *B* is exploited if *B*'s labour contribution (somehow measured) is more than proportional to *B*'s income (somehow measured). However, if no further restriction is placed on the way in which contribution and income are measured, nothing guarantees that our conditions of benefit (b) and power (c) are met. Indeed, *nothing guarantees that there is any causal interaction at all* between *A* and *B*. Take two autarkic communities which produce nothing but corn. There may be huge disproportionalities between labour expended (however measured) and amount of corn produced on either side. And yet there can be no exploitation (acceptably defined), since neither (b) nor (c) are met.

To ensure that *A* and *B* interact, there is no need, however, to insert this in an *ad hoc* fashion into the definition of exploitation. One can instead require that contribution and income be measured along the same dimension, and accordingly turn disproportionality into inequality. *A* is then an exploiter if the labour (somehow measured) *A* contributes falls short of the labour (measured in the same way) *A* appropriates through her income. And *B* is exploited if the labour contributed exceeds the labour appropriated. Disproportionality can here be turned into inequality because total contribution (in *living* labour of course – otherwise, non-workers could be exploited) equals total income (total *net* product expressed in labour terms). There is no way in which there could be exploitation in this sense without some interaction between the exploiters and the exploited. (How could an autarkic community contribute more – or less – labour than it appropriates?) Indeed, providing income is defined, as it must be, in terms of product *appropriated* (thanks to one's power), not just received, there can be no exploitation in this sense without (generally mutual) exercise of power. Such definition unquestionably implies that condition (c) is fulfilled.

The benefit condition (b), however, is not necessarily fulfilled. To see this, suppose you and I do the same sort of work (we grow corn together on a plot of land) for the same length of time and get paid the same number of bushels for the work we do. However, you work far more efficiently than I do. How does the definition of exploitation which is now being contemplated apply in this case? Let us measure each person's contribution in terms of labour actually performed. If we also measure each bushel of corn in terms of the work which actually went into it, it turns out that you exploit me if, for example, my pay (equal to yours) is made up solely of bushels which you have produced (not all of them, since that would make my pay bigger than yours), while your pay consists partly of all the bushels I have produced. In such a situation, you appropriate more labour than you contribute, even though (assuming moderate economies of scale) you would be better off without me. You exploit me, according to the definition considered, but you do not derive any benefit from my activity. The benefit condition is not met, and the definition, therefore, is unacceptable.

To guarantee the fulfilment of the benefit condition, it is essential to take productivity into account when measuring both labour contributions and the labour content of incomes. One simple way of doing this consists in asking of each labour contribution how much time it would have taken to produce the same output as it did if productivity had been at its social average for this type of work, i.e. how much *socially necessary labour* is involved in this contribution; and assessing each good in terms of the socially necessary labour or *labour value* it contains. This yields the familiar Marxian definition of exploitation in terms of 'surplus value':

> *A* is an exploiter if *A* contributes less labour-value than she appropriates through her income. *B* is exploited if she contributes more labour-value than she appropriates. (I)

This definition satisfies all three conditions (a)–(c). And, for the reasons spelt out above, concern with these constraints unavoidably drives to this definition (or to close variants of it) any attempt to define exploitation as an imbalance between labour contribution and income.[5]

5.5 The modal variant: necessary net value appropriation

However, this simple version of the net-labour-value-appropriation model of exploitation cannot possibly be satisfactory. Just imagine that the members of some society all work equally long, hard and productively and all earn the same monetary income. But they choose to spend their incomes on different bundles of goods. As soon as prices are not strictly proportional to labour values, some of this egalitarian society's members will turn out to be exploiters, and others exploited, simply because of the choices they happen to make *qua* consumers with identical incomes. Moreover, if some of the workers save part of their incomes, their exploitation status becomes indeterminate.

These difficulties can be solved, however, if we shift to a slightly different, 'modal' version of the same definition:

> *A* is an exploiter if *A* necessarily contributes more value than she appropriates through her income. *B* is exploited if she necessarily contributes more labour value than she appropriates.   (I*)

To determine whether *A* is an exploiter, one looks at the least labour-intensive bundle of goods whose price would exhaust *A*'s income. If the labour value of that bundle exceeds the socially necessary labour performed by *A*, *A* is a necessary-net-value-appropriator, and hence an exploiter according to this definition. To determine whether *B* is exploited, one looks, symmetrically, at the most labour-intensive bundle of goods which *B* could afford with her income. If the labour value of that bundle falls short of the labour value created through *B*'s work, *B* is a necessary-net-value-contributor, and hence exploited according to this definition.[6]

Many agents may be neither exploiters not exploited in this sense, in particular when there is a strong correlation between income and labour performed, and a poor correlation between prices and labour values. This definition being strictly stronger than the previous one, the three conditions (a)–(c) remain nonetheless satisfied. On the other hand, the definition is not so strong as to prevent any capitalist working a tiny amount from being an exploiter – as (a)–(d) did. A capitalist who hardly works and books huge profits is very likely to appropriate more labour value than he contributes even if all his income were spent on (precious but labour-poor) crude oil. Moreover, even if this were not the case and if, therefore, there were no exploiters, it would not follow that exploitation is absent, as many workers may be unable to afford even the cheapest bundle of goods embodying as much labour value as they contribute. Crowds of people may be exploited, according to this modal definition, even if no one can be called an exploiter.[7]

Does all this enable us to resolve our initial dilemma? Do we have a defensible definition which makes exploitation intrinsic to capitalism, but not to socialism? Note, first of all, that both definitions considered rely on the concept of labour value. And the very definition of this concept raises very serious difficulties as soon as we enter a world characterized by joint production and heterogeneous labour.[8] However, let us abstract from these difficulties for a moment, by imagining economies in which all labour is identical (or at least reducible to some basic type of labour with the help of coefficients reflecting skill acquisition) and joint production absent. *Actual* imbalance between labour value contributed and labour value appropriated (definition I) can then be said to obtain with certainty under capitalism. To the extent that a socialist society has full control over income distribution, such imbalance could in principle be eliminated under socialism, even though such elimination requires a close monitoring of each individual's productivity and is therefore most likely to be practically unattainable at any particular time. *Necessary* imbalance between value contributed and value appropriated (definition I*), on the other hand, is also bound to be present under capitalism, barring extreme situations which can be safely discarded,[9] while its absence from socialism is much easier to achieve, since it only requires a rough fit between (socially necessary) labour contribution and income.

This provides us with a precise formulation of a potential ethical advantage of socialism over capitalism. This formulation, however, is plagued with serious difficulties hinted at above. Admittedly, it is not true that the definition of exploitation to which we have been led requires the labour *theory* of value in any sense. We have seen that when prices deviate from labour values, definition (I) has uncomfortable implications, but these have been removed by the introduction of definition (I*). Both (I) and (I*), however, make essential use of the *concept* of value in the assessment of both contributions and incomes. And it is this concept which slips away in a world of intrinsic joint products, irreducibly heterogeneous labour and individually unmeasurable productivity. Instead of embarking on the messy business of attempting to solve these conceptual difficulties, let us examine instead whether they can be bypassed in one stroke, by exploring alternative ways out of our initial dilemma.

5.6 Roemer's solution: asset-based inequality

We did not want exploitation to be present in every instance of self-interested cooperation – and therefore present under socialism. Nor did we want exploitation to vanish as soon as capitalists did any amount of work – i.e. in any actual capitalist society. So we decided to make exploitation a matter of mismatch between the distribution of burdens and the distribution of advantages. This took us to the orthodox solution and its modal variant – a dead end for those who believe the concept of labour value should be left alone. However, there is a way of tackling simultaneously the problems raised by working capitalists and socialist cooperation without making any reference to labour values. It consists in focusing on the causal relation between the distribution of material assets and the distribution of income, and finds its most rigorous formulation in John Roemer's illuminating 'game-theoretical' approach to exploitation.

According to Roemer's explicit definition, a coalition A *exploits capitalistically* if A would do worse for its members by withdrawing with a per capita share of the means of production and organizing optimally, while A's complement would do better. And a coalition B *is capitalistically exploited* if B could do better for its members by withdrawing with a per capita share of the means of production, while B's complement would do worse.[10] Taken literally, this formulation is unacceptable. It implies, for example, that with significant economies of scale no group of people either exploits or is exploited. However, the intuition which it attempts to capture can be expressed in a way that does not generate such difficulties, using an alternative counterfactual formulation:

> A exploits capitalistically if A would be worse off than currently if society's means of production were equally distributed, everything else remaining unchanged and abstracting from both efficiency effects and price effects. B is capitalistically exploited if B would be better off than currently under the same circumstances.   (II)

What this counterfactual exercise is meant to capture is a causal notion of capitalist exploitation, understood as the specific and positive impact on the distribution of income, of an unequal distribution of property rights in the means of production, or, for short, as asset-based inequality. To get at this specifically distributive impact, it is necessary to discard efficiency effects – for example the fact that asset equalization may lead, via reduced incentives, to a smaller total income. And to make sure we are dealing with the positive side of the impact, it is also necessary to discard price effects – transfers of assets may affect relative prices in such a way that their beneficiaries actually become worse off as a result.

One of the attractive features of this causal notion of capitalist exploitation, whether in Roemer's or in the modified formulation, is that it lends itself easily to generalization. If one shifts attention from the unequal distribution of material assets to the unequal distribution of property rights over people and to the unequal distribution of skills, one gets (to use Roemer's labels) *feudal* and *socialist* exploitation respectively.[11] What matters most for our present purposes, however, is that the Roemerian definition (II), like the orthodox definition (I), though in a very different way, solves our initial dilemma. Capitalists who book huge profits and work a little are definitely exploiters according to (II), and *a fortiori* according to any broader definition of exploitation which has (II) as one of its disjuncts (e.g. feudal-or-capitalist-or-socialist exploitation). On the other hand, workers in a (genuine) socialist society could not possibly be exploiters in terms of (II), since socialism excludes by definition the private ownership of material assets. Exploitation in a broader sense, covering skill-based inequality, for example, is of course possible under socialism. But it is – arguably – not necessarily present in it. And in any case nothing forces us to extend our causal concept of exploitation in this way.

Have we found, thanks to Roemer, a defensible definition of exploitation which gets us out of our dilemma without saddling us with the intricacies of labour value? No, we have not. For definition (II) – and *a fortiori* any broadening of it along the lines indicated above – violates each of the three conditions (a)–(c) we had laid down as minimum requirements for any acceptable definition of exploitation. To see why the work condition (a) is not satisfied by Roemerian definitions, just imagine that I own less than average wealth and live an austere but idle life thanks to the interest payments derived from my modest wealth. I am capitalistically exploited according to (II), and yet I do not lift a finger. Definition (II), therefore, allows non-workers to be exploited and violates requirement (a). One might expect it to be easier for a causal definition of exploitation to meet the causal requirements (b)–(c). But such an expectation is ill-founded. The causal link on which definition (II) focuses is one *between assets and income* and has nothing to do with the benefit and power links *between the exploiter and the exploited* required by (b)–(c). It is perfectly possible for two autarkic subsocieties to exploit and be exploited, respectively, according to (II), even though neither of them exercises any power over or derives any benefit from the other.[12] What is being captured by Roemer-like definitions, therefore, may still play some part in a case for socialism against capitalism, but not in an exploitation-based case.

5.7 The Ricardian socialist solution: expropriation

Is it then true, after all, that an exploitation-based case against capitalism is bound to get stranded in the conceptual difficulties surrounding the notion of labour value? Not so, because there is yet another way of eschewing our initial dilemma.[13] To ensure that the not-quite-idle capitalist is an exploiter without thereby turning all socialist workers into exploiters, let us now adopt a decidedly microfocused approach. Instead of concentrating on the capitalists' systematic tendency to run a deficit on their labour-value account, or to take advantage of their superior wealth, it is possible to focus on the fact that they owe at least part of their income to something other than the labour they perform:

> A exploits B if A appropriates at least part of B's net product by
> virtue of anything other than A's current labour   (III)

Note that, according to this definition, appropriation rooted in wealth which is itself derived from past labour remains exploitative. For suppose part of the work I did last year consisted in making a tool. According to (III), I am an exploiter if I lend this tool out in exchange for a sum of money which more than compensates me for the wear and tear. But I am not if I use the tool to work more productively myself, and thus to appropriate through the sale of my products a greater share in other people's net product. In other words, whether my current capital is derived from past work or not is immaterial to the issue of whether using that capital to boost my income is exploitative or not. What does matter is whether the causal impact of my capital on what I can appropriate from others is effected in isolation (as in rents and interests) or jointly with the causal impact of my current work (as in capital-intensive self-employment).

Once again, our initial dilemma is solved. For someone to get an income without being an exploiter, according to this definition, it is not enough that she does some work. She must earn all her income *by virtue of* the work she does. And this is obviously too much to claim on behalf of any not-quite-idle capitalist. Further, any self-interested cooperation between workers, in particular in a socialist society, is not *ipso facto* exploitative according to definition (III), since in that case all claims to each other's products are precisely based on the labour one contributes. Moreover, the case for socialism and against capitalism which thus emerges can legitimately, and nearly tautologically, be labelled exploitation-based. The work condition (a) is clearly fulfilled, providing nothing can be called individual A's product if A has not worked towards it. And since there is appropriation of part of the net product, there is clearly a benefit for A, and equally clearly power exercised by A over B, bearing in mind the strong meaning given above (section 5.4) to the term 'appropriation'. Hence, all three requirements (a)–(c) are met, and we finally have what we were looking for: a defensible definition which makes exploitation intrinsic to capitalism without also making it intrinsic to socialism.[14]

Before specifying what is needed to turn this potential ethical case for socialism into an actual one – and thereby justifying the 'Ricardian socialist' label –, let us briefly pause to look at the logical relations between the various definitions we have considered. All entailments are represented by arrows in Figure 5.1. For a definition to be admissible, it needs to entail (a)–(c). For it to solve our initial dilemma, it must neither entail (a)–(d) (working capitalists), nor be entailed by (a)–(c) (socialist cooperation). Each of these relations has been explicitly dealt with in the above discussion.

Note, in addition, that the Roemerian definition (II) does not entail any of the others, if only because it is consistent with the absence of any interaction between the exploited and the exploiters. And it is not entailed by any of them, nor by (a)–(d), if only because appropriation by a non-worker may be made possible by her having wealth, without it being due to her having more than average wealth. (Since (a)–(d) entails (I), (I*) and (III), showing that (a)–(d) does not entail (II) suffices to show that (I), (I*) and (III) do not entail (II) either.) Further, (I*) and, a $fortiori$, (I) do not entail (III), since even people who derive all their income from their work may be significant net value appropriators (e.g. if someone with much lower productivity than others is paid the same as them). On the other hand (III) 'quasi-entails' (I), though not (I*), since it is only through an extraordinary fluke that the imbalance generated by virtue of (III) could be exactly offset by an imbalance of opposite sign in the area of labour incomes, in such a way that (I) would not obtain. Finally, (a)–(d) entails both (I*) – and hence (I) – and (III): a non-working appropriator is bound to be a net labour value appropriator, as well as to appropriate by virtue of something other than her labour.

5.8 Exploitation, patterned justice and entitlement

Each of the three perspectives examined and compared in this paper has come up with a potential ethical advantage of socialism over capitalism.

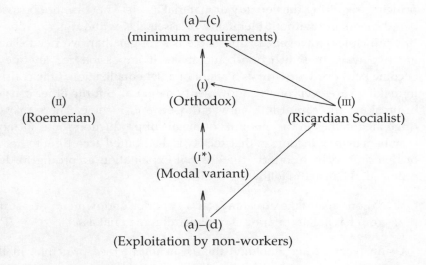

Figure 5.1   Entailments between exploitation concepts

To turn this potential advantage into an actual one, however, and thereby to provide the beginning of an exploitation-guided rebuttal of the libertarian challenge, we need to adduce – and justify – ethical principles which the presence of exploitation, as defined, necessarily violates. In this last section, I want to point out how deeply the principles required by the three perspectives differ from one another, without asking which one among them – if any – is ethically defensible.[15]

When exploitation is defined as it is in the orthodox perspective, what is needed to make it ethically wrong is some patterned principle of *equal* or fair *exchange*, where labour value is chosen as the normatively appropriate numeraire. Depending on whether the plain (I) or the modal (I*) version of the orthodox definition is chosen, this principle can be expressed as follows:

> Everyone must get from social cooperation just as much labour value as she contributes to it, or   (PI)

> Everyone must be able to get from social cooperation just as much labour value as she contributes to it.   (PI*)

When, instead, exploitation is defined as it is in a Roemerian perspective, what seems to be needed is another, very different patterned principle requiring the equality of material assets. There cannot be asset-based inequality without inequality of assets, i.e. without a violation of this principle. However, this principle is stronger than we need. There are two ways in which one could make it impossible for anyone to become better or worse off as a result of asset equalization. One consists in making sure everyone's endowments are equal. But the other consists in breaking the causal link between assets and income. There may be huge inequalities in the amounts of means of production some society's members own. If income in that society is distributed according to needs, or determined by a lottery, there is not exploitation according to definition (II). Hence, the following principle:

> No one may take advantage of a superior endowment, nor suffer from having an inferior endowment, in material assets.   (PII)

Using Nozick's terminology, this is an *unpatterned* principle, in the sense that it does not require the distribution of incomes to conform to any predetermined pattern. All it demands is that this distribution should not be affected by one particular factor, the (unequal) distribution of assets. In this respect, it resembles the standard libertarian 'entitlement' principle of distributive justice, which can similarly be construed as demanding that incomes be unaffected by one particular factor, namely coercion.[16] Nonetheless, some element of patterning is involved, in the sense that (PII) could not be violated without some deviation from equality (in asset ownership).[17]

This residual element of patterning disappears altogether as we turn to exploitation as defined in the third, Ricardian socialist perspective. Appropriation by virtue of something other than one's labour is shown to be wrong if one accepts the following principle:[18]

> Every worker is entitled to the whole of her product   (PIII)

This is one possible expression of the principle of distribution which was advocated by Thomas Hodgskin (1825) and other Ricardian socialists. It is closely associated historically with the notion, stigmatized by Marx (1875) in the opening sentences of the *Critique of the Gotha Programme*, that labour alone creates the product. But the latter notion is only one possible way of vindicating (with the further help of a creator-keeper principle) the ethical adequacy of (PIII). To be able to assert that only labour is entitled to the product, one is under no logical compulsion to assert that only labour creates the product.[19] On the other hand, application of (PIII) does presuppose that one can work out what part of the total product can be ascribed to each particular worker (which is different from determining each worker's marginal product). Attempts to solve this problem lead to tricky conceptual difficulties. But these need not bother us here, since however they are solved (PIII) leaves no room for appropriation on any ground apart from labour, and exploitation, as defined by (III) cannot but be wrong according to (PIII).

Unlike (PI), (PI*) and even (PII), the Ricardian socialist principle of distributive justice (PIII) is a pure entitlement principle. It differs from other pure entitlement principles such as Locke's or Nozick's (without the proviso), in that all entitlements stem from the current period: only labour currently performed gives rise to a title to any part of the net product of the current period. And it differs from such 'impure' entitlement principles as the Roemerian (PII), in that its violation is consistent with the non-violation of any equality principle whatsoever. Ricardian socialist exploitation, in contrast with both orthodox and Roemerian exploitation, *cannot* be viewed as a species of inequality. To see this, imagine a society in which all individuals are identical – in particular, they happen to possess identical skills and wealth, to perform the same type and amount of work with identical productivity, to earn identical wages and capital incomes, and to consume the same goods. In such a society, there could not possibly be net value appropriation $(I-I^*)$ nor asset-based inequality (II). But there will be expropriation, as defined by (III), as soon as capital incomes are positive. Since in such a fictional situation, any principle of distributive justice which can be formulated in terms of 'To each according to her ...' is of necessity satisfied, this also shows in all clarity that Ricardian socialist exploitation is not a matter of violating a pattern. It is purely a matter of (current-)historical entitlement.

Within the context of this chapter, this is an ironical result. In our search for an exploitation-based response to the libertarian challenge, we have discarded two of the three perspectives that seemed to hold some promise: the orthodox perspective because it was plagued with the irritating difficulties sticking to the concept of labour value, and Roemer's perspective because it turned out to be based on an indefensible definition of exploitation. The third perspective is the Ricardian socialist one, and it calls for an entitlement conception of distributive justice. This means that the only perspective we are left with requires the very sort of ethical principle which has been closely associated with the libertarian tradition. Whether or not there is an effective exploitation-based riposte to the libertarian challenge crucially depends on the ethical strength of the libertarians' favourite tool.

Notes

1 For a clear version of the first strategy, see esp. Wright (1956), discussed in section 9.8 below. See also Van Parijs (1992).
2 See Geras (1984) for a useful recent survey.
3 It is not obvious, however, that the rate of exploitation plays a useful role in this respect. Take the famous relation $r = e/(q + 1)$, which expresses, under some assumptions, the relations between the rate of profit (r), the rate of exploitation (e) and the organic composition of capital (q). The rate of profit is clearly of paramount importance for the dynamics of the capitalist mode of production, both because – if the workers do not save – it constitutes the maximum rate of accumulation and because it affects – via the expected rate of profit – the capitalists' propensity to invest. And the relation stated above seems to indicate that the rate of exploitation exerts a key influence on the rate of profit. However, it can be argued that the influence of the determinants of the rate of exploitation (length and intensity of the working day, wage rate, productivity) on the rate of profit can also be studied directly, without an unnecessary and rather confusing detour via the rate of exploitation.
4 Such a definition can be inferred from Marx's statement that the ratio of unpaid to paid labour can be viewed as a 'popular expression' of the ratio of surplus to necessary labour, itself the direct and exact expression of 'the degree of exploitation of labour by capital or of the worker by the capitalist' (see Marx 1867: 230–2, 556).
5 Such a definition cannot unambiguously be attributed to Marx, since his equation of the rate of exploitation with the rate of surplus value (i.e. the ratio of the labour value appropriated by the capitalists to the labour value appropriated by the workers) in an exchange economy (see Marx, 1867: 232) implicitly assumes that society can be neatly divided into two non-overlapping categories of capitalists and workers. When this assumption is dropped, one could conceivably generalize Marx's notion by taking the ratio of the value appropriated in the form of profits to the value appropriated in the form of wages – which leads to definition (III) of exploitation, to be introduced below. However, precise formulations of Marxian exploitation for non-dichotomic economies usually are variants of (I). For clear examples, see: 'The substance of exploitation is that there exist groups of people or classes which are able to obtain more goods on a permanent basis than can be produced with the amount of labour provided by the group' (von Weizsäcker 1973: 247): 'Any agent is defined to exploit his transaction partner if and only if the amount of abstract labour appropriated from the latter exceeds the amount supplied' (Holländer 1982: 871); and 'Marxian exploitation is defined as the unequal exchange of labor for goods: the exchange is unequal when the amount of labour embodied in the goods which the worker can purchase with his income is less than the amount of labor he expended to earn that income' (Roemer 1985: 30).
6 This modal definition of exploitation is proposed by Roemer (1982a: 121–3).
7 A sufficient condition for some workers to be exploited is that the firm whose products have, for whatever reason (low capital intensity, absence of monopolistic rents, sudden fall in demand), the lowest price/labour-value ratio makes positive profits. The workers of this firm do not earn wages which are sufficient to purchase the whole of their net product (otherwise, there would be no profits). And since this is, by assumption, the bundle of goods with the highest labour-value content they can afford, there is no way in which they can avoid being net labour-value contributors.
8 See e.g. Steedman (1977) and Armstrong et al. (1978) for a discussion of these difficulties.
9 Even if the (relatively weak) condition formulated in footnote 7 does not hold, many

other circumstances can bring about necessary-net-value contribution (e.g. the fact that not all workers can simultaneously buy the goods with the lowest price/labour-value ratio, or the fact that some highly productive workers may be very badly paid).

10 See for example Roemer (1982a: 202–11; 1982b: 94–7).

11 The relevance of this generalizability to the theory of social classes is explained in the next chapter.

12 Note that Roemer usually adds a condition of 'dominance' (1982a: 195, 237; 1982b: 91–2) or of 'dependence' (1982c: 285) to rule out exploitation by the (benefit-receiving) disabled and by a well-endowed autarkic island. The disabled, however, creates no problem when the withdrawal formulation is replaced by the *ceteris paribus* equalization formulation (a coalition of benefit-receiving disabled people would become worse off if it withdrew with a per capita share of the assets, but not if assets were equalized, other things – including transfer schemes – remaining unaltered). Suitably defined, the condition of 'dominance' can conceivably deal with the autarkic-island problem (which exists under both formulations), as well as with any situation in which either power or benefit is absent. But it could hardly deal with the 'exploited non-worker' problem, and constitutes in any case an *ad hoc* restriction quite alien to Roemer's central intuition. (It is of course possible to construct any number of 'admissible' definitions of exploitation by the *ad hoc* conjunction of conditions (a)–(c) and anything whatsoever consistent with these.)

13 I am here leaving out a further strategy put forward by Lawrence Crocker: 'I propose that the necessary and sufficient condition of exploitation is that there be a surplus product [difference between total product and what is paid in wages] which is under the control of a group which *does not include all the producers of that surplus* ... Whatever the nature of the dominant group, exploitation exists as long as *some producers are not part of it*, no matter what is done with the surplus – whether consumed, accumulated or thrown into the sea' (Crocker 1972: 205, my emphasis). Clearly, under such a definition, there can be no exploitation under (ideal) socialism, and even not-quite-idle profit-making capitalists are bound to be exploiters. Moreover, conditions (a)–(c) are met, no use is made of the concept of value, and a *prima facie* ethical argument can easily be concocted: 'The difference [between capitalism and socialism] is that under capitalism the deductions are controlled by a minority group which thereby dominates the structure and development of the economy and society. In the "cooperative society", even in its first phase, these decisions are collectively made' (Crocker 1972: 207). The relations between this proposal and those analysed in the main text are worth exploring in detail. To suggest briefly what I believe to be the key difficulty with this approach, let me just ask you to imagine the following situation. You are the only worker in a society which numbers 1,000 other members. At time 1, they alone decide what is going to be done with the surplus product. At time 2, you are enfranchised and all decisions about what is going to be done with the surplus product are now taken with a 1,000 to 1 majority. According to Crocker's definition, you are exploited at time 1, but no longer at time 2. Does this fit your intuition?

14 However, some caveats and qualifications are in order. In particular, one must make sure that socialism is defined in such a way that the workers – and not a bureaucracy *nor the community at large* – appropriate society's net product; and one must also abstract from 'sentimental exploitation' (where the source of power lies in the feelings the exploited has for the exploiter), which satisfies definition (III) but could not (acceptably) be eradicated from socialism any more than from any other mode of production. Furthermore, one may also have to discard the possibility of 'purely entrepreneurial capitalism', in which all capitalists would be managing their own firm and in which, therefore, some of their income would be due to their capital, but only put to use jointly with their labour (whether they work alone or employ waged workers). This would definitely be capitalism but, arguably, without exploitation. (In his 'feasible socialism', Alec Nove makes

108   Exploitation rejuvenated

room for small private entrepreneurs providing they work in their own firm. He argues: 'there would be no exploitation except in so far as a working owner-manager derives additional income from his employees (but then I exploit the secretary who is typing this page)' (Nove 1983: 212). What comes after 'but then' may not follow from what precedes it, but the implication is clear: such capitalist entrepreneurs do not exploit, what they get is not, as Nove puts it elsewhere (207), 'unearned income'. Terrell Carver (1987: section 3) analogously stresses the difficulty presented by owner-managers for the view that exploiting consists in benefiting from the workers' labour by virtue of being an owner. (If the owner-manager is made an exploiter, why not a capital-intensive self-employed person trading with a less capital-intensive self-employed person, e.g. a butcher buying a cleaning lady's services? We are then on a slippery slope. It will be very hard to stop before reaching Roemer's conception of capitalist exploitation *qua* taking advantage of one's superior endowment.)

15 Several chapters of Van Parijs (forthcoming) are devoted to this task. See also Van Parijs (1984).

16 See, for example, Rothbard's 'non-aggression axiom': 'The libertarian creed rests upon one central axiom: that no man or group of men may aggress against the person or property of anyone else' (Rothbard 1973: 23).

17 On the patterned/entitlement distinction and for an exploration of the space of possible entitlement theories, see van der Veen and Van Parijs (1985).

18 'If' but not 'only if'. Appropriation of part of the net product by people who have contributed no labour to it might conceivably be judged wrong on grounds other than distributive justice – efficiency, for example. But if exploitation is ethically wrong because it involves an unjust distribution of rewards between individuals, Ricardian Socialist justice is needed to match definition (III).

19 At one point, the latter principle seemed to be endorsed by Cohen (1980), who viewed the assertion that only labour creates what has value (not: creates value) as the foundation required by the moral indictment of exploitation. More recently, however, he has unambiguously dismissed this assertion on both exegetical and substantive grounds. (See expecially Cohen 1985.)

References

Armstrong, P., A. Glyn and J. Harrison. 1978. 'In defence of value: A reply to Ian Steedman', *Capital and Class* 5, 1–31.

Carver, T. 1987. 'Marx's political theory of exploitation', in A. Reeve, ed., *Modern Theories of Exploitation*, London: Sage, 68–79.

Cohen, G. A. 1980. 'The labour theory of value and the concept of exploitation', in M. Cohen, T. Nagel and T. Scanlon, eds., *Marx, Justice and History*, Princeton, NJ: Princeton University Press, 135–57.

    1985. 'Marx and Locke on land and labour', *Proceedings of the British Academy* 71, 357–88.

Crocker, L. 1972. 'Marx's concept of exploitation', *The Journal of Social Issues* 28, 201–15.

Elster, J. 1985. *Making Sense of Marx*, Cambridge: Cambridge University Press.

Engels, F. 1959 [1873]. *Zur Wohnungsfrage*, in K. Marx and F. Engels, *Werke*, vol. 18, Berlin: Dietz, 211–321.

Geras, N. 1984. 'The controversy about Marx and justice', *Philosophica* 33, 33–86.

Hodgskin, T. 1825. *Labour Defended against Capital, or the Unproductiveness of Capital Proved*, London.

Holländer, H. 1982. 'Class antagonism, exploitation and the labour theory of value', *Economic Journal* 92, 868–85.

Marx. K. 1962 [1867]. *Das Kapital*, vol. 1, Berlin: Dietz.

  1962 [1875]. 'Randglossen zum Programm der deutschen Arbeiterpartei', in K. Marx and F. Engels, *Werke*, vol. 19, Berlin: Dietz, 15–32.

Nove, A. 1983. *The Economics of Feasible Socialism*, London: Allen and Unwin.

Nozick, R. 1974. *Anarchy, State and Utopia*, Oxford: Blackwell.

Roemer, J. E. 1982a. *A General Theory of Exploitation and Class*, Cambridge, MA: Harvard University Press.

  1982b. 'Exploitation, alternatives and socialism', *Economic Journal* 92, 87–107.

  1982c. 'Property relations vs. surplus value in Marxian exploitation', *Philosophy and Public Affairs* 11, 281–313.

  1985. 'Why should Marxists be interested in exploitation?', in B. Chavance, ed., *Marx en Perspective*, Paris: Editions de l'Ecole des Hautes Etudes en Sciences Sociales, 29–50.

Rothbard, M. N. 1973. *For a New Liberty*, New York: Collier-Macmillan, 1978.

Steedman, I. 1977. *Marx after Sraffa*, London: New Left Books.

  1985a. 'Heterogeneous labour, money wages and Marx's theory', in B. Chavance, ed., *Marx en Perspective*, Paris: Editions de l'Ecole des Hautes Etudes en Sciences Sociales, 475–94.

  1985b. 'Robots and capitalism: a Clarification', *New Left Review* 151, 125–8.

van der Veen, R. J. and Van Parijs, P. 1985. 'Entitlements theories of justice. From Nozick to Roemer and beyond', *Economics and Philosophy* 1, 69–81.

Van Parijs, P. 1984. 'What (if anything) is intrinsically wrong with capitalism?', *Philosophica* 33, 85–102.

  1992. 'Basic income capitalism', *Ethics* 102, 465–84.

  (forthcoming) *Real Freedom for All. What (if anything) can justify capitalism?*

von Weizsäcker, C. C. 1973. 'Modern capital theory and the concept of exploitation', *Kyklos* 26, 245–81.

Wright, E. O. 1986. 'Why something like socialism is necessary for the transition to communism', *Theory and Society* 15, 657–72.

6. A revolution in class theory

Many Europeans of my generation – among them some of my closest friends – have never had a 'real' job. They have spent their adult life alternating between the dole and precarious, often government-sponsored jobs. And as they grow older, they have less and less hope that their situation will ever improve. The stark contrast between their position and, say, my own or that of most of my readers – a safe job with a decent wage, career prospects, pension rights, sizable perks and so on – has made me increasingly uneasy, not least because the dark side of this contrast has been growing with the arrival of each new cohort on European labour markets. If this deep split has, as I have come to believe, become a permanent feature of welfare-state capitalism, there is at least some intuitive appeal in looking at it as a cleavage between two classes.

Yet, faced with this phenomenon, standard class analysis has little to say. The central class divide in our capitalist societies, it says, is between capitalists and workers, between the owners of the means of production (and their agents) and those who operate the latter in exchange for a wage. Within this framework, the unemployed are classified as 'virtual' workers, who just happen to be temporarily out of work. Like 'actual' workers, their central complaint is the capitalists' monopoly of the means of production. And their struggle to improve their lot cannot but merge with the pursuits of the labour movement. If this were all class analysis could offer in the present context, it would be worrying indeed, since it is unpleasantly reminiscent of bourgeois apologetics at the time of the incipient labour movement, when the spokesmen for capitalist interests attempted to convince workers that the only privilege that mattered was landownership and that, therefore, the only real fight was against land-owners.

Is class theory, as developed in the Marxian tradition, bound to become

110

the 'scientific' guise of welfare-state capitalism's established working class? Or can it be revised and extended to provide an illuminating critical analysis of social relations in contemporary capitalist countries? I believe that it can, but that extensive alterations in the standard class-theoretical framework are required. Some key ingredients for the needed reconstruction have recently been adduced by Erik Olin Wright on the basis of John Roemer's theory of exploitation.[1] My main aim, in this chapter, is to rephrase and generalize the Roemer–Wright approach in such a way that it can be fruitfully applied to the issues raised above.

In the first two sections, I spell out the distinctive formal features of this approach, and in the third, I show how its most radical extension can cover domination as well as exploitation, and sex or race as well as 'productive' classes. Even when restricted to exploitation and to productive assets, however, the Wright–Roemer approach can accommodate the notion of organizational classes, Wright's most original contribution, and the closely analogous notion of job classes, which will be discussed in sections 6.5 and 6.6, respectively. In the last two sections, I argue that the concept of job classes provides an essential tool for understanding the specific class structure of welfare state capitalism and the new class struggle which will, under some conditions, develop on the basis of that class structure. Some recent contributions to the microeconomics of unemployment and the emerging European debate on basic income will prove to be of crucial importance for this discussion.

6.1 What do we want classes to be?

Conceptual discussions are pointless if we do not specify what job we want the concept under discussion to perform. Here I take it for granted that the purposes of class theory are not primarily normative. Consequently, we do not need to try to make sense of the claim that we must strive for a classless society – even though the class concept we end up selecting may be such that we can defensibly maintain that classes ought to be abolished. Instead, I assume that we are searching for a class concept that is:

> Relevant to the explanation of *consciousness* (ideology, values, attitudes) and/or *action* (lifestyle, political behaviour, social conflict).[2] 1.

But what is a *class* explanation of consciousness or action? I submit that the explanatory variable must at least be:

Hierarchical, in the sense that one can meaningfully say that one class is 'superior' to another.   2.

In other words, class has something to do with inequality. Moreover, the explanatory variable must also be:

Discrete, in the sense that belonging to a class is not just a matter of degree.   3.

In other words, even if class is defined by reference to some gradient (income, wealth), there must be some non-arbitrary boundary. These two conditions are still very liberal. They would be met, for example, by a classification that grouped people according to whether they can curl their tongues or according to whether they lived above or below sea level.

The class-theoretical research programme is, of course, more distinctive than this. It is rooted in a materialistic conception of history and hence requires classes to be defined in 'materialistic' terms. This can be understood in two distinct senses. One may mean that classes must be:

Concerned (by definition) with the distribution of *material advantages and burdens*, that is, of (a) income and work, but also possibly of (b) exercise of and submission to power,   4.

or that they must be:

Rooted (by definition) in the *property relations* that characterize the mode of production concerned.   5.

Property relations refer, for example, to the feudal rights enjoyed by the lords over their serfs or to the capitalists' private ownership of the means of production. Under either interpretation, this requirement of materialism implies that classes must be 'objective', in the sense that belonging to a class is a matter of situation rather than of consciousness or action.[3] If class were a matter of consciousness or action, class explanations, given the nature of the facts they are meant to explain, would become tautological.

Very schematically, it could be said that conventional definitions of class meet either condition (4) or condition (5), but never both. The conventional exploitation definition (workers versus profit earners) meets (4a). The conventional domination definition (workers versus their bosses) meets (4b); and the conventional ownership definition (those who own the means of production versus those who do not) meets (5). As we shall see, Wright's new conception of class has the advantage of simultaneously meeting (4) and (5), while elegantly generating a set of hierarchical and discrete classes that do not give rise to the 'embarrassment of the middle classes'. In other words, Wright's concept is materialistic in both senses mentioned above as well as hierarchical and discrete, and, unlike conventional definitions, it does not generate large intermediate categories that are hard to put to explanatory use. The method Wright uses to achieve this remarkable result is directly inspired by John Roemer's 'game-theoretical' concept of exploitation.[4] Let us carefully examine what it consists in.

6.2 The logical structure of class explanations

In the third part of his *General Theory of Exploitation and Class*, Roemer defines exploitation with the help of a 'withdrawal game'. A group is *exploited* (or *exploits*) if its members would become better off (or would become worse off) as a result of withdrawing from the economy. By varying the rules to which this withdrawal must conform, one can generate a number of institutionally specific types of exploitation. Feudal exploitation, capitalist exploitation, and socialist exploitation are distinguished by whether the withdrawers are allowed to depart, respectively, with their initial share of all assets, their per capita share of alienable assets (wealth), or their per capita share of inalienable assets (skills). Unfortunately, this formulation in terms of withdrawal games leads to a number of counterintuitive consequences, especially as we relax the restrictive assumption of a perfectly competitive economy with income-maximizing agents with which Roemer conducts his argument.[5]

Such difficulties can largely be resolved, however, if one interprets Roemer's game-theoretical definition as a simple conceptual *test* to check for exploitation under highly idealized circumstances (perfect competition, constant returns to scale, no incentive effects). The *definition* of exploitation, however, is to be phrased directly in terms of the *causal* influence of the distribution of various assets on the distribution of income (or of income-leisure bundles). In feudal exploitation, distribution of ownership over *people* affects the distribution of real income. In capitalist exploitation, the unequal distribution of ownership of the *means of production* influences the way incomes are distributed. And in socialist exploitation, it is the unequal distribution of *skills* that plays a causal role in shaping the distribution of income.[6] To this list, Wright adds *organizational* exploitation, which can analogously be defined by reference to the influence of an unequal distribution of organizational assets on the distribution of income. He accordingly defines as many classes as there are combinations of exploiter or exploited statuses according to these various definitions.

This general concept of class beautifully meets the various desiderata set forth in the previous section. It is hierarchical and discrete in the sense specified there: the non-arbitrary boundary between classes is determined by asking who would be better off and who would be worse off if the type of asset under consideration were equally distributed. It is also materialistic in the sense of both conditions (4) and (5). Since it refers to the distribution of income, it is clearly concerned, by definition, with material advantages. And since it refers to the distribution of assets, it is rooted, by definition, in the structure of property relations that characterizes a mode of production.

The logical structure of the class-theoretical research programme is thereby given a new, and rather attractive, shape. Contrary to simplistic presentations, class theory does *not* attempt to derive whatever aspect of consciousness or action it aims to explain (E) from the distribution of material advantages (M), using the simple causal scheme: $M \rightarrow E$. Nor does it attempt to derive its explanandum (E) from the distribution of a particular type of asset (A^*) – for example, the alienable means of production – to which it would give a special privilege at all times and places, using the simple causal scheme: $A^* \rightarrow E$.

Rather, the class-theoretical research programme consists in first asking, within a given historical context, which type of asset (A) exerts a major influence on the distribution of material advantages (M), and in next conjecturing that the control of that type of asset (A) therefore constitutes a major factor in the explanation of whatever aspect of consciousness or action one wants to explain (E), in particular of those aspects that command the future of the mode or production (attitudes and behaviour with respect to property rights).[7]

Hence, the underlying causal scheme can be represented as

$$(A \rightarrow M) \rightarrow (A \rightarrow E).$$

In other words, a class explanation entails the existence of three causal links. If the first link ($A \rightarrow M$) were absent – for example, if all material advantages were distributed by a lottery – there would be no classes. If the third link ($A \rightarrow E$) were absent – if the assets that shape the distribution of income did not shape consciousness and behaviour – the class explanation would be straightforwardly falsified. Moreover, even if the assets that shape the distribution of income also shape those aspects of consciousness and behaviour that interest us, the class explanation may still be false; the truth of such an explanation requires the assets to shape consciousness and behaviour *because* they shape the distribution of income – that is, it entails the existence of the central causal link in the formula given above.[8]

Thus, class is now defined in terms of income inequality.[9] But class so defined differs fundamentally from an income group, not just because the definition turns a continuous distribution into a discrete classification (those who would be better off and those who would be worse off if assets were equalized), but mainly because it filters out any aspect of the income distribution resulting from choice or luck rather than from the unequal distribution of some asset.[10] Class divisions are therefore closer to inequalities in the control over assets. However, belonging to the exploiting class (with respect to some particular asset) is not equivalent to having more than the average amount of that asset since assets may be left dormant instead of being used 'productively' to generate income. The owner of dormant assets would not be made worse off by asset equalization. The possession of assets is a potential and is turned into class membership only when this potential is used.

6.3 Class, domination and exploitation.

Erik Wright describes the move to this new concept of class, inspired by Roemer's approach to exploitation, as a shift from the domination-based to an exploitation-based concept of class. But this is a misdescription. For the gist of such a move is just as compatible with the former as with the latter.[11] There is no reason why, in the logical structure spelled out above, one should restrict the interpretation of material advantages (M) to income, or even to income-leisure bundles,[12] thereby leaving out *power*, construed as the (successful) giving of commands. Just as we can distinguish between capitalist exploiters and the capitalistically exploited in terms of whether they would have less or more income (with an unchanged amount of labour) if wealth were equalized, could we not distinguish between capitalist dominators and the capitalistically dominated in terms of whether they would have less or more power if wealth were equalized?[13] And what applies to wealth-based inequalities can easily be extended, *mutatis mutandis*, to inequalities deriving from the unequal distribution of other types of assets. What is essential to a Roemer-inspired approach is the fact that it focuses on the causal link between assets and material advantages, and not the particular type of material advantage it happens to select.

Of course, for such an extension of the class concept to be of any use, we need a well-defined concept of power. In particular, we need a concept that lends itself to measurement at least to the extent that it is in principle possible to say whether someone's power would be increased under various hypothetical arrangements. Note, however, that this implies no more than an *intra*-personally comparable and ordinal – though ultimately one-dimensional – concept. (We do not need to be able to say how much power an agent has or whether he/she has more power than another, but only whether his/her power increases or decreases.) Note, too, that income, especially but not exclusively in a non-monetary economy, is not an unproblematic concept either. (Think for example, of the fuzzy notion of a perk: should the enjoyment of a large desk or thick carpets, and not just that of a company car and business meals, count as part of a manager's income?)

Furthermore, the concept of power we need has to be analytically distinct from the various asset concepts. This looks particularly tricky when the assets concerned consist in ownership rights over people, control over the state, or organizational assets. The intuition that needs to be worked out, however, is that these assets – just like the ownership of wealth and skills – are titles or rights, to be enforced by legal or customary sanctions, whereas power, as a material advantage derived from one's ownership of assets, consists in actually getting one's commands obeyed, shaping what is produced and how. The test for analytical distinctness is that one must conceivably be able to hold those assets – to be a feudal lord or a manager – without actually giving the orders that the holding of these assets entitles one to give, just as the test for the analytical distinct-ness between wealth and income is that one must conceivably be able to be rich without earning any income.

If these conceptual difficulties can be solved – and I believe they can – the result will be a dual concept of class that extends Wright's concept while preserving the key feature of Roemer's notion of exploitation, namely the systematic connection between assets and material advan-tages. In other words, what Roemer's insight prompts is not a shift from a domination-based to an exploitation-based concept; it just happened that, being interested in exploitation, he naturally focused on one par-ticular type of material advantage – namely, income. Rather, what Roemer's insight prompts is a shift from definitions of class phrased either simply in terms of material advantages or simply in terms of assets to a definition phrased in terms of the causal link between advantages and assets. If asset-based power is as worthy of a place in a materialistic approach as asset-based income, there is no reason why such an approach should emphasize exploitation over domination.[14] For the sake of simplicity, however, the rest of this chapter is almost exclusively concerned with exploitation.

6.4 The radical extension: race and sex as class

Turning our attention from material advantages to assets, we can similarly ask why Wright restricts assets to the four rights he lists: over people, over means of production, over skills, and over organization assets. To give this question a rigorous answer, let us first turn to Roemer's original discussion of exploitation. Most of it focuses on two types of assets, wealth and skills (which he sometimes contrasts as alienable versus inalienable productive assets). There is nothing surprising about this selection. In a perfectly competitive market economy – the sort of economy most of Roemer's models are about – income, at equilibrium, is determined by marginal product. In such a context, only those items that 'contribute to production' can affect the distribution of income. *Skills* are simply all those productive items that cannot be detached from their bearers (and hence cannot be sold), whereas all other productive assets can be sold and are therefore subsumed under the concept of *wealth*. The real world, of course, only vaguely resembles this simple picture. Many systematic income differences – that is, differences that do not stem from choice or luck – cannot be accounted for by differences in skills or wealth, in however broad a sense.

Indeed, Roemer speaks about feudal exploitation in precapitalist societies and about status exploitation in socialist societies precisely to denote deviations from the income distribution that competitive markets would tend to generate. Whereas *feudal* exploitation occurs whenever feudal bondages affect the distribution of income, *status* exploitation occurs when special privileges (in income terms) accrue to someone because of membership in the communist party or position in the bureaucratic hierarchy.[15] The intuition behind feudal exploitation differs from that behind status exploitation in two ways: feudal exploitation is a personal relationship, and it is determined by birth, whereas those exploited by virtue of their lack of status in a socialist society need not be personally related in any way to their exploiters or prevented by virtue of their birth from acceding to the position of status exploiters. However, Roemer's wealth (or capitalist) exploitation covers cases in which there is a personal relationship involved (the exploitation of a wage worker by her/his employer) as well as cases in which there is nothing of the sort (two unequally wealthy autarkic communities), whereas his skills (or socialist) exploitation covers both the case of innate talents and that of acquired skills. Neither of the two differences between feudal and status exploitation can therefore consistently be used by Roemer as a basis for turning them into two distinct types of exploitation on a par with wealth and skills exploitation. Rather, consistency requires that one should construe feudal exploitation as a variety of status exploitation and define the latter – in a purely negative fashion – as income inequality stemming from the unequal distribution of 'non-productive' assets.

The plausibility of this reconstruction is enhanced if one considers that, according to Roemer (1982: 247), status exploitation can occur under capitalism as well. The so-called internal labour market makes for a hierarchy of wages within large firms that could hardly be said to mirror inequalities in skills and marginal products. In order to secure loyalty to the firm and strong work incentives under imperfect competition, promotion systems have been set up in such a way that income is strongly affected by seniority and by past performance. To take an extreme case, the best-paid job (which one only gets after a certain number of years in the firm and/or if one is believed to have worked harder than anyone else) might be one in which no skill is exerted and whose productivity is zero (say, sitting in a deep armchair smoking cigars and gazing through the window). Even a perfectly competitive capitalist economy with rational profit-maximizers – though not, of course, a perfectly competitive economy of independent producers – could contain such jobs.[16] Whether one can attain such positions, that is, whether one can become a status exploiter, may, of course, depend on the skills one possesses and has exerted in the past. But this does not turn status exploitation into a variety of skills exploitation, just as the fact that one's current wealth is the result of the past exertion of one's skills does not turn wealth exploitation into a variety of skills exploitation.

There are, of course, many other dimensions of status exploitation in this purely negative sense, most of which can be viewed either as constraints on the free operation of the market or as responses to imperfect information or transaction costs. For example, my Belgian citizenship gives me a number of income advantages over citizens of some other countries because citizenship determines, to a significant extent, where one is allowed to settle, which jobs one can apply for, or what benefits one is eligible for.[17] Similarly, the fact that in some remote past I got a degree – perhaps to certify that I had acquired some skills that have now been eroded away – also enables me to get higher benefits and better-paid jobs.

Moreover, a significant part of what is usually called sexual or racial *discrimination* can be given an analogous interpretation. True, the concept of productive skill could be stretched to cover the facts that a male executive does not risk career interruption by pregnancy or that a black shop assistant may turn away racially prejudiced customers. True too, much discrimination takes the form of the indirect influence of race or sex on income via selective access to skill acquisition. There is little doubt, however, that this attempt to reduce sex and race either directly to skill or indirectly to factors commanding skill acquisition leaves a considerable residue. Equally skilled men and women and blacks and whites frequently get unequal rewards because of their sex or race, even though they would not in a perfectly competitive economy.[18] In other words, there is specifically racial and sexual exploitation. Being (at least) as innate as feudal exploitation and as impersonal as citizenship or degree exploitation, both are varieties of status exploitation as defined above.

The notion of status exploitation then simply covers all types of income inequality attributable neither to luck nor to choice nor to inequalities in wealth or skills. Given the heterogeneity of this residual category, it is presumably wise not to define a single status-class divide (in terms of who would be better off and who worse off if the impact of status on income were neutralized). Rather, there should be as many class divides as there are factors systematically affecting the distribution of material advantages. The inhabitants of developed countries and those of the Third World, graduates and the uneducated, males and females, blacks and whites, can then constitute pairs of classes just as much as those who own considerable wealth and those who do not.[19] Which of these class divides is most relevant in a particular historical context simply depends on which factors most powerfully affect the distribution of income and power.

6.5 Productive assets and organizational classes

Wright (1985b: sect. 3), however, explicitly and firmly resists this radical extension of the Marxist notion of class, on the grounds that the materialistic class concept we are after should be concerned only with inequalities in material welfare stemming from unequal ownership of the *productive forces.* This restriction cannot possibly be justified by the expectation that the distribution of productive assets, in this sense, universally affects the distribution of material advantages more powerfully than race or sex, for example. Nor can it be justified by the belief that income or power inequalities deriving from inequalities in productive endowments are more objectionable or more conducive to ill-feelings than, say, sex-based or race-based inequalities. One can only hope to justify such a restriction, I believe, if one confines the explanandum of class theory to consciousness or action *related to a change in the mode of production*, the latter being defined in terms of property rights over the productive forces. Classes in this restricted sense cannot be expected to provide the sole basis for a materialistic theory of consciousness and action in general. But it can sensibly be argued that such a restriction is warranted if our primary aim is to understand why a society moves from one mode of production to another, because classes in this restricted sense partition society into different categories precisely according to whether they have a (*prima facie*) interest in a different mode of production.

Even if we accept this restriction, however, the Roemer–Wright approach can still yield a significant broadening of conventional class analysis along the assets dimension. How serious this restriction is depends on how narrowly the notions of productive forces and, hence, of mode of production are conceived. From the previous section, one might expect 'productive' classes to be defined in terms of wealth and skills exploitation and the residual category of status exploitation to be ejected from the realm of class. In addition to wealth classes and skills classes, however, Wright allows for classes defined by feudal exploitation – on the grounds that labour power is a productive force – as well as for classes defined by organizational exploitation – on the grounds that organization is a productive asset distinct from wealth and skill. Can this be sustained?

Take feudal exploitation first. Either one does *not* view the feudally exploited as part of the lord's property and interprets feudal exploitation as the serf's obligation to pay a due (in labour, goods, or money) to the lord. Such an obligation, as protected by custom and enforced, if necessary, by force, is bound to involve an influence on income distribution that is not reducible to wealth exploitation. But it plainly constitutes a standard case of *status exploitation* in the above (purely negative) sense. Although the lord's status can legitimately be construed as an asset – it is vested in him by the prevailing structure of property rights and commands access to material advantages – it cannot be regarded as a productive asset, that is something that, on a par with the means of production and the skills of labour power, contributes to the social product.

Alternatively, one may interpret feudal exploitation as an inequality of income that derives from the fact that some people own, at least in part, some other people and hence their labour power (on the slavery pattern). Feudal exploitation then becomes one aspect of wealth exploitation, along, say, with income inequality generated by the unequal ownership of horses. However, there is a sufficiently significant qualitative difference between such human wealth and other types of wealth to justify our assigning societies in which the ownership of other people is allowed (partial or total slavery) and societies in which it is banned, to different modes of production. (Similarly, a society that bans the private ownership of land though not that of other material means of production may be said to have a mode of production distinct from the one obtaining in a society in which all non-human goods can be privately appropriated.) The need to explain changes in the mode of production would then make it mandatory to allow for feudal (and possibly land) classes in this sense, instead of lumping everything together under the single heading of wealth classes. To sum up: if, as Wright insists, classes have to be defined in terms of income inequalities stemming from unequal control over productive forces, then either feudal classes are not classes at all or they constitute a sub-type of wealth classes, though one that may deserve separate treatment.

An analogous reduction to wealth exploitation is out of the question in the case of Wright's most novel category, *organizational exploitation*. Organization assets consist in 'controlling the technical division of labor, the coordination of productive activities within and across labor processes' (Wright 1985b: section 3). There is no doubt that the way in which the division of labour is organized can affect productivity to a tremendous extent and that those who do this organizing are thereby enabled to appropriate considerable material advantages (both in terms of income and, almost by definition, in terms of power). But it does not follow that organization assets constitute a distinct type of productive asset. Here again, two interpretations are possible. One could view the task of organizing the labour process as the exertion of a particular kind of skill. In a capitalist economy, this constitutes the specific job of the entrepreneur, who takes economic initiatives and brings capital and labour together to produce commodities. It is true that the entrepreneur's rewards cannot be reduced to capitalist or wealth exploitation: an entrepreneur might conceivably operate entirely with borrowed funds. It is also true that such rewards are very different, under capitalism, from most rewards for skills, insofar as they tend to be eroded by imitation and competition and have completely disappeared from (notional) equilibrium situations.[20] Yet, however peculiar the skill and however precarious the way in which it is rewarded, such organizational exploitation is, under socialism even more than under capitalism, just a special case of skills exploitation.

There is, however, another interpretation that does justify a distinct treatment. Imagine a situation in which the job of organizing production does not require any particularly scarce, valuable skill. If the person who happens to do it were replaced by any other ablebodied worker, there would be no noticeable difference. Nonetheless, the job is an essential one, and if it were not done, economic performance would be disastrous. This gives incumbents of such positions – on a par with the possessors of skills and wealth – a potential base for claiming material advantages, providing property relations are such that incumbency is firmly established. The essential difference between organization assets and skills concerns the nature of the sanction they confer on their holders: the disturbance of the production process in one case, the withdrawal of a precious input in the other. To the extent that market forces rule, the sanction associated with organization assets is kept within narrow bounds, as its use – the disruption of production – would threaten the very source – profits booked by selling the product – of the material advantages potentially accruing to those using it. Hence, returns to organization will be under constant pressure to disappear unless they are reinvigorated by the exertion of innovative skills. Under monopolistic capitalism, however, and even more under centrally planned socialism, organization assets are given considerable leeway to shape the distribution of material advantages.

Consequently, unlike feudal exploitation, organizational exploitation cannot be subsumed under either of Roemer's two types of productive-asset exploitation (based on wealth and skills) or dumped into the residual category of status exploitation. Organization assets do affect production, though not in the same way as 'withdrawable' factors of production. It makes sense, therefore, to incorporate them into the definition of a mode of production. And Wright's four-fold distinction (human means of production, material means of production, personal skills, organization) can be preserved as a meaningful and provocative conjecture about the sequence of dominant class divisions from slavery to bureaucratic socialism.

6.6 Jobs as assets and the microeconomics of unemployment

Without questioning Wright's restriction to productive assets (in his fairly broad sense), however, I want to argue that this typology is badly defective because it is blind to what tends to become the central class divide under what I shall loosely call welfare-state capitalism. Persistent involuntary unemployment provides my argument with its most natural point of departure. By definition, someone who is involuntarily unemployed is someone who possesses all the qualifications required to fill existing jobs and would be willing to do so for a wage lower than that paid to current incumbents. Consequently, the very existence of involuntary unemployment establishes that the holding of jobs influences the distribution of material welfare in a way that is not reducible to the influence of skills. But if involuntary unemployment is a purely transient phenomenon, both for society as a whole and for the individuals affected, the possession of a job cannot be viewed as a significant asset. This is, of course, exactly what standard models of perfectly competitive market economies imply. Such economies constantly tend toward an equilibrium state in which all those wanting to work have a job and earn a wage equal to their marginal product. Wealth and skills, in such a context, are highly important assets, but the holding of a job does not constitute an asset at all.

In contrast with this standard approach, some recent developments in economic theory (both radical and mainstream) have endeavoured to establish the possibility of equilibrium involuntary unemployment, even under perfectly competitive conditions. One of them, the so-called insiders-outsiders approach, is directly relevant to our present purposes.[21] It attempts to answer the riddle of persistent involuntary unemployment – why don't firms accept lower bids from outsiders instead of paying more than the market-clearing wage to their current employees? – by pointing (primarily) to the importance of hiring, training, and firing costs. Replacing an insider by an equally qualified, equally paid outsider is an expensive operation for a firm: severance pay to the worker being replaced, advertisements to find someone else, interviews, health checks, time spent teaching the job to the new recruit, initial mistakes due to lack of experience, and so forth may amount to a considerable cost that the firm saves by keeping its current employee. This provides the insider with possibly ample room to maneuvre to negotiate a wage exceeding both the outsider's reservation wage and his/her own.

How ample this room is depends on the size of the costs involved, and these in turn are largely a matter of institutional framework. The incentive for a firm to keep a worker at a wage significantly higher than what the unemployed would be willing to accept is, for example, much stronger if sacked workers are entitled to two years' severance pay than it is if the firm owes no compensation to the dismissed worker. How much of the maneuvring room thus created the workers will actually use depends on their bargaining power. Even a worker who bargains individually, with quitting as her/his sole weapon, may be able to win in higher wages a substantial portion of what it would cost the firm to replace her/him by an outsider. Collective bargaining and the use of such weapons as strikes and work-to-the-rule may further enhance this ability up to the point where insiders appropriate nearly all the firm saves by keeping them rather than hiring outsiders.[22]

It follows that some involuntary unemployment can be expected at equilibrium in any market economy relying on wage labour – there are always some hiring and training costs that will give rise, through the mechanism sketched above, to a discrepancy between the equilibrium wage (no endogenous pressure to change) and the market-clearing wage (demand matches supply). But this discrepancy, and the corresponding level of involuntary unemployment, will become significant only as the 'right to one's job' becomes institutionalized in various ways – in particular through statutory severance pay and recognition of the right to strike. Insofar as such a right is a central specific feature of welfare-state capitalism, this form of capitalism is inevitably characterized by a sizeable amount of involuntary unemployment and, hence, of material inequality deriving from the unequal distribution of job assets.

This conclusion receives further support from another, quite distinct, development in the microeconomics of unemployment, so-called efficiency wage theories. The central question is the same as above. What prevents market forces from eliminating involuntary unemployment? Why don't capitalist firms take advantage of underbidding by adequately qualified unemployed workers? The answer, however, is very different. This theory does not appeal to the difference between the bargaining positions of insiders and outsiders, but to the fact that productivity is affected by the wage level and that, therefore, the lowest wage the employer could get away with is not necessarily the profit-maximizing one. There are at least two reasons why this may be the case and, correspondingly, two main variants of efficiency wage theory.[23] The soft, *Maussian* variant claims that the profit-maximizing wage is higher than the market-clearing wage because workers who feel well treated by an employer from whom they receive a wage significantly higher than their reservation wage respond to this gift with a countergift in the form of keen performance.[24] The hard, *Hobbesian* variant claims instead that the firm's optimal wage rate exceeds the market-clearing rate because raising the workers' pay above what they could easily get elsewhere if sacked enhances their welfare loss in the case of dismissal and hence their incentive not to shirk.[25] As pointed out by proponents of both variants, the central claim of efficiency wage theory can also be expressed using the Marxian distinction between labour and labour power: paying as little as possible (the market-clearing rate) for a time unit of labour power (with given skills) generally does not amount to paying as little as possible per unit of labour effectively performed since a higher payment per unit of time may enable the capitalist, for either of the reasons mentioned above, to extract from each unit of labour time a significantly greater amount of actual labour.[26]

It follows that, even in the absence of any attempt by insiders to take advantage of their superior bargaining position, the capitalists' profit-maximizing behaviour drives a wedge between equilibrium wages and reservation wages, thus turning involuntary unemployment into an intrinsic feature of any capitalist economy. Here again, however, this feature can be expected to grow more significant with the development of the welfare state. Shapiro and Stiglitz (1984: 434), for example, point out that one of the implications of their (Hobbesian) model is a positive relation between the unemployment rate and unemployment benefits (or other welfare payments). The reason for this is not, as conventionally asserted, that high benefits slow job search and thereby boost voluntary unemployment, but rather that high benefits soften the sanction of dismissal by reducing the welfare differential between being employed at a given wage and being unemployed. The higher the benefits, the theory predicts, the higher the efficiency wage, and hence (other things remaining equal) the higher the level of unemployment.[27] It hardly needs saying that this expectation is further strengthened if, as is usually the case, benefits are financed out of wages. Consequently, insofar as the distribution of the welfare state can be construed, at least in part, as a rise in the level of benefits (say, as a proportion of GNP per capita), efficiency wage theory warrants the expectation that welfare-state capitalism will be endemically plagued by a particularly high level of involuntary unemployment.[28]

This is not the place the discuss how well these two approaches fit the available data on unemployment, how much of the latter they explain, or to what extent they compete with or supplement other accounts based, for example, on the deficiency of aggregate demand or on rationing. If the analysis stemming from either of the above approaches is correct, however, the distribution of (irreducible) job assets significantly affects the distribution of material welfare in any capitalist economy – as opposed to a market economy without wage labour – and this influence becomes ever more significant as the welfare state develops, whether in the form of an increasingly entrenched right to one's job or (somewhat paradoxically) in the form of a rising level of unemployment benefits. One can accordingly define a *job exploiter* (a *job exploited*) as someone who would be worse off (better off) if job assets were equally distributed, with the distribution of skills remaining unchanged and all efficiency effects being assumed away.[29] Job exploitation thus defined provides a further item on Wright's list of class divisions. Like feudal, capitalist, skills, and organizational exploitation, it denotes a way in which the unequal control over some productive forces generates inequalities in the distribution of material welfare.[30]

6.7 The class structure of welfare-state capitalism

Just how significant is this job class division under advanced welfare-state capitalism? Does the unequal distribution of job assets generate inequalities in material welfare to anything like the same extent as the unequal distribution of capital does? Is there any sign that it affects consciousness and behaviour, in particular collective action aimed at changing the corresponding property relations? Should a class struggle between those endowed with a job and the jobless be expected to play an increasingly prominent role under welfare-state capitalism?[31]

To tackle these questions, let us first ask in which counterfactual situation the material welfare of the millions of West Europeans who are currently receiving unemployment or welfare benefits would be most enhanced: in a situation in which capital income were equally divided among all adults or in a situation in which labour income were equally shared among all those wanting to work? There is no doubt as to the answer: the unemployed would gain much more from a redistribution of jobs than from a redistribution of wealth.[32] Admittedly, this is only a very rough estimate of the significance of job assets. On the one hand, it overestimates that significance quite considerably by assuming skills to be evenly distributed between the employed and the unemployed.

Although the gap between the educational level of the average worker and that of the average unemployed person has narrowed strikingly in the past ten years of massive unemployment,[33] it is still far from having closed completely. Consequently, the simple test described above captures the effect of some redistribution of skills as well as of job assets. On the other hand, there are also a number of reasons why this test greatly underestimates the real impact of job assets. First, it completely ignores the indirect incomes associated with having a job, mainly pension rights, to which the unemployed fail to gain entitlement. Second, it reduces the material welfare derived from having a job to the wage attached to it. But being unemployed does not just mean a cut in one's standard of living. It also means a loss of social integration and self-respect, which badly affects the material welfare of the people affected – in particular, their health.[34]

Most important, however, this test completely ignores the unequal distribution of job assets *among the employed*. There is, of course, a world of difference between a part-time, casual, poorly paid job, and a full-time, well-protected, and well-paid one. Some of the differences simply reflect the fact that people are at different stages in their careers. Others directly reflect inequalities in skills or inequalities in the control over organizational assets. But many, possibly most, of the differences are irreducibly rooted in what happens to be the distribution of 'ownership' over jobs. Both the insiders-outsiders approach and efficiency wage theories predict wage differences among workers with identical skills; for example, as a function of intersectoral differences in hiring and firing costs or in the cost of monitoring performance.[35] Whether the underlying mechanism involves the unequal bargaining power attached to different jobs (insiders-outsiders approach) or the unequal interest the employer has in paying more than the reservation wage (efficiency wage theories), it is the holding of the job itself that is the source of the relevant material advantages.

One implication of this remark is that it is not just the unemployed who would gain from an equalization of job assets. Another is that even the purely static impact of such equalization becomes difficult to assess with any precision. Such an overall assessment is required, however, if one is to be able to compare the current significance of class divisions based on different types of assets. To establish that the job divide has now become more significant than the class divide, it is not enough to show that the jobless would gain more from a redistribution of jobs than from a redistribution of wealth – just as showing that the propertyless would gain more from the latter than from the former would not suffice to establish that capital ownership remains the central determinant of the class structure. What needs to be shown is that a greater share of the inter-individual variation in material welfare can be (causally) explained by the distribution of job assets than by the distribution of capital assets. Needless to say, these remarks do not pretend even to start seriously investigating the empirical validity of this conjecture. But they suffice to show, I hope, that at least in some of the most developed welfare-state capitalist countries, the claim that the job class division has become the central component of the class structure makes enough sense for such an investigation to be worth undertaking.

6.8 The new class struggle

Suppose that, for some countries at least, such a claim can be established. Should one then expect the central class struggle under welfare-state capitalism to be one between those with a stable, decently paid job and those deprived of access to such a job, rather than, say, between capitalists or manager-entrepreneurs and workers? For this to happen, a movement of the *job poor* – the unemployed and the casually employed – needs to get off the ground and formulate a coherent social project that would remove the property relations from which they suffer. But however deep the job class divide, is there not ample ground for scepticism about the possibility of mobilizing the job poor into collective action and of giving such action a coherent positive objective?

Even if the job poor are a class in the objective sense considered here, it is frequently argued that they will never become a class in a subjective sense; that is, that they will never acquire class consciousness or organize class action.[36] The unemployed and casual workers form a heterogeneous group, which they are often not aware of belonging to, let alone proud to be members of. Dole queues, unlike factories, do not lend themselves to the sort of interaction that can lead to collective demands and actions. Unlike workers, who can strike, the unemployed have no weapon they can use in support of their claims. Those among them who are able to organize and mobilize the others are 'good' enough to get a real job and leave the class.[37] All these arguments point to genuine practical obstacles in the way of the rise of a movement of the job poor. The most serious obstacle, however, may be of an ideological nature. What is the social model, the change in property rights, that the job poor should be fighting for in order to abolish or reduce inequalities stemming from the unequal distribution of job assets?

In a way, centralized socialism provides the most straightforward answer to this question. Only a system in which the means of production are centrally controlled could in principle ensure that job assets are equally shared by all those wanting to work. However, even leaving aside the possible cost in terms of other values (such as freedom), the risk that even the asset poor may end up worse off as a result of the implementation of such a system (taking all dynamic effects into account, not just the static effects considered when applying the criterion for exploitation) is now broadly perceived in our societies as an overwhelming one. Indeed, the notion that centralized socialism has a seriously adverse effect on efficiency gains further credibility if a legal right to a (decent) job is made an intrinsic component of it – as it needs to be in the present context.[38]

Instead of dwelling on this controversial, but academic, issue, let us ask whether there is an alternative; that is, whether there is any way of drastically reducing job-asset-based inequalities within the framework of a decentralized economy, either capitalist or market socialist. A general and significant cut in maximum working hours (with matching cuts in gross wages), as advocated in Europe by some of the unions and parties that claim to have the interests of both employed and unemployed workers at heart, may seem to fit the bill. However, both theoretical considerations and empirical data on the history of work-sharing policies raise doubt about their ability to do much to solve the problem of mass unemployment without such a heavy loss in efficiency that even their 'beneficiaries' would end up worse off.[39]

Instead of trying to equalize job assets, one may then (reluctantly) turn to neutralizing the effects of their unequal distribution – just as the working-class movement has turned away from the objective of socializing capital to that of raising the share of wages. In the case of job assets, however, this sort of strategy seems to contain an internal contradiction. For as one increases the incomes of the jobless – unemployment benefits and welfare payments – is one not bound, by virtue of the mechanism sketched above in connection with efficiency wage theories, to increase their numbers? When trying to improve their current, disadvantaged station, the jobless would then be forced to worsen their chances of leaving it. Given that this strategy does nothing about the non-pecuniary advantages of having a job – or about inequalities among the employed – the net result of any effort in this direction looks bound to be an *increase* in job-related inequalities in material welfare.

This quick run through three possible objectives for a movement of the job poor may suggest that such a movement is doomed for lack of any coherent positive project. But what about the following, fourth possibility, which is now coming to the fore in those European countries in which an organized unemployed movement has more or less managed to get off the ground?[40] The proposal is to give every permanent inhabitant, whether waged, self-employed, or jobless, a completely unconditional 'universal grant' or 'basic income' sufficient to cover at least fundamental needs.[41] At first sight, this is no more than a slight variant of the previous strategy for attenuating the pecuniary inequalities generated by the unequal distribution of jobs. However, there are a number of crucial differences, one of which is particularly relevant in the present context. An adequate basic income does not mean just a reduction in the cost of not having a job. It also means that everyone is now given the real possibility of creating, alone or with others, her/his own job. Why? Because the very notion of what constitutes a (paid) job is substantially altered as a result of fundamental needs being unconditionally covered. A job must no longer be an activity yielding an income sufficient to cover at least these needs; and creating one's own job, therefore, no longer requires an amount of capital out of proportion to what the vast majority can afford.[42] Even with a substantial basic income, however, job assets could still be very unequally distributed among the employed (including the self-employed). Nevertheless, whether under capitalism or, *mutatis mutandis*, under market socialism, the basic income strategy offers the unemployed (and 'poorly employed') movement a way of attempting to systematically reduce the privilege conferred by job assets while *expanding* (unlike the previous strategy) the circle of those with access to a job. Moreover, through a general increase in every individual's bargaining power on the labour market, it also means a gradual erosion of the inegalitarian impact of job assets among the employed.

If the argument sketched in the preceding paragraph is correct, the ideological obstacle to class struggle along the job-asset dimension is now removed. What about the practical obstacles mentioned earlier? There are good grounds for believing that something like the introduction of a basic income – first at a modest level and without total replacement of current social transfers – is itself the key condition for the building of a strong movement in the service of the strategy described above. Such an institution would provide those wishing to set up an organization along these lines with the minimum amount of financial security and undisturbed leisure they need for this purpose. More important, it would homogenize a large number of people currently split into numerous categories with no perceived common interest (the registered unemployed, welfare claimants, low-paid workers, housewives, students, pensioners on a low pension). And it would dramatically curtail the current vulnerability of the unemployed movement to upward mobility (getting a job would no longer amount to leaving the group) and to stigmatization (no need to be ashamed of receiving what everyone receives).[43] In stating that the existence of something like a basic income is the key condition for the building of a strong movement pursuing the basic-income strategy, I am not implying that the latter is stuck in a vicious circle. The degree of universality of the grant system that is here claimed to be a prerequisite for the building of a strong job-poor movement and – even more so – the grant levels involved can fall far short of those such a movement should aim for.

Is there any chance that this prerequisite will be met anywhere on earth in the foreseeable future? One favorable factor is the current crisis of the welfare state. On both the Left and the Right, there is widespread frustration and discontent with its complexity, intrusiveness, administrative cost, and frequent counterproductivity. This provides a background on which a plan for radical reform has a fighting chance. But who is going to fight, given that it cannot be the movement that the success of this fight would make possible? It is hard to believe that the basic impulse will come from mainstream parties on the Right or on the Left, whose interests are too closely linked to those of big business and the established trade union movement. My guess is that the only serious hope in the near future lies in the emerging Green parties' ability both to survive and to bring this demand to the forefront of their platforms. The importance these parties attach to solving the unemployment problem without counting on the resumption of rapid growth and the relative value their typical members ascribe to 'leisure' (including unpaid work) as against 'consumption' (or purchased goods) combine to make it likely that most of their members will find the idea of a basic income most congenial and well worth fighting for.[44]

Whether this fight will prove successful, I do not know. Nothing in the extended framework for class analysis developed in this chapter enables us to say whether it will. What this framework has made possible is the identification of a new class divide that has – I conjecture – become even more important than the standard division between capitalists and workers in those capitalist societies in which the welfare state is most developed. This identification has prompted questions about the conditions under which class struggle along these lines could take shape.

Tackling these questions has, in turn, led to a novel interpretation of the historical significance of the European Green movement. If this line of thinking is, even approximately, on the right track, the revolution set in motion by the Roemer–Wright approach amounts to much more than academic hairsplitting. It is of central importance for a proper understanding of the fate of Western societies.

Notes

1 Wright (1985a, 1985b), Roemer (1982a, 1982b).

2 As Jon Elster (1985a: 335–6) notes, Marx himself primarily used the concept of class to explain collective action. Marx also tended to view the explanation of behaviour by class in terms of simple convergence between the class map and the behavioural map of a society (see Elster, 1985b: section 2). In both respects, the present characterization of the class-theoretical research programme is broader: it leaves room for class explanations of individual behaviour, and it allows for a more complex causal link between class and behaviour.

3 There is no lack of 'subjective' definitions of class in this sense among authors who explicitly distance themselves from the Marxist tradition. See, for example, in note 36 below, the grounds on which Dahrendorf and Gorz refuse to grant class status to the unemployed.

4 And *not* by Roemer's own class concept, to which I return below (see note 14). What I here call the Roemer–Wright approach to class (based on Roemer's game-theoretical treatment of *exploitation*) must not be confused with what I call below the Roemer–Elster approach to class (based on Roemer's 'endogenous' analysis of *class*).

5 See the *Politics & Society* (11 [1982]) symposium around Roemer (1982b).

6 For a more detailed justification of this reconstruction of Roemerian exploitation, see van der Veen and Van Parijs (1985) and chapter 5 above.

7 As Mino Carchedi pointed out to me, this provides a neat interpretation of the old Althusserian distinction between 'dominance' and 'determination in the last instance'. Which type of asset – and hence which class struggle – is dominant $(A \rightarrow E)$, varies from one mode of production to another, but is determined throughout history by an invariant criterion. This criterion gives dominance in this sense to whichever type of asset most powerfully influences the distribution of material advantages $(A \rightarrow M)$. For a formally analogous but substantially different interpretation of Althusser's 'determination in the last instance', see chapters 1 and 2 above.

8 Note that the truth of $M \rightarrow E$, though sufficient for the truth of $(A \rightarrow M) \rightarrow (A \rightarrow E)$, is by no means entailed by it. Class theory, as characterized here, is not committed to asserting that assets affect behaviour *because* assets affect income *and* income in turn affects behaviour. Singly or in combination, the three causal links that class theory consists in asserting do not even entail that income affects behaviour or that there is any statistical correlation between income and behaviour. For an old, but still very useful clarification of this point, see Costner and Leik (1964).

9 Talking about an asset-based income inequality is just a convenient shortcut. Unequally distributed ownership of asset A can conceivably affect income, and exploitation can therefore be present, even though income is distributed in a perfectly equal way. This can happen because the influence of asset A on income could (by a fluke) be exactly offset by the influence of other assets (whose ownership would need to be inversely correlated with that of A) or by the play of individual preferences and luck.

10 One's present assets may result from past luck or choice. When assets are distinguished from choice and luck as major influences on income, some time scale is implicitly brought

in. Restricting ourselves to the two extreme possibilities, we must decide whether the equalization thought experiment that enables us to determine which class someone belongs to should operate on 'initial' or on 'current' endowments. In the case of wealth, for example, should one equalize what people have received and can still be expected to receive (leaving out choice and luck) over their whole lifetimes? Or rather, should one equalize the wealth people happened to have, say, at the beginning of this month? For explanatory purposes, one major advantage of the first option is that it enables class theory to discriminate between the young with good and bad ('structural') prospects, instead of lumping (nearly) all of them together into the wealth-exploited class. One major advantage of the second option is that it puts into the wealth-exploiting class those who have accumulated wealth through a combination of choice and luck (i.e. hard work, persistent thrift, and good fortune), while putting those whom luck and choice have left with very little of their initial assets into the wealth-exploited class. Realizing the importance of the time scale selected does not blur the distinction between assets on the one hand and choice or luck on the other hand. But it does make it necessary to specify whether reference to initial assets or reference to current assets makes the concept of class more fruitful as far as the explanation of consciousness and action is concerned.

11 Moreover, Roemer's concept of exploitation itself arguably has little to do with exploitation, as the term is commonly understood. I argue in chapter 5 that any defensible explication of our (or indeed Marx's) notion of exploitation must fulfil at least three conditions: A exploits B only if (1) B works, (2) A gets a benefit from B, and (3) A exerts power over B. Not one of these conditions is fulfilled by Roemer's definition, which allows a non worker to be exploited – for example, someone choosing to live austerely on the meagre interest yielded by a smaller than average capital endowment is, according to Roemer, capitalistically exploited. Roemer's definition also allows for two autarkic communities to exploit and be exploited because of unequal endowments, even though neither of them derives any benefit from or exerts any power over the other. Hence, although I shall for convenience continue to do so below, using the term *exploitation* to refer to Roemer's concept is misleading. So, too, if only for this reason, is describing Wright's redefinition of class as a shift to an exploitation-based concept. In the text, however, I ignore this semantic issue.

12 Agents may trade income off against leisure, and the unequal distribution of assets may therefore substantially affect the distribution of material advantages by generating massive inequalities in leisure time while hardly affecting the distribution of income. (Imagine, for example, a society in which people choose to work just enough to get a subsistence income and some of whose members control an amount of wealth just sufficient to give them that income without working at all. In such a situation, wealth equalization would not make anyone better or worse off in income terms. It would only lead some people to work less (or to take on more attractive jobs) and other people to work more (or to take on less attractive jobs) than before, in order to maintain the same income level. For formal models along these lines, see Roemer 1982a: part 1.) To take this possibility into account, one needs only to modify the counterfactual exercise slightly. Instead of simply asking whether people's incomes would increase or decrease as a result of asset equalization, one must now ask this same question *assuming that* everyone keeps doing the same job for the same length of time.

13 Consider a hypothetical situation in which all incomes are equal, not by virtue of people's preferences (some of them would like to earn more than the equal-income share), but by virtue of the system's basic rules: taxes are collected in such a way that both the post-tax return on capital and the post-tax wage rate are zero. (For a description of such a system and an argument that it could work, see Carens (1981: part 1)). In such a situation, the wealth-equalization test (whether in its simpler version or in the modified version described in the preceding note) would lead to the conclusion that, even though

wealth is very unequally distributed, there is no wealth-based exploitation. At the same time, wealth-based domination may be ubiquitous. Those who own the factories get no post-tax return on their capital, but they may well exert considerable power over the workers they hire, even though the latter find their jobs so attractive that they are willing to take them at a zero net wage.

14 As mentioned earlier (note 4), Wright's concept of class, based on Roemer's concept of exploitation, differs from Roemer's concept of class, recently taken over and generalized by Jon Elster (1985a: section 6.1). Roemer (1982a: chapters 2 and 4) defines class (in a capitalist society) in terms of whether people's optimal course of action consists in selling their labour-power, in hiring someone else's labour-power, or in being self-employed (or a combination of these). This is not a purely behavioural definition, but a *modal* definition in terms of a relation between people's assets (which determine, jointly with people's preferences, what is their optimal course of action) and their overt behaviour. It can be generalized to any type of economy: 'A class is a group of people who by virtue of what they possess are compelled to engage in the same activities (working or non-working, renting or hiring land, capital or labour, giving or receiving orders) if they want to make the best use of their endowments' (Elster 1985a: 331; see also section 2). Why not adopt this general definition instead of the one used in the present chapter?

It is important to note, first of all, that the above definition uses the expression 'compelled' in a very weak and unusual sense: being compelled does not consist in having no other option or in having no other tolerable option, but simply in having no better option. In this sense, a Rockefeller who plays at being a proletarian is not just someone who does something (selling his labour power) he is not compelled to do, but ipso facto also someone who does not do something (hiring workers) that he is 'compelled' to do. Such people are absent from Roemer's models. But there are many of them in the real world: people who fail to optimize – for example, by hiring no one when, given their endowments (and imputed references), they should, or by remaining idle when optimality (on their part *and* on everyone else's) would require them to work. This leads to a dilemma. Either we define classes in terms of what people are 'compelled' to do, whether or not they actually do it, in which case we end up with 'workers' who have never worked and 'employers' who have never hired anyone – not a promising point of departure for treating the issues mentioned at the beginning of this chapter – or we define classes as categories of people who do something they are compelled to do (or, somewhat more strongly: people who do whatever they are compelled to do *because* they are compelled to do it). In this case, we end up with huge grey areas containing many more than one crazy Rockefeller. This dilemma, which does not arise with the Roemer–Wright approach, points, in my view, to a serious defect in the Roemer–Elster general concept of class and provides a major reason for rejecting it.

Elster, however, objects to the Roemer–Wright approach on two distinct grounds. First, he claims, an exploitation approach is bound to be either too coarse-grained or too fine-grained. Too coarse-grained, if classes are just a matter of exploiting or being exploited – which prevents us from distinguishing between capitalists and landowners, for example. Too fine-grained, if classes are made a matter of degree of exploitation, which does not give a better basis for a non-arbitrary discrete classification than does income distribution (see Elster 1985a: 323–4). However, the Roemer–Wright version of the exploitation-based approach allows us to make as many qualitative distinctions as there are types of assets we want to distinguish. Moreover, it provides – no more but no less than the Roemer–Elster approach – a non-arbitrary device for turning the continuous distribution of assets into a small number of discrete categories.

Second, Elster (1985a: 328) argues that 'exploitation status does not serve as a motivation for collective action, since no one in a society knows exactly where the dividing line between exploiters and exploited should be drawn'. Note again, however, that this applies much less to the Roemer–Wright exploitation concept than to the standard one (in terms of net value appropriation). It is, of course, in most cases extremely difficult to assess whether someone's income would be higher or lower than it is now if all assets of a given type were equalized. How much income some individual ends up with depends on the complex dynamics of incentive effects, on possibly counterintuitive price effects, and on the individual's own preference structure. But Roemer's exploitation criterion abstracts from these intricacies and must do so in such a way that it comes down, in practice, to simply checking whether the individual concerned owns more or less than the average amount of the type of asset under consideration. For most types of assets and most individuals, which side of this dividing line they are on should be pretty clear. Indeed, this criterion is likely to apply unambiguously in many more cases than the Roemer–Elster criterion, as soon as one fully takes into account that the latter is not a behavioural definition but a modal one: one cannot determine someone's position by looking at what (s)he does; one needs to look at what (s)he has and work out in this light what is optimal for her/him to do. Many cases will, of course, be unproblematic (you cannot rent out land if you have none, or hire workers if you cannot provide them with tools), but the number of uncertain cases cannot but be greater under this criterion than under the Roemer–Wright exploitation criterion. Consequently, if Elster's objection were sufficient to destroy his target, it would be more than sufficient to blow up the position from which he is shooting. (Roemer's proof of a systematic correspondence between class and capitalist exploitation does not invalidate this conclusion. The correspondence derives from the connection between wealth on the one hand and both class and exploitation in Roemer's sense on the other hand. But since Roemer's class partition is more fine-grained than his exploitation partition, it is clear, even in this particular case, that class status is harder to assess than exploitation status.)

15 See Roemer 1982a: 199–202, 243–7.
16 For a subtle attempt to reconcile marginal-product payment (as far as career profiles, not synchronically given incomes, are concerned) with internal wage hierarchies, see, however, Malcomson (1984: 486–507). If all internal wage hierarchies can be analysed in this way, intra-firm 'status exploitation' vanishes as soon as the appropriate time scale is selected.
17 See chapter 7, section 7.2 for an elaboration of the notion of citizenship exploitation and a discussion of its relevance.
18 A tricky case arises when the causal link between, say, sex and income, is not provided by legal restrictions or collective bargaining power, but by preference schedules (in the broadest sense, encompassing normative expectations, gender ideology, and the like): think of 'the belief of male workers, employers, and women workers themselves that there existed a woman's job and a woman's rate' (Lewis 1985: 114). Exploitation is an asset-rooted, and hence not a preference-rooted, inequality of income. But what if asset differences generate differences in preferences?
19 In some contexts, it may be equally meaningful to differentiate wealth classes as well. For example, when land has a special standing and cannot readily be exchanged against other forms of wealth (produced means of production), it makes sense to speak of land classes.
20 See the Austrian School's analysis of entrepreneurial profits (e.g. Kirzner 1973).
21 See, for example, Solow (1985), Lindbeck and Snower (1985, 1986).
22 If they appropriated the whole of it, it would become in the firm's interest to sack everyone and recruit a new lot of workers from the pool of the involuntarily unemployed.
23 Here I ignore other possible rationales for the causal connection between wage rate and productivity: impact on physical productivity (workers can work better when they are better fed), recruitment of more productive workers (whose reservation wage is higher),

impact on the rate of turnover, etc. See Malcomson (1981), and Lindbeck and Snower (1985: section 3).

24 See Akerlof (1982).

25 See esp. Malcomson (1981); Shapiro and Stiglitz (1984); and Bowles (1985).

26 See Akerlof (1982: 147) and Bowles (1985: 19–20).

27 See Shapiro and Stiglitz (1984: 434). The net effect of an increase in benefits is not just the sum of the voluntary unemployment generated in one way (search theory) and of the involuntary unemployment generated in another way (efficiency wage theory) since higher benefits may turn a significant part of the earlier involuntary unemployment into voluntary unemployment.

28 Ironically this means that the attempt to compensate those who suffer from the lack of job assets leads to an increase in the number of those who lack them *and* suffer from this lack. The fact that unemployment benefits reduce the number of the involuntarily unemployed (and the involuntariness of their unemployment) *with a given number of jobs and given wages* is perfectly compatible with their boosting considerably the number of the involuntarily unemployed, once the effects of higher (efficiency) wages and fewer jobs are taken into account.

29 Job asset equalization is not to be confused with the equalization – or neutralization – of what Wright (1985a: 76) calls *credentials*. Both the 'ownership' of jobs and the restriction of access to certified skills can be viewed as posing 'barriers to entry' and thereby enabling employed workers to appropriate more than the return to their skills that would occur in a pure market model. Like skills, however, and unlike job assets, credentials are attributes that individuals can take from one job to another and that one may, therefore, want to subsume under a broadened version of skills.

30 One might conceivably deny 'job classes' the dignity of classes on the grounds that jobs do not really constitute productive forces in the sense in which people, land, tools and skills do. However, such a denial cannot be sustained once organizational assets have been allowed. Job assets and organizational assets are closely analogous. Both types of assets can exert a significant influence only to the extent that the rule of 'market forces' is constrained – hence their absence in standard neoclassical models. Both presuppose the exertion of some skills, but neither reduces to skill ownership. Insofar as they are carefully distinguished from the provision of the skills they presuppose, neither of them can be said to 'contribute to production' in a strict sense, even though the control of both types of assets can profoundly affect production, if only through the nuisance value they confer on those who possess them.

31 For interesting analyses of the specific nature of class relations under welfare-state capitalism quite different from the one proposed here, see Krätke (1985) and de Beus (1986).

32 In a typical welfare-state capitalist society such as Belgium, the officially unemployed have an average monthly income of about $390 (1982 figures). If (declared and undeclared) post-tax capital income were distributed equally among all adults, each of them would receive an estimated additional $120 every month, bringing their income up to $510. The average monthly income of employed people is $740. If all jobs (and their incomes) were divided equally among all those wanting to work, each would get $690 (total income from work or benefits divided by the number of people currently employed or claiming benefits). For the officially unemployed, this amounts to an average increase of $300 per month, i.e. more than double the increase they can expect (statically speaking, of course) from an egalitarian redistribution of wealth. The difference would be even larger if the unofficially (but involuntarily) unemployed had also been taken into account: most of them get far less than the average $390 of the officially unemployed, and many of them (mostly housewives) received nothing at all. For them, of course, the income gains from the redistribution of paid work would be even greater.

(I thank Paul-Marie Boulanger for helping me work out these estimates on the basis of Belgium's national accounts figures.)

33 See, e.g., Vanheerswynghels (1987), for the case of Belgium.

34 Such effects are well documented by numerous sociological studies; see, e.g. Jahoda, Lazarsfeld, and Zeisel (1933); Sinfield (1981) and Schnapper (1981).

35 See, e.g. Malcomson (1981: 849); and Shapiro and Stiglitz (1984: 434).

36 See, e.g., Ralf Dahrendorf's (1986: 32) unambiguous statement: 'The unemployed are not a class'; or André Gorz's (1980) description of this category as a 'non-class or non-workers'.

37 For a beautiful first-hand report and an illuminating analysis of many of these difficulties, see Jordan (1973, 1988).

38 This is one implication of the efficiency wage theories presented above, as pointed out, e.g. by Jon Elster (1988: section 5).

39 For a well-documented, sympathetic, but sobering assessment of the chances of work-sharing policies in a broad sense, see Drèze (1986). To indicate briefly the nature of the difficulties I believe lie at the core of the working time reduction strategy, let me ask four questions. How can you significantly reduce the working time of the low paid without either pushing them below the poverty line or pricing them out of their jobs by raising their (relative) hourly wages? How can you absorb most of the jobless in those trades in which unemployment is high without creating unmanageable bottlenecks – as well as sizable rents – in many other trades? How can you be fair to waged workers without imposing costly controls on the working time of the self-employed? And how can you impose compensatory new hirings without inducing useless (and possibly fatal) hiring and training costs in many firms that are currently hoarding labour? See Van Parijs (1991b) for further discussion.

40 See, e.g., Hogenboom and Janssen (1988), and Albert (1986).

41 This proposal is not new, of course. What is new is the broader perspective in which it has been put (see chapter 8 below), and, above all, the intense interest and broad support it is beginning to attract throughout Europe (see Van Parijs 1987).

42 See the various arguments in favour of basic income from the viewpoint of small firms and the self-employed, well summarized in Nooteboom (1986).

43 This conjecture gets some empirical support from the fact that countries – most typically the Netherlands – where support for the basic income strategy is comparatively widespread, especially among the unemployed organizations, are also those countries in which welfare state benefits are most universal (child benefits, basic state pensions, minimum guaranteed income, etc.). See, the country-by-country survey presented at the First International Conference on Basic Income (Miller, ed. 1988).

44 This is no political fiction, since most European Green parties now include the proposal of a basic income in their platforms, as does the Green-Alternative Group in the European parliament. For more details and some qualifications, see Van Parijs (1986, 1987, 1991a).

References

Akerlof, George A. 1982. 'Labor contracts as partial gift exchange', in *An Economic Theorist's Book of Tales*, Cambridge: Cambridge University Press, 145–74.

Albert, Pierre. 1986. 'Un système pour redonner la dignité aux chômeurs: l'allocation universelle', *Partage* 31, 19–21.

Bowles, Samuel. 1985. 'The production process in a competitive economy: Walrasian, Neo-Hobbesian, and Marxian models', *American Economic Review* 75, 16–36.

138   Exploitation rejuvenated

Carens, Joseph. 1981. *Equality, Moral Incentives and the Market*, Chicago: University of Chicago Press.
Costner, Herbert L. and Robert K. Leik. 1964. 'Deductions from "Axiomatic Theory"', *American Sociological Review* 29, 819–35.
Dahrendorf, Ralf. 1986. 'Für jeden Bürger ein garantiertes Mindesteinkommen', in *Die Zeit*, 17 January, 32.
de Beus, Jos W. 1986. 'Schept sociale zekerheid een nieuwe klasse?', in J. W. de Beus and G. A. van Doorn, eds., *De reconstrueerde samenleving*, Meppel (NL): Boom.
Drèze, Jacques. 1986. 'Work sharing: some theory and recent European experience', *Economic Policy* 3, 546–619.
Elster, Jon. 1985a. *Making Sense of Marx*, Cambridge: Cambridge University Press.
Elster, Jon. 1985b. 'Three challenges to class', in J. E. Roemer ed., *Analytical Marxism*, Cambridge: Cambridge University Press, 141–61.
Elster, Jon. 1988. 'Is there (or should there be) a right to work?', in Amy Guttman, ed., *Democracy and the Welfare State*, Princeton (NJ): Princeton University Press, 53–78.
Gorz, André. 1980. *Adieux au prolétariat*, Paris: Le Seuil. (English translation: *Farewell to the Working Class*, London: Pluto, 1983.)
Hogenboom, Erik and Janssen, Raf. 1988. 'Basic income and the claimants' movement in the Netherlands', in A. G. Miller ed., *Proceedings of the First International Conference on Basic Income*, London: Basic Income Research Group; Antwerp: Basic Income European Network, 237–56.
Jahoda, Marie, Lazarsfeld, Paul F. and Zeisel, Hans. 1933. *Die Arbeitslosen von Marienthal*, Frankfurt: Surkamp, 1975.
Jordan, Bill. 1973. *Paupers: The Making of the New Claiming Class*, London: Routledge and Kegan Paul.
    1988. 'Basic incomes and the claimants' movement', in A. G. Miller, ed., *Proceedings of the First International Conference on Basic Income*, London: Basic Income Research Group; Antwerp: Basic Income European Network, 257–68.
Kirzner, Israel M. 1973. *Competition and Entrepreneurship*, Chicago: University of Chicago Press.
Krätke, Michael. 1985. 'Klassen im Sozialstaat', *Prokla* 58, 89–108.
Lewis, Jane. 1985. 'The debate on sex and class', *New Left Review* 149, 108–20.
Lindbeck, Assar and Snower, Dennis J. 1985. 'Explanations of unemployment', *Oxford Review of Economic Policy* 1, 34–59.
    1986. 'Wage setting. Unemployment and insider-outsider relations', *American Economic Review* 76, 235–9.
Malcomson, James M. 1981. 'Unemployment and the efficiency wage hypothesis', *Economic Journal* 91, 848–66.
    1984. 'Work incentives, hierarchy, and internal labour markets', *Journal of Political Economy* 92, 486–507.
Miller, Anne Glenda ed., 1988. *Proceedings of the First International Conference on Basic Income*. London: Basic Income Research Group; Antwerp: Basic Income European Network.
Nooteboom, Bart. 1986. 'Basic income as a basis for small business', in *International Small Business Journal* 5 (3), 10–18.

Roemer, John E. 1982a. *A General Theory of Exploitation and Class*, Cambridge, Mass.: Harvard University Press.

1982b. 'New directions in the Marxian theory of exploitation and class', *Politics & Society* 11, 253–88.

Schnapper, Dominique. 1981. *L'Epreuve du chômage*, Paris: Gallimard.

Shapiro, Carl and Stiglitz, Joseph E. 1984. 'Equilibrium unemployment as a worker discipline device', *American Economic Review* 74, 433–44.

Sinfield, Adrian. 1981. *What Unemployment Means*, Oxford: Martin Robertson.

Solow, R. 1985. 'Insiders and outsiders in wage determination', *Scandinavian Journal of Economics* 87, 411–28.

van der Veen, Robert J. and Philippe Van Parijs. 1985. 'Entitlement theories of justice: from Nozick to Roemer and beyond', *Economics and Philosophy* 1, 69–81.

Vanheerswynghels, Adinda. 1987. 'Les Jeunes, leurs chômages, leurs emplois, *La Revue Nouvelle* 85, 403–10.

Van Parijs, Philippe. 1986. 'L'Avenir des écologistes: deux interprétations', *La Revue Nouvelle* 83, 37–48.

1987. 'Quel destin pour l'allocation universelle?', *Futuribles* 106, 17–31.

1991a. 'Impasses et promesses de l'écologie politique', *Esprit* 171, 54–70. (Also in F. De Roose and P. Van Parijs, eds., *La Pensée écologiste*, Brussels: De Boeck Université, 1991, 135–55.)

1991b. 'Basic income: a green strategy for the new Europe', in Sara Parkin, ed., *Green Light on Europe*, London: Heretic Books, 166–76.

Wright, Erik O. 1985a. 'A general framework for the analysis of class structure', *Politics & Society* 13, 385–423.

1985b. *Classes*, London: New Left Books.

7. Marxism and migration

Through the inequalities it generates, through the opportunities it provides, through the ever faster transport and communication it facilitates, world capitalism has brought about an unprecedented pressure towards the migration of both capital and people across national boundaries. Free movement is obviously a major factor in equalizing conditions on a world scale. On the other hand, it is in the interest of the affluent countries' capitalists, who are found to gain from the availability of cheap immigrant labour and of investment opportunities abroad. And it is, on the contrary, against the interest of the affluent countries' workers, whose jobs and living conditions are most likely to suffer from the presence of immigrants and whose bargaining power is bound to be badly affected by capital's credible threat to move out.

So, what constitutes a coherent, defensible ethical standpoint about this increasingly acute issue? Can the Marxist tradition be of any help in articulating such a standpoint? Does it contain conceptual resources that could be fruitfully recycled for this purpose?

7.1 Four Marxist stances

When screened with this question in mind, the Marxist tradition can readily be shown to display four distinct – indeed mutually exclusive – attitudes.[1]

1. *The task and achievement of Marxism is to unveil the laws of history. This provides no room whatever for raising ought-questions or engaging in ethical debates.* As Marx himself puts it in a famous passage, notions of right and wrong merely reflect the current mode of production. They do not provide standards for judging it. True, this does not prevent a Marxist from talking about the migration of people and capital, nor indeed from

asking whether such migration is 'necessary'. But he will then be asserting, for example, that immigration was needed to satisfy metropolitan
capitalism's needs for additional labour-power, or that capital exports
serve the 'function' of counteracting the tendency for the rate of profit to
fall.

2. *There is room for ought-questions, but at the most basic level, there is no
specifically Marxist answer.* For Marxism – or whatever there is in Marxism
that is still usable – is not a normative system, but an analytical framework. When discussing matters of migration, therefore, Marxists do have
policy recommendations to make on the basis of an analysis that can
claim to bear some relation to Marx's admittedly sketchy remarks on the
subject. But these recommendations take for granted policy objectives
that are no different from those of a 'global realist' for example.

3. There *is* room for ought questions, and there *is* a specifically Marxist
answer to them: we ought to fight for a socialist revolution, itself a
precondition for the ultimate achievement of full communism. *But on
such short or medium-term issues as the migration of people and capital, ethical
considerations are trumped by instrumental considerations.* Whether a claim,
an action, a policy is right or wrong is entirely determined by whether it
helps society along towards the socialist revolution, for example by
strengthening working-class solidarity. Appeals to the *raison de classe*
have here displaced any claim to fairness or morality.

4. Lastly, there *is* room for ought questions, and there *is* a specifically
Marxist answer to them: socialism leading to communism. *Moreover, the
same ethical considerations which warrant the choice of this long-term aim also
provide guidance for the ethical discussion of more immediate issues such as
migration of people and capital.*

In the remainder of this chapter, I shall say no more about the first
stance, because I believe it is absurd, nor about the second stance, because
it does not construe Marxism as an ethical tradition. I shall hardly say
more about the third stance, because it is blatantly untenable. Why is it?
Not because it is purely consequentialist – global utilitarianism might be
untenable, but not blatantly so. Nor because there is an inconsistency
between the cosmopolitan commitment of people favouring universal
socialism and the narrowly nationalistic recommendations often required
by the tough-minded pursuit of socialism in one country – *reculer pour
mieux sauter* is part of the stock and trade of strategic thinking. What is
disturbing about this third stance at work is rather, more specifically, that
it ruthlessly justifies sacrificing the interests of any number of current
proletarians – for example, the potential Irish immigrants who should be

kept out if the solidarity of the English working class is to be salvaged – for the sake of a hypothetical future event the fruits of which none of them is likely ever to enjoy.[2]

Hence it is on the fourth stance that I shall concentrate in the rest of this chapter. The fact that this stance does not square with some, or even most of what Marx had to say on the subject, and hence that it may not be deemed 'recognizably Marxist', is of decisive importance to the exegete, but of hardly any interest to the recycler. For one to be entitled to call Marxism that which is being recycled, it is enough that some aspect of some self-described Marxist tradition serves as one major source of inspiration. This condition, I believe, is uncontroversially fulfilled in the following discussion.

7.2 Citizenship exploitation

Among Marxist notions with ethical connotations, exploitation is second to none in either theoretical or practical prominence. According to the conventional definition, a group of people is exploited (exploits) if it contributes more (less) labour value – i.e. socially necessary labour – to production than it appropriates, or, more generally, than it can (must) appropriate, through its income. The notion of labour value which plays a central role in this definition raises a number of serious conceptual difficulties which have jettisoned the respectability of the conventional notion of exploitation. This is one of the reasons why John Roemer (1982; 1989) has undertaken to provide an alternative definition that would make no use whatever of the notion of value. Another reason is that the alternative definition seems to him to capture better the ethical intuition behind the notion – which makes it particularly relevant to our present purposes.

Roemer (1982: part 3) calls his definition the 'property-relations definition' of exploitation and characterizes it in game-theoretical terms. No game theory is required, however, to understand the intuition underlying it. A group is 'capitalistically exploited' (capitalistically exploits), on Roemer's definition, if it would be better off (worse off), other things remaining unchanged, if wealth were equalized. There is capitalist exploitation, in other words, if the unequal distribution of the means of production or, more generally, of alienable wealth, causally affects the distribution of income or, more generally, of material welfare. This notion can easily be extended beyond the case of capitalist exploitation by considering other types of assets. Roemer speaks of 'feudal exploitation' to refer to the effect on income distribution of the fact that some people own or partly own other people. And he speaks of 'socialist exploitation' to refer to the income-distributive effect of the unequal distribution of skills. The fundamental Marxist ethical imperative then consists in abolishing in turn these various forms of exploitation – first feudal, next capitalist, finally socialist. There is no reason, however, why the list should stop here: any other factor that affects the distribution of material welfare can in principle be used to define a new dimension of exploitation.[3]

This takes us straight to the heart of our subject. For in a borderless and frictionless world market economy, only endowments in wealth and skills will affect the equilibrium distribution of rewards. But if capital is less than perfectly mobile, and if people are not free to move to the areas where job prospects and wage rates are highest, then a third type of asset may affect the distribution of income more powerfully than wealth and skills. Depending on which country you are a citizen (or, sometimes, just a resident) of, your expected income can vary dramatically. I shall accordingly say that a group is 'citizenship-exploited' (a citizenship-exploiter) if its expected income would go up (down) in the event that citizenship were equalized, i.e. if no special prerogative were attached to being a citizen of any particular country. Like feudal exploitation, citizenship exploitation pulls the distribution of income away from what it would be under pure market conditions, where only productive assets (wealth and skills) elicit differential rewards.[4] The Marxist ethical imperative requires that this form of exploitation too should be abolished. This generates at least a *prima facie* presumption in favour of anything that erodes the differential advantages attached to citizenship, most obviously the free movement of both people and capital.

7.3 Unequal exchange: three interpretations

Let us now sharpen this conclusion by briefly scrutinizing the widely used notion of 'unequal exchange'. Drawing more or less explicitly on Marx's (1863: 106) elliptic remarks about the 'commercial exploitation of poor countries by rich countries', various authors have tried to analyse the relationship between developed and less developed countries as a systematically unequal exchange of goods. This systematic inequality may conceivably be due, first of all, to systematically asymmetric 'departures from perfectly competitive conditions'.[5] If metropolitan firms can take advantage of monopolistic or monopsonic positions to a larger extent than peripheral firms, the true value of goods travelling from the periphery to the centre will systematically exceed that of the centre-produced goods against which they are being traded. It is debatable whether such asymmetry is an intrinsic feature of the relation between rich and poor countries. It is one, in any case, which theoreticians of unequal exchange have tended to assume away, by postulating perfect competition.

On a second interpretation, the inequality in the exchange derives from 'unequal capital intensities'. Take a situation in which international trade is perfectly competitive, while capital and labour are not free to move across borders. The countries with a higher (lower) capital/labour ratio will then maximize their income by specializing in more capital-intensive (labour-intensive) production, and the equilibrium prices will be such that the socially necessary labour incorporated in the goods imported by the capital-rich country will exceed that incorporated in the goods it exports. The control over more dead labour makes it possible for one country to appropriate through competitive trade more labour value than it gives away, i.e. to exploit its trading partner according to the conventional definition recalled in the previous section.[6] Arguably, this second picture offers a somewhat better approximation of what is actually going on between rich and poor countries, even though one must bear in mind that, for present purposes, natural resources must be assimilated to capital. One essential feature of the picture, however, is the lack of free movement for labour and capital, a feature explicitly ruled out in standard statements of the theory of 'unequal exchange'.

This leads to a third interpretation, where differences in wage levels are given the key role. In Arghiri Emmanuel's (1969) original formulation, capital is assumed to move freely across borders, in such a way that the rate of profit tends to be equal all over the world. Since capital is perfectly mobile, one can no longer expect rich countries to systematically specialize in capital-intensive activities, and poor countries in labour-intensive activities. Labour, however, is not similarly mobile, and this lack of mobility – so Emmanuel believes – makes it possible to have very different wages for equally productive labour. Competitive trade with unequal wages is bound to generate unequal exchange, now understood as departure from the exchange of goods embodying equally precious bundles of factors, not necessarily from the exchange of equal amounts of socially necessary labour.

Unfortunately, this third interpretation is inconsistent. As Roemer (1983: sections 3–4) has neatly shown, there is a strict isomorphism, in a frictionless world, between capital mobility and labour mobility. Whether you leave capital free to move and confine labour within closed borders, or free labour and confine capital, in either case both the rate of profit and the wage rate will be equal at equilibrium all over the world. In this sense, the international capital market and the international labour market are perfect substitutes, functional equivalents. The real world, of course, is far from frictionless in the required sense. In particular, movement of capital and labour is not fully determined by a straightforward maximization of expected profits or wages. But as frictions enter the picture and hinder either the free migration of capital or the free migration of people, both the tendency towards a uniform rate of profit and the tendency towards a uniform wage rate are attenuated.

In this light, Emmanuel's assumption of perfect capital mobility and equal rates of profit appears plainly inconsistent with his assumption of unequal wages. Yet there is one way of reconstructing the analysis so as to restore consistency. It consists in assuming – contrary to Emmanuel's (1969: 205; 1975: 351) own explicit statements – that differences in wage levels are matched by differences in labour productivity. There is then no tension left between equal profit rates and unequal wages. Produc- tivity differences need not be due to 'intrinsic' features of the various countries' labour power. They may be related to physical circumstances (the fertility of the soil, the climate) or to cultural conditions (the work ethic, the relation to time) which account for the fact that the 'same' labour-power is unequally productive in different contexts. (There may or may not be in addition an 'efficiency wage' positive feedback: those who get lesser wages because they are less productive are also less productive because of the poorer living conditions under which they have to live because of their lesser wages.) Such differences are com- patible with perfect capital mobility, and also with 'open borders' for labour, but not with perfect labour mobility: something must durably prevent workers from taking advantage of the open borders, by moving to places where physical and cultural conditions make for both higher productivity and higher wages. This may simply be the fact that wages are not the only thing in the world they care about, and that attachment to their native place and culture may make them forgo a significantly higher money income.[7]

If differences in wages match differences in productivity, one can safely predict that, with a given capital content, more labour will be embodied in the goods exported by the poor countries than in the goods against which they are traded at competitive prices. But not only does this 'unequal exchange' fail to qualify as an exchange of unequal amounts of labour value: less productive labour corresponds to a lesser amount of socially necessary labour. It can no longer be construed either as an exchange of goods embodying unequal amounts of precious factors: less productive labour is economically less precious than more productive labour. Poor countries, therefore, are not cheated by 'unequal exchange' under the third interpretation (appropriately reconstructed). It is not only the case that poor countries gain (in welfare terms) from this exchange, possibly more than their trading partners. It is not only the case that making the exchange more 'equal' in terms of amounts of embodied labour may be counterproductive, as rich countries may find it advantageous to turn to the next best home-produced substitute.[8] Making the exchange more 'equal' in this sense would even make it less fair on any sensible evaluation of what is being exchanged.

It does not follow, of course, that there is no unfairness associated with the coexistence of high and low-wage countries. But this unfairness is best expressed not as unfair exchange or commercial exploitation between the two sets of countries, but rather as an unequal distribution of assets, here of whatever it is that accounts for the systematic differences in labour productivities.

7.4 Capital mobility and the fundamental injustice of world capitalism

What are the implications of this rather abstract discussion of 'unequal exchange' for our ethical discussion of the transnational migration of people and capital. Firstly, if citizenship exploitation is defined in terms of job prospects and wage levels (for people with a given productivity), we have seen that, in a 'frictionless' world economy, it could be abolished by either the opening of all borders to the migration of capital, or the opening of all borders to the migration of people. Now, it has often been pointed out that a massive uprooting of people under the pressure of economic necessity does not sound like a terribly clever way of attempting to deal with international economic inequalities.[9] The good news encapsulated in Roemer's isomorphism is that, at least in a 'frictionless' economy, there is no need for this painful process, because there is a perfect substitute for it. This is not a massive altruistic transfer of resources in the form of 'development aid', but the unconstrained movement of capital in search of higher profits. This sounds particularly good news today, as we keep hearing that money is becoming increasingly slippery and that its movements are ever harder to control, so that –

whether we like it or not – borders are more open to capital flows than they have ever been.[10]

In the real world, 'frictions' will of course prevent capital movements from getting rid of citizenship exploitation altogether. Paramount among them is the 'political risk' associated with investment in 'unstable' countries. Lower equilibrium wage rates will prevail in those countries in which firms will need a higher rate of profit or lenders a high rate of interest to offset the risk of expropriation, destruction, labour unrest, default, etc. But as more 'artificial' obstacles to capital movements are removed, a country's marginal gain from increased stability (or, more generally, from investor-friendliness) will grow, and hence also its incentive to reduce political risk. This will strengthen the tendency towards a uniform rate of profit and uniform wages rates, thus further reducing citizenship-based inequalities without any need for the migration of people.

A second implication of the above discussion is that even if citizenship exploitation were completely abolished (whether through free capital migration or through free labour migration), the unfairness inherent in a world capitalist economy would not be eradicated. Removing all obstacles to the transnational migration of capital (or people) would allow workers in poor countries to share in the benefits currently enjoyed by workers in rich countries by eroding all those wage differentials that are not the reflection of unequal labour productivities. But of two countries with equally large populations, one would keep appropriating a larger share of the world product because of the superior wealth held by its citizens (be it invested abroad) or because of the superior productivity of its workforce (whether due to its skills or to environmental conditions). The forms of exploitation intrinsically linked to capitalism, therefore, would remain undiminished.

On this basis, it is tempting to infer that it is not such 'imperfections' of the world capitalist economy as the existence of closed borders, that constitute its 'fundamental' injustice. But we must beware of not being carried away by sheer rhetoric. Nothing in what has just been said rules out that citizenship exploitation may be more relevant than wealth-based or skills-based exploitation in either or both of the following senses. Citizenship status may exert a quantitatively more powerful influence on the distribution of material welfare than wealth status or skill status. Moreover, reducing by a given amount the material advantages associated with citizenship (by letting capital out, admittedly not by letting people in) may also be more feasible, or less counterproductive, than reducing by the same amount those associated with wealth or skills. There are circumstances, therefore, under which the Marxist ethical imperative, construed as the abolition of exploitation, should assign priority to the promotion of international capital mobility (to get rid of citizenship exploitation) over the struggle for socialism (to get rid of wealth exploitation).

7.5 Popular sovereignty

I have assumed so far that the reason why Marxists favoured socialism is that it would enable us to get rid of capitalist exploitation, itself an instance of a broader phenomenon of exploitation, which the central Marxist ethical principle tells us must be abolished. Some Marxists could meaningfully argue, however, that what underlies their commitment to socialism is not their concern with exploitation but their concern with popular sovereignty. Popular sovereignty can be defined as the actual capacity to implement a democratic polity's preferred choice among technically feasible options.[11] It is obviously limited by the private ownership of the means of production. Suppose, for example, that it would be technically possible to introduce tougher norms of environmental protection or work safety at a slight cost in terms of average income, and that this is what a majority would like to happen. The negative effect on profits that would result from such measures, however, may trigger off private capital flight or a domestic investment strike on such a scale that the price to be paid for the measures (in terms of national income) becomes prohibitive. A democratically preferred and technically feasible option is thus made unfeasible by the response of private capital owners. Some may rejoice at this welcome discipline, but not those who find popular sovereignty an important objective. Under public ownership of the means of production – so the pro-socialism argument goes – this shrinking of society's feasible set would be avoided, and popular sovereignty would be enhanced.

If popular sovereignty is the aim, other measures falling short of or going beyond the nationalization of the means of production are equally legitimate. If socialism is not possible, or if introducing it would be counterproductive, the democratic will's room for manoeuvre may be expanded by hindering the exit of capital, perhaps by imposing exchange controls or a tax on repatriated profits. And once socialism has been introduced, one may further expand this room for manoeuvre by hindering the exit of skilled labour, perhaps through a stingy rationing of exit visas or through the compulsory reimbursement of what the state spent on an emigrant's education. We can now see that the implication for the transnational migration of people and capital is exactly the opposite of the one that emerged from the perspective explored in the previous three sections. If what matters is the abolition of all forms of exploitation, including citizenship exploitation, there is a strong presumption in favour of open borders. But if what matters is the protection of popular sovereignty, there is an equally strong presumption against them. Are the underlying perspectives inescapably inconsistent, or is there a possibility for reconciliation?

My own view is that the two perspectives are contradictory if the objectives they focus on – the abolition of exploitation, the protection of popular sovereignty – are conceived as aims in themselves. But unlike the abolition of exploitation, I do not believe that popular sovereignty can sensibly be defended as more than an instrumental objective, if only because it clashes by its very nature with individual sovereignty: the more the individual's room for manoeuvre is shrunk – for example, by restricting the free choice of occupation, of working time, of residence, of religion, etc. – the less constrained the popular will. Nevertheless, I do believe that popular sovereignty is an important consideration, and one that plays a key role in what I regard as the only cogent justification of socialism (if there is one). What needs to be protected, however, is not popular sovereignty *tout court*, but the collective capacity to pursue such a specific substantive aim as everyone's real freedom to lead her/his life as s/he wishes. *If* the pursuit of this aim is necessarily thwarted by the private ownership of capital, then we have a strong case for at least a partial socialization of the means of production.[12]

Let us now return to the transnational migration of people and capital. To deal with this issue, it is obviously of decisive importance to know who 'everyone' is in the above formulation of the substantive objective for the sake of which popular sovereignty can legitimately be protected at the expense of some aspects of individual freedom. If 'everyone' is just everyone inside the borders of some country or federation of countries, then the argument for closed borders is straightforward: if the viability or the deepening of the European (or Canadian or Wisconsin) social-democratic model is helped by obstacles to human inflow or monetary outflow, then such obstacles are evidently legitimate. But if the 'everyone' whose real freedom one is concerned with covers every member of mankind – as it must, if consistency with the condemnation of citizenship exploitation is to be reestablished – then the justification of closed borders, if there is one, needs to take a more subtle form. The effective fight against inequalities in both wealth and job assets in rich countries requires the introduction of social transfers, indeed, arguably, of social transfers of an unconditional (non-work-related) kind. The viability of such transfer systems in one country is likely to be contingent upon some restriction on the emigration of capital and is bound to be contingent upon a major restriction on the immigration of people: there is no way in which such systems could survive if all the old, sick and lazy of the world came running to take advantage of them. The reduction of domestic wealth or job exploitation, it seems, clashes head on with the reduction of citizenship exploitation.

I suggest the following combined strategy as a workable compromise among the two sets of considerations. Let capital (and technology) out towards the low-wage countries, only making some trouble when the country concerned does not respect trade union rights or democratic decision procedures. A gradual erosion of citizenship exploitation can be expected, while mechanisms for the erosion of both wealth- and job-exploitation inside the poorer countries are being fostered. As a result the economic and political pressure for the immigration of people will decrease, ultimately to the extent that closing the borders would be pointless. In the meanwhile, however, do not let people in too easily from poorer countries – because capital migration is a less painful process, because the least advantaged, being less mobile, are not likely to benefit, and above all because it would undermine any serious attempt to equalize, be it locally and partially, wealth and job assets. Such local equalization, it may be argued, can be justified even by reference to those with least real freedom in the world. For it demonstrates that a strongly redistributive economy is more than a fancy dream, and it thereby provides a tangible model both for redistributive strategies in each country and for a first-best fully individualized transfer system on a world scale which would provide each citizen in the world with her/his share of the value of aggregate material wealth and jobs. Does this sacrifice too much of the interests of the least advantaged in today's world for the sake of pursuing an uncertain long-term goal?

Notes

1 The first three of these attitudes are exemplified in Brown (1992) and Hübner (1992). This chapter originates in a commentary on these papers and owes them a great deal.
2 See Elster (1985: 117–18).
3 This point is argued in chapters 5 and 6 above.
4 The analogy between feudal serfs and citizens of poor countries, emphasized for

example by Ann Dummett (1992) and Joseph Carens (1992), is thereby given a systematic framework.

5 This interpretation is akin to the notion of international exploitation elaborated, for example, by Kolm (1969: esp. 853–4) and Cooper (1977: esp. 81–2).
6 For an explicit model, see Roemer 1983: section 2.
7 This is usually taken into account even in the most simplistic economic models of labour migration. See e.g. Stark (1991) for a recent survey.
8 As stressed for example by Barry (1979: 65–7).
9 See, for example, Carens (1992).
10 See, for example, Strange (1992).
11 See Przeworski and Wallerstein (1986).
12 For further discussion of this issue, see esp. Wright (1986), Roland (1988), Van Parijs (1991a, 1991b, 1992) and chapter 9, section 9.8 below.

References

Barry, Brian. 1979. 'Justice as reciprocity', in E. Kamenka and A. E. S. Tay, eds., *Justice*, London: Edward Arnold, 50–78. (Reprinted in *Democracy, Power, and Justice. Essays in Political Theory*, Oxford: Oxford University Press, 1989.)

Brown, Christopher. 1992. 'Marxism and the transnational migration of people: ethical issues', in Brian Barry and Robert E. Goodin, eds., *Free Movement*, Hemel Hempstead: Harvester Wheatsheaf, 127–44.

Carens, Joseph H. 1992, 'Migration and morality: a liberal egalitarian perspective', in Brian Barry and Robert E. Goodin, eds., *Free Movement*, Hemel Hempstead: Harvester Wheatsheaf, 25–47.

Cooper, R. N. 1977. 'A new international economic order for mutual gain', *Foreign Policy* 26, 66–120.

Dummett, Ann. 1992. 'The transnational migration of people seen from within a natural law tradition', in Brian Barry and Robert E. Goodin, eds., *Free Movement*, Hemel Hempstead: Harvester Wheatsheaf, 169–80.

Elster, Jon. 1985. *Making Sense of Marx*, Cambridge: Cambridge University Press.

Emmanuel, Arghiri. 1969. *L'Echange inégal*, Paris: Maspero, 1975.

1975. 'Réponse à Charles Bettelheim', in Emmanuel 1969, 342–415.

Hübner, Kurt. 1992. 'Transnational migration of money and capital – a Marxist perspective', in Brian Barry and Robert E. Goodin, eds., *Free Movement*, Hemel-Hempstead: Harvester Wheatsheaf, 145–54.

Kolm, Serge-Christophe. 1969. 'L'Exploitation des nations par les nations', *Revue Economique* 20, 851–72.

Marx, Karl. 1863. *Theorien über den Mehrwert*, vol. 3, Berlin: Dietz, 1960.

Przeworski, Adam and Wallerstein, Michael. 1986. 'Popular sovereignty, state autonomy, and private property', *Archives Européennes de Sociologie* 27, 215–59.

Roemer, John E. 1982. *A General Theory of Exploitation and Class*, Cambridge (Mass.): Harvard University Press.

1983. 'Unequal exchange, labor migrations and international capital flows: a theoretical synthesis', in P. Desai, ed., *Marxism, the Soviet Economy and Central Planning*, Cambridge (Mass): MIT Press, 34–60.

1989. 'Second thoughts on exploitation', in K. Nielsen and B. Ware, eds.,

Analyzing Marxism, supplementary volume 15 of the *Canadian Journal of Philosophy*, 257–66.

Roland, Gérard. 1988. 'Why socialism needs basic income, why basic income needs socialism', in Anne Miller, ed., *Proceedings of the First International Conference on Basic Income*, Antwerp: BIEN and London: BIRG, 94–105.

Stark, Oded. 1991. *The Migration of Labour*, Oxford: Blackwell.

Strange, Susan. 1992. 'Ethics and the movement of money: realist approaches', in Brian Barry and Robert E. Goodin, eds., *Free Movement*, Hemel Hempstead: Harvester Wheatsheaf, 1992, 232–47.

Van Parijs, Philippe. 1991a. 'Maîtrise, marché et société industrielle', *Revue Philosophique de Louvain* 89, 36–46.

   1991b. 'Inéluctable, liberté', in J. M. Chaumont and P. Van Parijs, eds., *Les Limites de l'inéluctable. Penser la liberté au seuil du troisième millénaire*, Brussels: De Boeck Université, 125–52.

   1992. 'Basic income capitalism', *Ethics* 102, 465–84.

Wright, Erik O. 1986. 'Why something like socialism is necessary for the transition to something like communism', *Theory and Society* 15, 657–72.

Part IV
Forward without socialism!

8. A capitalist road to communism

(JOINTLY WITH ROBERT J. VAN DER VEEN)

Prospects for the Left look bleak indeed. Electoral disasters (on the British pattern) and policy U-turns (on the French pattern) have reinforced the suspicion that socialism may forever remain out of reach. Even worse, actually existing socialist societies have repeatedly failed to provide an attractive picture of socialism. Compounded by mounting disillusionment with the achievements of state intervention in the West, this failure has shaken many people's faith in the very desirability of socialism.

In this chapter, we argue that this predicament provides no legitimate ground for dismay, cynicism or despondency – not because true socialism is different, or because it is possible after all, but because the Left need not be committed to socialism. We believe there is another way forward, a radical alternative to socialism, that combines feasibility and desirability to a surprising extent and that is, therefore, well worth considering.

This belief is unorthodox enough. It implies, among other things, that the 'working class', even broadly defined, is not the social force that the Left should systematically identify and side with.[1] Nonetheless, the arguments we shall put forward in support of this belief are fairly orthodox. Indeed, we believe they are fully consistent with Marx's ultimate views on the sort of future we should struggle to realize, as well as with his claim that material conditions determine which struggles make historical sense. Our putting forward these arguments does not mean we are fully convinced by the conclusion to which they lead. But we *are* fully convinced that a serious discussion of this sort of conclusion and argument is urgently needed.

There is one question about our scenario that many readers are likely to ask and to which no reply can be found in this chapter: granted, if only for the sake of the argument, that the path we sketch is economically feasible as well as ethically desirable, where are the social movements and political forces that are both willing and able to help our societies along it? We believe that this question is of the utmost importance and that some lineaments of an answer exist.[2] But we also think that the questions we tackle here are logically prior, and hence that it is with them, and not with political feasibility, that we should be concerned in the first place. We have sympathy for those – mainly economists – who say one should not waste time investigating the ethical desirability of a scheme that is not economically workable. And we understand those – mainly philosophers – who say there is no point in investigating the economic feasibility of a proposal that is ethically unacceptable. But denying the usefulness of investigating either economic feasibility or ethical desirability before having established, or at least discussed, a scheme's political chances, is unwarranted and irresponsible. For what is politically feasible depends largely on what has been shown to make economic and ethical sense. In any case, our ambition is not to provide a fully-fledged plea – at several junctures, we shall point out important gaps that need to be filled – but merely to set the stage for a meaningful discussion about whether the transition path described is, if feasible, desirable and, if desirable, feasible.

8.1 Does communism require socialism?

From a Marxian standpoint, 'socialism' is not an end in itself. It is a means, indeed the best means or even the only means, to reach true communism. The term 'socialism' here covers what Marx calls the lower stage of communism in the *Critique of the Gotha Programme*. It refers to a society in which workers collectively own the means of production – and in which therefore they collectively decide what these should be used for and how the resulting product should be distributed, namely according to the principle: 'To each according to his labour.' 'Communism', on the other hand, refers to the higher stage of communism, as characterized in the *Critique of the Gotha Programme*. It is defined by the distribution principle: 'From each according to his abilities, to each according to his needs' – which implies at least that the social product is distributed in such a way (1) that everyone's basic needs are adequately met, and (2) that each individual's share is entirely independent of his or her (freely provided) labour contribution.[3] Socialism, as defined, implies that 'exploitation' is abolished – workers appropriate the whole of the social product – while communism, as defined, implies that 'alienation' is abolished – productive activities need no longer be prompted by external rewards.

Why then do we need socialism? Why can't we move straight into communism? There are two standard answers to these questions. One is that communism is utopian as long as man is what capitalism has made him: we need socialism to reshape man, to get rid of his selfishness, his *Selbstsucht*, and to turn him into the altruistic person communism requires. The second answer is that communism is bound to fail under conditions of scarcity: we need socialism to develop the productive powers of humankind and thus create the state of abundance in which alone communism can flourish. Both these answers consist in a conjunction of two propositions: (1) the possibility of communism depends on the development of altruism/productivity, and (2) such development is better served by socialism than by capitalism, by the collective ownership of the means of production rather than by their private ownership. Both answers fail, we believe, because at least one of the propositions of which they consist is indefensible.

One may well doubt that (democratic) socialism is better than capitalism at promoting altruism, i.e. that involvement in collective decision-making about production would make people less selfish than they are in a system in which production decisions are mediated by the market. For the sake of argument, however, let us suppose that this is the case. This does not give socialism a decisive advantage over capitalism as a way of approaching communism, because the latter does *not* require altruism. (Indeed, if it did, those who reject communism as irredeemably utopian would be right.) To see this, let us look more closely at how the transition to communism is supposed to proceed.

Even at the lower stage of communism, as Marx describes it in the *Critique of the Gotha Programme*, part of the social product is distributed according to needs – whether to meet the individual needs of those unable to work or to fulfil collective needs. The transition to full communism can then be viewed as a gradual increase of the part of the social product distributed according to needs *vis-à-vis* the part distributed according to labour contributions.[4] Progress along this dimension does require that material rewards should gradually lose their significance, but does not entail that workers should be increasingly driven by altruistic motives. To start with, non-material rewards (respect, esteem, prestige, fame, glory and the like) could be substituted for material ones as a way of motivating people to perform the required amount of work.[5] Moreover, the content of work, its organization, and the human relations associated with it could and should be so altered that extrinsic rewards, whether material or not, would be less and less necessary to prompt a sufficient supply of labour. Work, to use Marx's phrase, could and should become 'life's prime want'.[6]

By proceeding along this dimension – the improvement of work up to the point where it is no longer work – the transition to communism need not rely in any way on the development of altruism, nor indeed on any other transformation of human nature. It takes people and their preferences as they are, but alters the nature of (paid) work up to a point where it is no longer distinguishable from free time. Even if we grant that only socialism can turn people into altruistic beings, therefore, it does not follow that socialism is indispensable to reaching communism.

Though socialism is not needed to get rid of selfishness, it may still be needed to get rid of scarcity. For as Marx repeatedly stressed, the growth of the productive forces (in a sense to be specified below) plays an irreplaceable role in the transition scenario sketched above. More precisely, productivity growth defined as an increase of output per unit of effort – taking both the length *and* the unattractiveness of labour into account – is essential to make room for a substantial improvement in the quality of work, and hence for an increase in the proportion of the social product that can be distributed regardless of labour contributions.[7]

The question, then, is not whether productivity growth, in the relevant sense, is indispensable to the advent of communism – it certainly is – but rather whether socialism is superior to capitalism as a means of achieving productivity growth. Marx did believe that there is a decisive argument to this effect. In both the 1859 *Critique* and in various passages of *Capital*, he argues that the development of the productive forces is *fettered* under advanced capitalism: the productivity of labour grows at a rate that is lower than it would be if relations of production were changed, i.e. if socialism were substituted for capitalism. This is because profit maximization, which competition forces capitalists to seek, does not necessarily coincide with the maximization of labour productivity or – what comes down to the same thing – with the minimization of the amount of labour that is required directly (as 'living labour') or indirectly (as 'means of production') to produce one unit of output. Suppose a technique that uses comparatively much capital (or indirect labour) and little living (or direct) labour performs better, according to the latter criterion, than another technique, which requires more direct labour but less capital. It may nonetheless be against the capitalist's interest to introduce it, essentially because, when using direct labour, he need pay only the workers' wages, but when using indirect labour, the price he must pay includes not only the wages of the workers who performed it, but also the profits derived from it by the capitalists who employ these workers. Hence there are techniques that would enhance the productivity of labour but which will never be introduced under capitalist relations of production. This argument plays an absolutely crucial role in Marx's overall vision of history, because this 'fettering' of the productive forces is the fundamental reason why, in his view, capitalism is but a transient mode of production. Marx gives no other argument in support of his claim that capitalism fetters the development (as distinct from the use) of the productive forces. And nothing but such fettering can, according to historical materialism, necessitate the replacement of capitalism by socialism.[8]

This argument is flawed, however, not because capitalism really does select techniques so as to maximize the productivity of labour, but because a rational socialist planner would not do so either. This is the case, first of all, because labour is not the only primary factor. Natural resources are scarce, and how much of them various possible techniques use up is clearly relevant to making a rational choice among them. Moreover, even if labour were the sole primary factor, selecting techniques in such a way as to maximize labour productivity would be justified only under very special conditions, if one is to maximize utility from consumption per capita for a given working time. (And what is the point of producing if not to consume, and the point of consuming if not to derive utility from it?) That there may be situations in which choosing the technique that minimizes labour time makes no sense becomes obvious if you consider the following example.

Suppose you have ten more years to live. You now produce your bread with a highly labour-intensive technique. If you build a mill, the labour time required, whether directly or indirectly, to produce one loaf of bread will be cut by half. Nonetheless, if it takes you ten years to build the mill, you will wisely stick to your less 'productive' old ways. Moreover, even if you lift the assumption of a finite time horizon (which makes some sense for a rational planner) and disregard the transition period from one technique to another (to consider so-called 'steady states'), it can still be shown that the maximization of labour productivity is only defensible as a criterion of technical choice if both the rate of accumulation and the rate of time preference are zero, i.e. if there is no growth and future consumption is valued as much as present consumption. When these strong conditions do not hold, rational socialist planning will deviate from such a criterion by attributing a greater weight to labour that needs to be performed one or several periods in advance of the production of consumption goods. (How great the weights need to be depends on the rates of accumulation and of time preference). In so doing, socialist planning uses a criterion that need not coincide with, but is bound to approximate pretty closely, capitalist profit maximization. Consequently, if rational socialist planning is the appropriate baseline for comparison, no significant 'fettering' can be expected from technical choice under profit-maximizing capitalism.[9]

Thus, the central theoretical argument in favour of socialism's superiority for productive development is flawed. Moreover, the empirical evidence is hardly encouraging. On the opposite side, apologists of capitalism are keen to stress that the rules of the capitalist game provide producers with strong incentives to introduce productivity-enhancing innovations. Indeed, they often force them, if they are to survive at all, to fight off the routine and inertia into which they would sink under a mellower system, and to further develop the productive powers of humankind. If 'abundance' in some sense is a key condition for the realization of communism and if the development of the productive forces, as understood above, constitutes the way of reaching it, should not a rational pursuer of communism frankly opt for capitalism? Of course, capitalism as such offers no guarantee that the quality of work will be improved, that more and more will be distributed according to needs, or that increased productivity will be reflected in reduced effort rather than in growing output. But as we shall see shortly, one key institutional change *within* capitalism could turn such tendencies into endogenous features of the system.

8.2 Is socialism morally superior?

Before describing this institutional change and examining its consequences, let us briefly pause to consider an alternative tack that defenders of socialism might want to take. The whole discussion so far assumes that the superiority claimed for socialism over capitalism is of an instrumental nature: socialism is (normatively) superior to capitalism because it is a better instrument for helping society along on the road to communism, whether by promoting the development of altruistic dispositions or by fostering more effectively the growth of labour productivity.

But there is another, *directly* ethical way of justifying socialism against capitalism: not as a more effective way of getting somewhere else, but as *intrinsically* more just, and therefore better, than capitalism. After all, as pointed out earlier, it follows from the very definition of (ideal) socialism that it abolishes exploitation. One may therefore expect exploitation to be much less present, if at all, in actual socialism than in any version of capitalism we may dream of. And this in itself may suffice to justify our preference for socialism over capitalism, especially when one realizes that communism only constitutes the notional and unreachable end of a transition that is bound to drag on forever, even under the most favourable circumstances. Even if capitalism could take us more safely or faster in the direction of communism, therefore, it may still be wise to choose socialism, because choosing capitalism would have the intolerable implication that exploitation would be with us forever.

This objection presupposes that exploitation can be precisely defined so that it is possible both (1) to say that exploitation is intrinsic to capitalism, and (2) to construct a cogent case in support of the claim that exploitation is ethically unacceptable. And showing that this is possible is far trickier than is commonly assumed. Nonetheless, we believe the objection is a serious one and one that deserves careful consideration.[10] In this chapter, however, we want to stick to a fairly orthodox Marxian framework. And for Marx, questions of justice and other ethical considerations were, if relevant at all, secondary. What really matters, when assessing a mode of production, is not how fairly the social product is shared out, but how effectively productive development is spurred in the direction of full communism. We therefore keep to the instrumental perspective adopted in the previous sections, and now turn to the question of how capitalist development could be geared to the advent of communism.

8.3 Two types of guaranteed income

Capitalism as such does not imply that any part of the social product should be granted to anyone who contributes neither labour, nor capital, nor natural resources. But it does not exclude it either. It does not exclude the possibility of a *social income* whose recipients need not contribute anything to production at the time they receive it. It is of crucial importance, however, to distinguish between different formulas of social income in this sense.

Some of them are just indirect wages. They involve an indirect connection with labour contribution. For example, the right to a social income may be restricted to those who are unable to work or unable to find work, as is roughly the case with unemployment benefits in advanced capitalist countries. Or it may be extended to people who freely choose not to work, but subject to the proviso that they have in the past performed some specified amount of labour, as in Edward Bellamy's utopia recently revived, in less rigid versions, by Gunnar Adler-Karlsson, André Gorz and Marie-Louise Duboin.[11] In all such cases, labour – or at least the willingness to work – remains the basis of the entitlement to a social income, and increasing the size of the latter cannot be construed as a move toward distribution according to needs.

Other formulas, however, grant a genuine *guaranteed income*: the connection with labour contribution is completely severed. This is the case, for example, when any household whose income from other sources falls below some specified minimum is entitled to a transfer payment that makes up for the difference – which is roughly the way in which basic social security actually works in several advanced capitalist societies. And it is also the case when every individual, whatever his or her income from other sources, is entitled to a completely unconditional *universal grant* or *basic income*, the level of which depends only on such variables as age and degree of handicap (as rough proxies for basic needs) – an old idea advocated by Bertrand Russell[12] that has recently become the focus of growing interest throughout Western Europe.[13]

In the case of these last two formulas, it makes sense to say that an increase in the level of the social income moves us closer (*ceteris paribus*) to communism, as defined by distribution according to needs. In both cases, it is possible to say that in any economy (defined by its technological level, its stock of labour power and capital, and the preference schedules of its members) some positive levels of a guaranteed income are sustainable, while others are not. And in both cases, it is therefore in principle possible to determine a maximum sustainable level of the guaranteed income (with given technology, stocks and preferences), which the pursuit of communism within capitalism should constantly aim for.[14] Nonetheless, it is of paramount importance to see that the consequences associated with these two versions are by no means the same: whereas the former version would lock the transition to communism in a dead end, the latter provides a promising way of effecting it.

The key point is that a *make-up guaranteed income* – whereby transfer payments are added to income from other sources up to the level of the guaranteed income – not only stigmatizes all those who 'live off benefits'. It also unavoidably imposes a minimum wage: no one will accept a job (even a job one would much like to do, though not for nothing) for less than the guaranteed income, because accepting it would mean becoming financially worse off than one would be without working (due to the cost of child care, of transport to and from work, etc.). At first sight, this seems to be a consequence we should welcome. But as soon as the make-up guaranteed income reaches a level that is not negligible, it catches all those whose skills are such that they could not market them for a higher wage, in the so-called unemployment trap. Moreover, it constitutes a strong disincentive against sharing out the jobs of those whose part-time work would only earn them less or little more than the guaranteed income. Obviously, the higher the relative level of the guaranteed income, the more people get caught in the unemployment trap, and the more one's choice is restricted to working a lot (to make it 'worth it') and not working at all (and 'living off' the others' work). Capitalism with a substantial make-up guaranteed income, therefore will be attractive neither to those who will feel excluded from work nor to those who will feel they bear all the burden. Moreover, it will be very expensive, financially speaking, because the taxes required to support it will need to be raised from a shrinking tax base.

If, on the other hand, the guaranteed income takes the form of a *universal grant*, unconditionally awarded to every citizen, things are different indeed. Because citizens have an absolute right to this grant whatever their income from other sources, they start earning additional net income as soon as they do any work, however little and however poorly paid it may be. Combined with some deregulation of the labour market (no administrative obstacles to part-time work, no compulsory minimum wage, no compulsory retirement age, etc.), the universal grant would make it possible to spread paid employment much more widely than it is now. Consequently, if the guaranteed income takes this form, its growth need no longer generate acute tensions between the overworked who feel exploited and the jobless who feel excluded. Moreover, it also follows – however paradoxical it may seem – that awarding a decent basic income to all may be, under appropriate conditions, much 'cheaper' (in terms of marginal tax rates), and therefore more realistic, than awarding it only to those who 'need' it.[15]

8.4 Universal grants and the transition towards full communism

Consequently, if communism is to be approached within a capitalist society, it must be by way of raising as much as possible the guaranteed income in the form of a universal grant. Note that this maximization could be conceived in either absolute or relative terms. Maximizing the guaranteed income in absolute terms could be justified on the basis of John Rawls's well-known 'difference principle': it would amount to eliminating all income inequalities that are not required if the least advantaged – here identified as those who have no income, in cash or kind, apart from the guaranteed minimum – are to be as well off as possible.[16] Such an elegant way of combining the imperatives of equality and efficiency may seem attractive to many.[17] But it does not coincide with the Marxian objective of abolishing alienation, which implies instead, at least as a first approximation, that the guaranteed income should be maximized in *relative* terms. Communism is achieved when the whole social product is distributed irrespective of each person's contribution, *not* when the share each gets irrespective of his contribution reaches some absolute threshold.

Of course, whatever the level of technology, the amounts of labour and capital available, and individual preferences, it is always 'possible' to set the universal grant (and hence the tax rate) at 100 per cent of per capita disposable income, i.e. to tax all gross incomes so that everyone has the same net income after taxes. But this would, in all likelihood, generate such a dramatic fall in the supply of both capital and labour, and hence in the size of the social product, that per capita income (now equal to the universal grant) would no longer cover fundamental needs. Consequently, the Marxian criterion should be construed as implicitly imposing a constraint on the maximization of the relative share of society's total product distributed according to needs: this share should be and remain large enough, in absolute terms, to secure the satisfaction of each individual's fundamental needs. Due to insufficient technical progress, insufficient capital or skill accumulation, or excessive aversion to working or saving, some economies are unable to meet this constraint. But others may have reached a state of 'abundance' in the weak sense that an unconditional guaranteed income could viably cover everyone's fundamental needs. As productivity (in the comprehensive sense, which takes the unattractiveness of labour into account) increases, the maximum relative share of the guaranteed income compatible with this constraint increases steadily, up to the point where 'abundance' is reached in the stronger sense that all fundamental needs could sustainably be met without labour being differentially rewarded.[18]

We do not believe that advanced capitalist countries have achieved anything like abundance in this strong sense required for the implementation of full communism. But we do believe that they have achieved abundance in the weaker sense specified above: they could grant each of their members a sustainable universal grant – though not necessarily a sustainable make-up guaranteed income – that would be sufficient to cover his or her fundamental needs. Of course, such a claim, once made precise (what are 'fundamental needs'?), can only be established by informed simulation and actual experiments. It is not the purpose of this chapter to undertake the important task of assessing this empirical claim. In the remaining pages, we want to focus instead on the following question. Let us suppose that the empirical claim just made is correct. Let us suppose, in other words, that technology, capital stocks and preferences are such, in advanced capitalist countries, that it is possible to provide everyone with a universal grant sufficient to cover his or her 'fundamental needs' without this involving the economy in a downward spiral. How does the economy evolve once such a universal grant is introduced?

A precise answer to this question would obviously require that one specify the way the universal grant would be financed (indirect or direct taxation, progressive or proportional), the way it would be modulated according to age, the extent to which it would replace or supplement other public expenditures, and so on. In very general terms, however, it can be said that introducing such a universal grant need not cancel capitalism's endogenous tendencies towards productivity increases. But it would twist these tendencies so that productivity in the comprehensive sense (amount of effort, rather than simply of labour time, per unit of product) will be promoted more effectively than before. For the workers' unconditional entitlement to a substantial universal grant will simultaneously push up the wage rate for unattractive, unrewarding work (which no one is now forced to accept in order to survive) and bring down the *average* wage rate for attractive, intrinsically rewarding work (because fundamental needs are covered anyway, people can now accept a high-quality job paid far below the guaranteed income level). Consequently, the capitalist logic of profit will, much more than previously, foster technical innovation and organizational change that improve the quality of work and thereby reduce the drudgery required per unit of product.

The growth of productivity in this comprehensive sense does not guarantee that the economy will move toward communism as defined above. It only provides a necessary condition for it. When less drudgery, less disutility, is required to produce a given social product, more of the latter *could* be distributed according to needs rather than according to contributions, without this reducing the absolute level of the universal grant. Whether and to what extent the relative share of the universal grant will actually rise, however, depends on whether and how far this possibility is seized through political decisions to raise the average rate at which gross income is (directly or indirectly) taxed. It is obvious that nothing of the sort will be done if growth is the overriding objective. *If instead there is a political will to use increased productivity for changing the distribution pattern (and thereby reducing the effort prompted by differential rewards) rather than for increasing output, capitalist societies will smoothly move towards full communism.*

8.5 From supply-side economics to political ecology

The 'Laffer curve' of supply-side economics provides us with an effective (though oversimplified) device for depicting the range of choices open to a society.[19] For a given technology, a given pattern of individual preferences between income and leisure, and a given (potential) labour force, one can picture both the amount of effort elicited from the population and (consequently) the total product as decreasing functions of the tax rate (supposed to be uniform). On the other hand, total receipts, which are given by the total product multiplied by the tax rate, and coincide (to keep things simple) with the part of the total product distributed in the form of a universal grant, first increase and then decrease as the rate of tax rises. Note, however, that the total product (or income) we are talking about here only corresponds to the *taxable* product (or income). As the tax rate increases, the actual total product may well fall at a much slower rate, as people replace market production by household production, monetary by non-monetary transactions, and consumption outside the firm (wages) by consumption within the firm (say, comfortable offices and business trips).

A policy that gives a guaranteed income for all a high priority could be guided by at least four distinct principles: it could attempt:

(1) to maximize the total product (both actual and taxable) under the constraint that the universal grant should reach a given minimum level (*growth-oriented criterion*);
(2) to maximize the absolute level of the universal grant (*Rawlsian criterion*);
(3) to maximize the relative level of the universal grant (as a proportion of total taxable income) – which amounts, under our assumptions, to maximizing the tax rate – under the constraint that its absolute level should not fall below some given minimum level (*Marxian criterion*); and
(4) to maximize equality, as approximated by the ratio of the universal grant to the actual total product, subject again to the (not necessarily

binding) constraint that the universal grant does not fall below some minimum level (*equality-oriented criterion*).

The tax rate set in accord with criterion (4) must necessarily lie some-where between the tax rates set in accord with criteria (2) and (3). For suppose that actual income and taxable income behave in nearly the same way, i.e. that, as the tax rate goes up, people tend to replace activities yielding taxable income by pure leisure. Then the ratio of the universal grant to taxable income will hardly be different from the ratio of the universal grant to actual income, and maximizing equality (criterion (4)) will then practically be equivalent to maximizing the rate at which market incomes are taxed (criterion (3)). At the other extreme, suppose that taxable income is strongly affected by changes in the tax rate, while actual income is hardly affected at all – i.e. that taxable production is nearly fully replaced by (just as unequally distributed) non-taxable pro-duction. Then the ratio of the universal grant to the actual total product mirrors closely the absolute level of the universal grant, and maximizing equality (criterion (4)) is then practically equivalent to maximizing the tax yield (criterion (2)). One possible configuration of the four choices is given in Figure 8.1.

The Y curve represents the level of a country's taxable social product. The G curve represents the part of that product absorbed by taxes (the total tax yield). The shape of these curves indicates how the labour force will respond to changes in the tax rate t when the entire tax yield tY is redistributed among the general population by means of a universal grant (i.e. when tY equals G). As the tax rate rises from 0 to 100 per cent, the workers' incentive to supply productive effort will decline steadily to 0, and (assuming a given technology) the taxable social product Y will fall correspondingly.

To explain the shape of the Laffer curve (the tax yield curve G), consider the net effect of a small rise in the tax rate. Raising the tax rate increases the proportion of the taxable social product going to grant recipients (the redistributive effect) but also reduces the amount of labour supplied, and therefore the size of the taxable social product itself (the incentive effect). The relative impact of these two effects, and hence the net effect of the small rise of t on G, vary with the absolute level of the tax rate. If t is relatively low, the redistributive effect will dominate the incentive effect: the rise of t will be greater than the fall of Y it induces, and therefore the level of the universal grant G will rise as the tax rate rises above 0. If t is relatively high, however, the incentive effect will

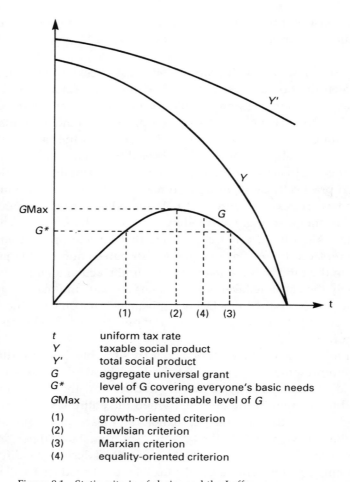

Figure 8.1   Static criteria of choice and the Laffer curve

dominate the redistributive effect, and G will fall as t rises to 100 per cent. At a tax rate located somewhere between 0 and 100 per cent, the incentive effect will exactly offset the redistributive effect. This is $GMax$, the peak of the Laffer curve.

Figure 8.1 describes a state of abundance in the weak sense that the maximum sustainable level of the universal grant exceeds the minimum level required to cover everyone's fundamental needs. In such a state, as argued earlier, the most obviously Marxian criterion is criterion (3): pursuing communism means that the tax rate is raised as high as possible, but not high enough to jeopardize the satisfaction of everyone's funda-

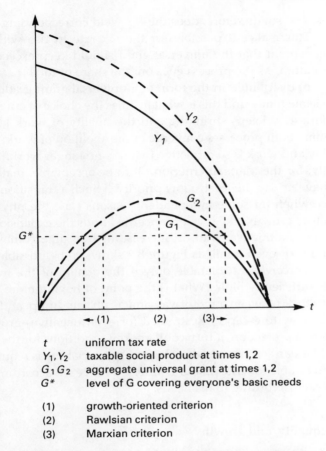

t	uniform tax rate
Y_1, Y_2	taxable social product at times 1, 2
$G_1 G_2$	aggregate universal grant at times 1, 2
G^*	level of G covering everyone's basic needs

(1)	growth-oriented criterion
(2)	Rawlsian criterion
(3)	Marxian criterion

Figure 8.2 Possible transitions to communism, as productivity rises over time

mental needs. Yet the diagram makes it clear that this choice can be justified neither in terms of making those who are worst off as well off as possible, nor in terms of equality. What criterion (3) does guarantee, however, is that the 'realm of freedom' will be expanded as much as possible without letting the universal grant fall below what is required to satisfy fundamental needs. By requiring the minimization of taxable income under this constraint, criterion (3) ensures that work, and in particular unpleasant work, is discouraged as much as possible. In other words, it promotes the expansion of freedom both in the sense of shortening the average working day and in the sense of improving the average quality of work. As productivity (in the comprehensive sense) grows (see Figure 8.2), the total product generated by a given amount of effort increases, and so, therefore, does the tax yield corresponding to a given tax rate. This makes it possible for the tax rate to rise without violating the constraint that the universal grant should keep exceeding the chosen minimum. As the process goes on, the share of total (taxable) income that is not distributed in the form of a universal grant gradually shrinks. At the same time – and this is what justifies the choice of criterion (3) – the working day keeps shrinking and the quality of work keeps rising. At the limit, both processes converge in the abolition of work: free time fills the day and work is so attractive that it is no longer work.[20]

Consequently, for the Marxian criterion (3) to be acceptable, material growth must have, to say the least, a low priority.[21] Such a transition has the best chance when for some independent reasons (say, the physical and social 'limits to growth') the society concerned finds the expansion of GNP sufficiently unattractive. And an increase of free time combined with a stagnation (or even a fall, as Figure 8.2 shows to be possible) of incomes can be perceived as tolerable only if the quality of the living environment is sufficiently high. (What is the point of having more free time if you live stuck between a motorway and a rubbish dump, and get no additional money to escape?) Restrained (or even negative) growth and environmental protection, it turns out, are key conditions for the full success of our Marxian scenario. And ecologism, not socialism, is required if we are ever to be able to write on our banners: 'From each according to his abilities, to each according to his needs!'

8.6 Freedom, equality, and growth

Still, one may doubt whether the 'Marxian' criterion (3) is really the most appropriate criterion. First, as already mentioned, the choice of criterion (3) may not be the most *egalitarian* one. Expanding the 'realm of freedom' may mean that an increasing part of society's wealth is produced outside the formal sector, in the form of self-production, mutual help, volunteer work, etc. And nothing guarantees that the benefits of this production will be evenly spread: a childless old-age pensioner stuck in a third-floor flat in an anonymous city is not likely to get as large a share of this 'autonomous' production as vigorous young people living in a rural area and firmly integrated in a closely knit network of neighbours, relatives and friends. Precisely because of the growth of the 'autonomous' sphere, therefore, even full communism would go hand in hand with quite a high level of avoidable inequality. This may incline us to favour criterion (4). But it need not. If what really matters to us – as it arguably did to Marx

– is the expansion of freedom, the abolition of alienation, we need not be bothered by the persistence of substantial inequalities, at least as long as everyone's fundamental needs are covered.

A second and stronger argument against criterion (3) is that the expansion of freedom should not mean only an increase in the quantity of free time *vis-à-vis* working time and an improvement in the quality of work, but also an improvement in the *quality of free time*. And the latter is nothing but the degree to which people are able to fulfil their desires in their free time – which is itself closely related to the level of production (stripped of externalities). Two possibilities must be distinguished here. Suppose, first, that what matters (as regards the quality of free time) is only the extent to which those who are *worst off* can fulfil their needs. One could then choose any criterion in the range between criteria (3) and (2). At one extreme, the 'Marxian' criterion (3) requires only that the quality of free time enjoyed by those who are worst off should not decrease, while the 'Rawlsian' criterion (2) requires that the quality of their free time should be as high as possible, at the cost of a lower share of free time in total time or of a poorer quality of working time. But suppose, next, that what one cares about is the quality of the *average person's* free time. One could then, at one extreme, maximize production under the constraint that the universal grant remains sufficient to cover fundamental needs, i.e. select our 'growth-oriented' criterion (1), with the further proviso that, as productivity grows, the amount of effort required for production should not increase (i.e. the other dimensions of the realm of freedom should not shrink). At the other extreme, one could initially choose our 'Marxian' criterion (3) but with the proviso that, as productivity rises, total income should not go down. There is, clearly, a trade-off between the freedom to satisfy one's needs and freedom from drudgery. The more importance one attaches to the former, the more inclined one will be to retreat from the austere criterion (3) toward the more expansive criterion (2) or even (1).

Such a retreat receives further support if one brings in, thirdly, the causal link between growth and productivity. Restrained or negative growth, as implied by the 'Marxian' criterion (3), may conceivably hinder labour-saving and labour-quality-improving innovations to such an extent that the potential for any further transition may be undermined. Using criterion (1) and maximizing growth forever, on the other hand, means that this potential builds up without ever being used. Here again there is a trade-off: between using all the existing potential to maximize freedom from drudgery for the current generation and refraining from doing so in order to improve the prospects for the next generation – assuming higher production does not deplete other resources that generation would need.

If one aims to expand the realm of freedom, the choice of the appropriate tax rate may thus be, even at this abstract level, a rather complex matter. The optimal transition towards communism may not be the one that proceeds by simply maximizing the tax rate – and thus minimizing drudgery. It may be argued that the choice of the tax rate should not only be constrained by the provision of a universal grant covering everyone's fundamental needs, but that it should be further constrained by the need to keep (actual) inequality within bounds and by the need to keep growth at a sufficiently high level for productive development to continue.

But suppose something like a universal grant is introduced – because of the intolerable consequences of having no guaranteed income system at all and because of the perverse effects associated with alternative formulas. The choice of the tax rate (and hence of the level of the universal grant) will of course not be determined by any abstract optimality calculus, whether conducted in a Marxian framework or not. It will be determined by power relationships in the context of current material conditions. It is these material conditions – basically, rapid labour-saving technical change combined with compelling constraints on economic growth – that will turn the capitalist transition to communism from a utopian dream into a *historical necessity*, not in the sense that it will happen automatically, no matter what people think or do, but in the sense that, given the material conditions, human rationality can be relied upon to generate, sooner or later, political forces that will bring it about. A crucial part is played in this process by the exploration of alternative futures, by the investigation of their possibility and desirability – the central component of human rationality. Consequently, however sketchy and tentative, the argument of this chapter is of a piece with the historical necessity it ends up asserting.

Notes

1 This claim does not contradict the view – to which we adhere – that, by definition, the Left systematically sides with those who own nothing but their labour-power (if that).

2 See chapter 6, section 6.8 above, chapter 9, sections 9.6 and 9.7 below.

3 Note that 'communism', as defined, does not entail collective ownership of the means of production by the workers, i.e. 'socialism' as defined above. But it does entail collective ownership of the social product by society as a whole: while the owners of means of production, labour-power and skills decide whether and how to put them to productive use, society appropriates all income flows in order to distribute them 'according to

needs' to all its members. This constitutes the etymological justification for our 'thin' definition of 'communism'.

4 For a formal model of this transition from socialism to communism, see van der Veen (1984).

5 See Carens (1981). If the motivation to work is provided by fear of non-material penalties (social disapproval, contempt, resentment, etc.), it is questionable whether alienation has really been abolished.

6 Using Sen's (1979) terminology, it must be conceded that any society, whether capitalist or socialist, that effectively guarantees a minimum consumption level, if only to those who are unable to work, needs to rely to some extent on 'sympathy' (giving weight to other people's preferences) or 'commitment' (letting moral considerations override one's preference). However, the possibility of increasing the part that is being distributed independently of labour contributions by no means requires *increasing* reliance on sympathy or commitment.

7 See van der Veen (1991: chapter 4) for a very simple model in which the exact nature of relations between the rise in productivity, increase in the proportion of the social product distributed according to needs, and expansion of the realm of freedom, can be rigorously explored.

8 For a lucid discussion of the concept of 'fettering', in particular in the distinction between use-fettering and development-fettering, see Cohen (1983a). Some might think that Marx's work contains (implicitly) a distinct argument (based on the theory of the falling rate of profit) that could do the job far better than the explicit argument here considered. But the difficulties raised by this theory are fatal to it, as argued in chapters 3 and 4 above. Moreover, the argument derived from it would equally apply to socialist economies – indeed, even more so if Marx's explicit argument discussed in the main text were correct: if socialism did not filter out some of the capital-intensive techniques that are not viable under capitalism, the organic composition of capital would rise faster and the rate of accumulation would fall more rapidly under socialism than under capitalism.

9 The formal points are made by von Weizsäcker and Samuelson (1971); Samuelson (1973) and Samuelson (1982). For illuminating discussions of their relevance to the Marxist view of the difference between capitalism and socialism, see Roemer (1983) and Elster (1985: sections 3.2.2 and 5.1.3).

10 See Van Parijs (1984), van der Veen (1987; 1991: chapter 5) and chapter 5 above.

11 See Adler-Karlsson (1979), Gorz (1983, 1985) and Duboin (1984).

12 Russell (1918: 891).

13 In English, see, for example, Jordan (1973, 1985), Cook (1979), Roberts (1982), Miller (1983), Ashby (1984). For surveys of the discussion in various European countries, see Boulanger et al., eds. (1985), Miller, ed. (1988).

14 Or so it seems. Several qualifications are introduced below.

15 This point is developed in De Villé and Van Parijs (1985).

16 See Rawls (1971: sect. 13); and, for a more scrupulous analysis of the relationship between this 'Rawlsian' criterion and Rawls's own views, Van Parijs (1991).

17 See, for example, Elster (1985: 230), who argues that Rawls's difference principle is better than the labour contribution principle as a second best to distribution according to needs. See also van der Veen (1991: chapter 3) who argues that this 'Rawlsian' criterion provides a legitimate interpretation of Marx's ruling principle of communism, 'the full and free development of every individual'.

18 This stronger sense is akin to the one Steedman (1982) gives the term. The distinction could also be made in terms of a contrast between individual and collective freedom, which Cohen (1983b) uses in a different context. Under weak abundance, every single individual is (not just formally) free not to do any paid work, but only because a sufficient number of individuals do not make use of this freedom (individual freedom).

Under strong abundance, this condition no longer applies: everyone retains the freedom not to do any paid work, even if no one else engages in it (collective freedom). See chapter 10 below for a more systematic analysis.

19 Simplifications include the abstraction from any public expenditure other than the universal grant, and the absence of capital stock constraint.

20 For further discussion of the growth of the 'autonomous' sphere see Gorz (1980: 142–55) and Van Parijs (1985: section 2).

21 As one advocate of some form of universal grant puts it: 'If we want to enter the realm of freedom, then it is absolutely certain that we must impose limits on ourselves as regards the amount of material goods' (Adler-Karlsson 1979: 63). Van der Veen (1991: section 4.3) shows that material growth must be kept low (close to zero growth of per capita income) even if the 'Rawlsian' criterion (2) is adopted.

References

Adler-Karlsson, Gunnar. 1979. 'Probleme des Wirtschaftswachstums und der Wirtschaftsgesinnung: Utopie eines besseren Lebens', *Mitteilungen zur Arbeits- und Berufsforschung* 4, 481–505.

Ashby, Peter. 1984. *Social Security after Beveridge: What Next?* London: National Council for Voluntary Organizations.

Boulanger, Paul-Marie, Philippe Defeyt and Philippe Van Parijs, eds. 1985. *L'Allocation universelle: Une idée pour vivre autrement*, special issue of *La Revue Nouvelle* 81, April.

Carens, Joseph H. 1981. *Equality, Incentives and the Market*, Chicago: University of Chicago Press.

Cohen, G. A. 1983a. 'Forces and relations of production', in B. Matthews ed., *A Hundred Years of Marxism*, London: Lawrence and Wishart, 111–35.

1983b. 'The structure of proletarian unfreedom', *Philosophy and Public Affairs* 12, 3–33.

Cook, Stephen. 1979. 'Can a social wage solve unemployment?', Birmingham: University of Aston Management Centre, Working Paper no. 165.

De Villé, Philippe and Philippe Van Parijs. 1985. 'Quelle stratégie contre la pauvreté? Du salaire minimum garanti à l'allocation universelle', *La Revue Nouvelle* 81, 361–72.

Duboin, Marie-Louise. 1984. *Les Affranchis de l'an 2000*, Paris: Syros.

Elster, Jon. 1985. *Making Sense of Marx*, Cambridge: Cambridge University Press.

Gorz, André. 1980. *Adieux au prolétariat*, Paris: Seuil.

1983. *Les Chemins du paradis: l'agonie du capital*, Paris: Galilée.

1985. 'L'Allocation universelle: Version de droite et version de gauche', *La Revue Nouvelle* 81, 419–28.

Jordan, Bill, 1973. *Paupers: The Making of the New Claiming Class*, London: Routledge and Kegan Paul.

1985. *The State Authority and Autonomy*, Oxford: Blackwell.

Miller, Anne G. 1983. 'In praise of social dividends', Edinburgh: Heriot-Watt University, Department of Economics, Working Paper no. 1.

Miller, Anne G. ed. 1988. *Proceedings of the First International Conference on Basic Income*, London: Basic Income Research Group; Antwerp: Basic Income European Network.

Rawls, John. 1971. *A Theory of Justice*, Oxford: Oxford University Press, 1972.

Roberts, Keith. 1982. *Automation, Unemployment and the Distribution of Income*, Maastricht: European Center for Work and Society.

Roemer, John E. 1983. 'Choice of technique under capitalism, socialism and Nirvana: reply to Samuelson', University of California, Davis, Department of Economics, Working Paper 213.

Russell, Bertrand. 1918. *Roads to Freedom: Socialism, Anarchism and Syndicalism*, London: Allen and Unwin.

Samuelson, Paul A. 1973. 'Optimality of profit-including prices under ideal planning', *Proceedings of the National Academy of Sciences* 70, 2109–22.

1982. 'The normative and positivistic inferiority of Marx's value paradigm', *Southern Economic Journal* 48, 11–18.

Sen, Amartya. 1979. 'Rational fools', in F. Hahn and M. Hollis, ed., *Philosophy and Economic Theory*, Oxford: Oxford University Press, 87–109.

Steedman, Ian. 1982. 'Some socialist questions', University of Manchester: Department of Economics, unpublished.

van der Veen, Robert J. 1984. 'From contribution to needs. A normative-economic essay on the transition towards full communism', *Acta Politica* 18, 463–492. (Reprinted as chapter 10 of van der Veen 1991.)

1987. 'Can socialism be non-exploitative?', in A. Reeve, ed., *Modern Theories of Exploitation*, London: Sage, 80–110. (Reprinted as chapter 12 of van der Veen 1991.)

1991. *Between Exploitation and Communism. Explorations in the Marxian Theory of Justice and Freedom*, Groningen: Wolters-Noordhoff.

van der Veen, Robert J. and Philippe Van Parijs. 1985. 'Capitalism, communism and the realm of freedom: a formal presentation', Université Catholique de Louvain: Département des Sciences Economiques, Working Paper 8501.

Van Parijs, Philippe. 1984. 'What (if anything) is intrinsically wrong with capitalism?', *Philosophica* 34, 85–102.

1985. 'Marx, l'écologisme et la transition directe du capitalisme au communisme', in B. Chavance, ed., *Marx en perspective*, Paris: Editions de l'Ecole des Hautes Etudes en Sciences Sociales, 135–55.

1991. 'Why surfers should be fed. The liberal case for an unconditional basic income', *Philosophy and Public Affairs* 20, 101–31.

von Weiszäcker, Christian C. and Paul A. Samuelson. 1971. 'A new labor theory of value for rational planning through use of the bourgeois profit rate', *Proceedings of the National Academy of Sciences* 68, 1192–4.

9. Universal grants versus socialism

(JOINTLY WITH ROBERT J. VAN DER VEEN)

'Society cannot underwrite the pet ideas of each and every enthusiast who offers a panacea for our problems' (Elster 1986: 720). We could not agree more. There is nothing wrong with entertaining pet ideas, and even less with displaying enthusiasm. But society would be crazy to give ideas for radical reforms a try without subjecting them first to a ruthless critical debate regarding both feasibility and desirability. This is why we attach such great importance to the sort of discussion published in the symposium issue of *Theory and Society* devoted to the argument of chapter 8.

The latter presented and defended a 'capitalist road to communism', which can be helpfully decomposed into two stretches, both of which run within capitalism all the way. What we will call the *first transition* refers to the move from welfare-state capitalism to *universal-grant capitalism*, i.e. to the replacement of a great deal of current social security arrangements and labour legislation in advanced capitalist countries by a grant sufficient to cover fundamental needs and awarded in a totally unconditional fashion to every individual.[1] What we will call the *second transition* starts where the first transition leaves off and leads to *communism*, i.e. to a situation in which the social product is distributed entirely in the form of unconditional grants, possibly modulated in terms of such proxies of objective needs as age or disability ('to each according to his needs'), without anyone being coerced into performance ('from each according to his abilities'). In our article, we claimed essentially that both these transitions were desirable – even on Marxian grounds – and feasible, at least economically.

All of our critics argue that some at least of these claims raise very serious problems. But whereas some (Berger, Przeworski) seem nonetheless inclined to believe that something along the lines of our proposal is the most promising way forward, the others reject it in favour of some form of 'feasible socialism' *à la* Nove,[2] whether with (Nove, Wright) or without (Carens, Elster) a universal grant.[3] In this reply, we shall review and discuss succinctly what we regard as their most significant objections to our 'capitalist road to communism', taking each of the two transitions in turn and looking in either case at the issues of desirability, economic feasibility and political feasibility.

9.1 The end of solidarity?

Berger, Nove, Przeworski and Wright all join us to assert that our first transition, if feasible, would be desirable indeed. Carens, however, is far less keen. And Elster is frankly hostile. Carens (1986: 679) does agree that it would in principle be preferable to implement a guaranteed income through universal benefits rather than in a make-up version.[4] But he has strong misgivings about our proposal because of an important element that he says is missing in our view: a 'sense of commitment to the collective', which he also calls 'socialist motivation'. The latter is desirable, according to Carens (1986: 684–5), both because it makes incentive problems tractable in an egalitarian society and because it expresses a 'moral ideal', a 'moral vision of human beings as interdependent and connected, with duties to, as well as rights against, one another', in one word: 'solidarity'. This is what justifies, in his eyes, that one must institutionalize the 'principle of the social duty to contribute', for example by restricting the right to a full income share to 'those working full time or unable to work through no fault of their own', while 'others who were capable of work but chose not to do so might receive a reduced share'.[5]

We gladly concede that 'a sense of commitment to the collective', along with any other variant of the work ethic, makes moves towards egalitarianism (whether on our road or any other) economically easier, and that behaviour driven by such a sense is ethically superior to purely selfish behaviour. Our proposal, however, was emphatically not about motivational change but about institutional reform. The question Carens must ask is whether there is any reason why solidarity should play a smaller part in motivating individual behaviour under universal grant arrangements than when a duty to work is institutionalized. People who would contribute nothing in the former case are presumably people who only work in the latter because they are forced to, not out of 'commitment to the collective'. Why should the removal of the compulsion to (selfishly) earn one's living systematically erode the motivational force of solidarity?

Is it not possible to argue instead that it would free those who are sensitive to such a value to spend much more time on solidarity-driven actions (say, voluntary work for an anti-apartheid organization)? It cannot just be taken for granted that a proposal that does not require the development of such motivation automatically undermines it.[6]

What Carens is getting at, however, should perhaps be understood differently. Under the sort of institution he favours, which hardly differs in this respect from the core of the social security system characteristic of welfare-state capitalism, redistribution operates, in principle, from the lucky to the unlucky but *not* from the industrious to the lazy. Under universal-grant arrangements, on the other hand, redistribution operates, roughly, from those who perform paid work to those who do not. This *need* not be a redistribution from the industrious to the lazy – because its net beneficiaries may be keen but unable to get a paid job *and* because they may perform very considerable amounts of unpaid work. But, even in principle, it *can* be. And this is exactly why universal grants – unlike Carens's grants to those unable to work and unlike welfare-state benefits – cannot be justified as expressing solidarity (an issue quite different from whether they encourage behaviour motivated by solidarity). Does this weaken the ethical appeal of our scheme? From one angle, it certainly does not. For net contributors who give their consent to an unconditional transfer system no doubt show more generosity than solidarity requires, because net beneficiaries need no excuse for taking advantage of what such a system offers them ('no questions asked'). In this sense, our scheme is morally grander than one that merely expresses solidarity and is, therefore, stuck halfway between unconditional generosity and pure selfishness. From another angle, however, our scheme may well look morally repugnant in comparison to one based on solidarity. For is it not despicable that some should be able to be parasites out of choice? The moral condemnation of this possibility – rather than dubious conjectures about the motivational impact of introducing universal grants – is probably the true basis of Carens's misgivings about our proposal.

9.2 Injustice and the uncertainty of large-scale reform

If this is indeed the case, Carens's ethical objection to universal grants is of essentially the same nature as Elster's. For the first reason why Elster (1986: 709, 719) does not think much of the desirability of our proposal is that it 'completely lacks the potential for being ... wedded to a conception of justice'. Indeed, it 'goes against a widely accepted notion of justice: it is unfair for able-bodied people to live off the labour of others'. We strongly disagree with the former statement – our proposal stems directly from our conception of justice – and believe that the second statement, though true, carries little weight because the plausibility conditions of the notion of justice to which it appeals are in the process of disappearing.

To indicate in what sense and to what extent our proposal is wedded to a conception of justice, we shall confine ourselves to three brief remarks. Firstly, what is 'unfair' about living off the labour of others when everyone is given the same possibility? Facing this possibility, some will choose to do no or little paid work, while others will want to work a lot, whether for the additional money or for the fun of working, thereby financing everyone's universal grant. If the latter envy the former's 'idleness', why don't they follow suit?[7] Formal fairness is at least as well respected when everyone enjoys the freedom not to work as when no one does, as would be the case in a socialist society strictly ruled by the principle 'To each according to his labour.' And it is definitely better respected when everyone is granted that freedom than when this freedom is the privilege of a small minority, as it is in all existing capitalist societies, whether with or without a substantial welfare state.

Secondly, it is of crucial importance to bear in mind that, under advanced welfare-state capitalism, access to (paid) labour has become a privilege.[8] Contrary to what Elster (1986: 712) seems to take for granted, unemployment is not just a matter of inefficiency, but also of injustice. The introduction of the universal grant must be viewed as a way of sharing out the advantages currently attached to the holding of a ('real') job. What cries out for it in our eyes, and on the sort of grounds neatly exposed by Przeworski, is protracted structural unemployment, not *qua* sub-optimal use of productive resources but *qua* unfair exclusion of an increasing proportion of those living under welfare-state capitalism. In a word, the very persistence of involuntary unemployment shows that there is a persistent imbalance of benefits in favour of the employed.[9] Our proposal constitutes one way of getting rid of this morally intolerable imbalance. But there are other ways, which are consistent, unlike our proposal, with the upholding of a compulsion to work, most conspicuously (at least in the current European context) a dramatic reduction in standard working time. Why prefer the universal grant?

Again, the issue is complex, even leaving feasibility aside. But ultimately it comes down – and this is the third point we want to stress – to the relative importance we attach to liberty.[10] A universal grant cannot be justified by reference to solidarity (in favour of the 'unlucky') or to any desert principle (nobody 'deserves' it). It can only be justified in terms of real freedom from toil for everyone.[11] Once such freedom has become possible (an assertion to be discussed shortly), it needs much more than a quick reference to a 'widely accepted notion of justice' to convince those who attach a high price to (real) freedom that this opportunity should be forgone and the subjection to paid work maintained.

This is particularly so in a context in which the plausibility of Elster's particular 'notion of justice', is dwindling at a fast pace, and in which, therefore, the weight of his second statement quoted above is being eroded. We do not deny that the notion that 'he who does not work shall not eat' still has staunch defenders on the Right, of course, but also on the Left.[12] And we do not want to interpret the fact that only two of our six critics hold this position as evidence that similar proportions hold in society at large. But we want to stress the importance of three distinct trends that concur to undermine the claim that work (or at least willingness to work) alone entitles one to any part of the social product.

Firstly, the women's movement has led to a *revaluation of unpaid work*. If one agrees that there are some productive activities (typically, but not only, the bearing and rearing of children) of which it is undesirable that they should become paid work,[13] if one insists that people should be (genuinely) free to specialize in such activities for part or all of their lives if they so wish, and if one also insists that those who do so should nevertheless not be reduced to the status of a 'dependant', then there is no way in which one can stick to the principle that only those who perform (paid) work – or have done so or give evidence that they would gladly do so – are entitled to an income of their own. It is no serious objection to this claim to say that the right to the minimum income could be restricted to those performing activities socially recognized as useful, whether paid or unpaid, as opposed to pure parasites who do nothing useful at all. For restricting the right to the minimum income in this way amounts to turning so-called unpaid work into paid work (with the monitoring of duration, intensity and efficiency this implies), because the payment of the minimum income would be contingent upon its performance in the same way as the payment of wages is contingent upon the performance of standard paid work. It is hard to see why the reasons that make it undesirable to turn some activities into paid work would fail to apply just because the payment is not called a wage.

Secondly, *technical progress* has immensely attenuated the truth contained in the impression that what is being produced by a worker, the income she or he generates, is owed entirely, or principally, to that worker's efforts. Nor does this only apply to those workers who operate sophisticated machinery. If you compare the real incomes of self-employed barbers in Amsterdam and in Calcutta (working equally hard and using tools that hardly differ), you will get a hint about how little is actually due to the worker's effort, rather than to technical development and capital accumulation in the economy in which she or he happens to work. When the size of one's income has so little to do with the work performed, how can one oppose the introduction of a universal grant on the ground that capitalists would then no longer be the only people capable of getting an income without working?[14]

Finally, *privatization and destruction* of the remaining commons by industrial society have left whoever does not get a monetary income with such meagre possibilities for subsisting independently, that it hardly seems shocking to ask those who get the highest benefits from such a system to compensate the less lucky for what they are deprived of as a result.[15] This argument is particularly strong when, as is currently the case under welfare-state capitalism, many of those who derive income from their work occupy jobs that many of those out of work would be glad to occupy. For all these reasons, we believe very little weight should be given to the 'widely held notion of justice' to which Elster gives such a decisive role – far less at any rate than would be needed to make us shy away from wanting to give everyone the freedom not to work as soon as this has become economically possible.

However, there is another, quite distinct ground on which Elster (1986: 719) questions the desirability of our proposal. The case we make for it, he rightly says, is of a consequentialist nature,[16] and, as always with large-scale reforms, 'the alleged effects are surrounded by massive uncertainty'. This, we take it, is not only meant to affect the political feasibility of our proposal, but its very desirability. To be able to stop at this point, however, Elster must be either desperately pessimistic about the present state of the social sciences or happily complacent about the present state of social affairs. We do not believe he is either, as is evidenced by the fact that he himself considers at some length the likely consequences of self-management and of Weitzman's share economy (Elster 1986: 712–19). As far as universal-grant capitalism is concerned, however, he finds it sufficient to state that 'there is an abundance of actual or potential proposals of equal plausibility' (Elster 1986: 720), without bothering to consider the specific consequentialist case we make. Elster's useful discussions of local/global, partial/net, static/dynamic, and transitional/steady-state consequences are all important for us to bear in mind when arguing for our proposal, as we believe, along with Przeworski (1986: 705) that 'no proposal is better than the specific effects it would engender'. But to sweep universal grants onto the garbage heap of the history of fantasies, it will not do simply to say what sort of difficulties might in principle affect any large-scale proposal. One must take the trouble of spelling out in what way this particular proposal is likely to go wrong according to the standards to which one is committed. Failing this, we keep believing more than ever that introducing an adequate universal grant, if at all feasible, would be highly desirable.

9.3 Weak abundance

But precisely, is universal-grant capitalism really feasible, even leaving political considerations aside? Put more rigorously, has *weak abundance* been reached, i.e. is a universal grant at a level sufficient to cover everyone's fundamental needs sustainable in advanced capitalist countries, taking all the economic agents' responses into account? Obviously, this question cannot be answered without having some idea of what 'fundamental needs' consist in – an issue about which several of our critics insist that more should be said. What we mean by 'fundamental needs' is not to be defined as an objectively assessable 'biological minimum', if there is one. (Would it cover, for example, weekly cancer checks or costly heart operations at any age?) Nor is it defined as what the government – or whichever administration is in charge of the poor, or even public opinion – decrees to be the 'social minimum'.[17]

Fundamental needs are rather a matter of people's preferences (wants, desires, etc.) and hence subject to historical and cultural variation, even though they are not identical to such preferences. That people choose to work in order to earn additional income at a given level of the universal grant does not prove that the latter fails to meet their fundamental needs. However, that they would accept a highly unpleasant full-time job for a pay, say, equal to the unconditional grant they receive would be strong evidence that the latter is indeed insufficient. This suggests one possible criterion for an *adequate* universal grant: it would consist in identifying the level of the grant (in the form of an optimal combination of collective consumption and individual cash transfer) which would cause people to turn down a job answering this description, even if they lived on their own.[18] We have not (and no one, to our knowledge, has) worked out what the level of such an adequate grant would be in advanced capitalist countries. But we will conjecture, as Przeworski (1986: 698) does, that it corresponds to about one-half of per capita domestic income in those countries (compared to about 30 per cent of GDP currently spent on welfare in OECD countries).[19]

Is a universal grant at such a level economically sustainable? Elster does not take up the issue. Berger and Nove do not seem to see this as a major problem. But Carens, Wright, and Przeworski do and look upon our optimism in this matter with various degrees of scepticism. All three of them would agree that advanced capitalist countries can afford an adequate universal grant (as estimated above) in a purely static sense: added to the existing government expenditure on items other than income transfers (which averages about 20 per cent of GDP in OECD countries), the financing of the universal grant would not exceed their current national income. But our critics object that the national income may no longer be sufficient once all economic agents will have fully adjusted to the institutional change.[20]

Whether this is the case essentially depends on how the suppliers of the main factors of production react to the availability of the grant itself and to the implied changes in the marginal rates of tax on the incomes they derive from putting these factors to productive use. As these rates of tax rise, they may choose to supply less of the factors they own: capitalists may consume or hoard what they previously saved and invested, and workers may choose to work less or to do more attractive jobs. Moreover, capitalists and workers may choose to keep putting their resources to productive use, but in a way that enables them to avoid taxation: capitalists find loopholes in the tax laws or enter illegal business, workers turn to home production or to the black economy. Finally, both capitalists and workers may also choose to move out in search of a place in which less of their incomes is being taxed away.

9.4 Will idleness flourish?

Let us first consider the threat to weak abundance that may come from labour's response. Both Carens and Przeworski refer to econometric studies on the effects of taxes and transfers on the supply of labour and on aggregate income in the United States. On this basis, Przeworski (1986: 701) conjectures that introducing a universal grant at an adequate level – which implies, he reckons, that taxes increase by about 20 per cent of GDP – can be expected to 'reduce the supply of labour by a magnitude that, without productivity changes, would reduce aggregate income by more than five per cent'. The truth of this conjecture, as Przeworski is well aware, would not invalidate our claim that weak abundance has been reached. For by no means does this claim entail that introducing an adequate universal grant would have no negative effect on aggregate income. Moreover, as Przeworski (1986: 700) himself is anxious to emphasize, this sort of conjecture must be taken with the greatest caution, given the wealth of risky assumptions used in the process of deriving it. Several reasons converge in making it particularly hazardous to use existing econometric studies in order to sharpen our expectations about the consequences of introducing a universal grant.

Firstly, it is important to realize that what matters to the economic agents' response is not the proportion of the national product taxed away, but rather the agents' marginal incomes. And these two variables are not so closely related that any rise in the former implies a fall in the latter. If, for example, a uniform negative income tax system is replaced by a universal grant system guaranteeing the same minimum income and financed by a proportional tax on extra income, the proportion of aggregate income taxed by the government will go up very substantially, even though the marginal rates of tax, the distribution of net incomes, and hence the supply of labour and the level of aggregate income undergo no change whatsoever.[21] We are not claiming of course that the rise in the tax level required to introduce an adequate universal grant in OECD countries is exactly of this type. But a large part of it is. And speculations about the impact of such introduction that are based on estimates of the elasticity of the aggregate supply of labour with respect to the average tax rate are simply blind to this fact.

Secondly, one must be very cautious when inferring from a fall in the aggregate supply of labour to a fall in aggregate income under conditions of massive *excess* labour supply. Mass unemployment should give enough leeway for tax increases that significantly reduce the aggregate labour supply without markedly affecting the level of aggregate income. And this leeway is even further increased if, as is expected, productivity keeps rising faster than output in the coming years, thus generating the 'jobless growth' that Przeworski (1986: 695) rightly views as a central element in the background of our proposal. Consequently, even if one is convinced, as Carens (1986: 683) is, that universal grants would lead many workers to reduce their earnings significantly, nothing whatsoever needs to follow as far as aggregate income is concerned.

It may be objected that a significant part of the current excess supply of labour is fake, as it really consists in voluntary unemployment. But this is no strong objection. Indeed, it leads to a third consideration that further limits the relevance of the results mentioned above. For the 'voluntariness' of this unemployment, if we want to call it that, is largely due to the extremely high marginal rates of tax (often 100 per cent or over) that are faced by recipients of welfare payments and unemployment benefits and that it is one of our proposal's primary aims to abolish. The marginal rates of tax on some incomes will certainly go up if an adequate universal grant is to be introduced. But nothing rules out that the resulting fall in the labour supply of some workers currently earning a high wage might be compensated by the increase in the effective labour supply of many more currently debarred from any sort of work by prohibitive marginal rates of benefit withdrawal. It so happens that the studies referred to, in particular those relating to the negative income tax experiments, are concerned with the United States, where this unemployment trap, due to lower benefits, is shallower than in Europe. Hence, any argument based on those studies is likely to overestimate substantially the difficulties our proposal would meet if it were introduced in Europe, where we think it has in any case (and partly for this reason) a much higher chance of reaching the political agenda.[22]

This is *not* to say, however, that the supply of labour is something we need not worry about. For there are also reasons why one should expect conjectures based on existing econometric studies to *under*estimate the impact that the introduction of a universal grant would have on aggregate income. Firstly, note that the level of most current transfer payments – especially pensions, unemployment benefits, and many disability benefits – is heavily dependent on whether and to what extent one has worked in the past. Cutting (wholly or partly) this causal link, as the (total or partial) replacement of such transfers by a universal grant would, may well have on the labour supply an effect that far exceeds what can be inferred from currently observed relations between tax rates and labour supply. If your post-tax income from work is reduced in order to finance conditional transfer payments, to which you are only entitled if you work – and are taxed – now, your willingness to work (and to report your work on your tax form) will be less affected than if your post-tax income is similarly reduced to finance universal transfer payments, to which you are entitled regardless of whether and how much you (are known to) have worked.

Secondly, even if it can be shown that the total number of hours people work is not going to drop significantly – indeed, even if it can be shown that it will rise substantially – we are not necessarily safe on the labour supply front. For the introduction of a universal grant may generate a massive substitution of less 'productive' for more 'productive' work. One of the main arguments we give for our proposal is that it makes economically viable a large number of intrinsically attractive but poorly productive jobs: jobs that people would accept even for the small amount of income they yield, once their fundamental needs are covered by income from another source. But our proposal may become the victim of its own success in this area. People may work just as much, or even more, than before, while earning through their work lower gross incomes. The universal grant and the implied tax rates may have made it wise for them to substitute (untaxed) 'consumption' at work for (taxed) consumption out of work – rather than leisure for work, thereby reducing the tax base in a different way.

There is no question that these are important issues, which deserve serious consideration. Unfortunately, and precisely because of the structural differences just mentioned between the two systems, even simulations using the most sophisticated techniques and the most reliable and disaggregated data on current elasticities are unable to generate reliable predictions as to how aggregate income will be affected as a result of the universal grant's impact on the labour supply. Moreover, for the general sort of reason well set out by Elster (1986: 710–11), experiments on a limited space and time scale would not yield results that could be generalized to a society-wide reform. There is no alternative to trying the proposal itself. This need not involve massive and irresponsible societal experimentation, because one could start, as in a proposal recently made by a commission officially appointed by the Dutch government, with a genuine but 'partial' universal grant (i.e. one insufficient to cover the fundamental needs of someone living alone), while a major part of the social security system subsists in its present, conditional form.[23]

Of course, just as a large change in the small, a small change in the large need not tell us what a large change in the large would lead to (Elster 1986: 710). But although some of the effects can only be expected to be significant once an adequate grant is in force (for example, major savings in administrative costs), there is no argument we can think of that would prevent a substantial though partial basic income, combined with the maintenance of part of the existing social security system and labour regulations, from having ('in the small') the sort of consequence a larger grant would have: the unemployment trap would not be suppressed, but its depth would be reduced, improvement of the quality of work would be fostered, though only moderately, and so on. This sort of experiment provides the only decisive way of undermining our critics' scepticism. And it is also the only way in which they can hope to shatter our optimism on this point, which remains totally unscathed in the light of the figures they mention and of what can be inferred from these figures about the dynamic impact of the introduction of an adequate universal grant under welfare-state capitalism.

9.5 Will capital vanish?

More serious, it would seem, is the threat to weak abundance that comes from the side of capital. Both Carens and Wright believe this threat is fatal to our proposal, while Przeworski is less sure. As Wright (1986: 662) suggests, one of the main differences between labour and capital is the latter's superior mobility. When tax rates go up, both labour and capital may of course decide to move out, thus threatening the collection of a tax yield sufficient to finance an adequate universal grant. But distances that are quite long to travel for labour power, because of language boundaries, personal ties, difficulties in getting one's credentials recognized, etc., are not quite so long for financial assets.[24] Consequently, whereas tax rates on labour income as high as 80 per cent may still be well within the bounds of the supply-siders' 'normal range' – i.e., further increases of the rate would not depress the supply of labour to such an extent that the tax yield would be reduced –, tax rates as low as, say, 10 per cent on capital income (net of inflation) may already belong to the 'prohibitive range' – that is any further increase of the rate will depress the domestic supply of capital to such an extent that the tax yield from capital income taxation would fall.[25] Hence, the attempt to finance an adequate universal grant through increased taxation of both labour and capital income may soon run into intractable difficulties, due to gradual, though massive, disinvestment.

To prevent such disinvestment, one may attempt, as Wright (1986: 663) suggests, to break the noted asymmetry between labour and capital without going all the way to a full-fledged socialization of capital. The most obvious way of doing so is to restrict narrowly the free movement of financial capital, in such a way that the risk of capital flight is drastically curtailed. How this can be done effectively is a tricky matter, which is familiar enough to advocates of a democratic transition to socialism and is now beginning to receive serious treatment.[26] Of course, even though the capitalists would still be able to get income from the assets they own and to move them around as they please inside the area concerned (and possibly, within limits, outside it), such measures would imply some degree of social control over capital and hence, as Wright (1986: 663) stresses, at least a tinge of 'socialism'. Moreover, it is by no means fanciful to imagine that they will trigger off a process that can only end, barring a U-turn, in nationalization of the means of production on a grand scale. For with drastic restrictions on the export of capital, it is not only likely that foreign investment will dry up altogether, but also that domestic investors will band up in a more or less concerted way to get the measures lifted. Assuming it is indeed correct that an open capitalist economy is unable to durably provide an adequate universal grant without introducing such measures, then only socialism can viably make room for such a grant – if anything can.

Is it so obvious, however, that the introduction of an adequate universal grant would scare capital away? First of all, nothing forces us to tax all income, whatever its source, at the same rate. An adequate universal grant might conceivably be financed by a high tax on wages, while not taxing profits at all. Or alternatively one could tax profits only to the extent that they are consumed, for example by replacing the income tax by an expenditure tax or by giving high tax relief on new investment.[27] In order to evaluate this strategy, it is essential to bear in mind the distinction between *tax burden* and *tax incidence*. Suppose the tax burden on capital – the rate at which profits are taxed – is zero, while an adequate universal grant is being financed out of a 70 per cent labour tax. Under such conditions, there is no reason, at first sight, to fear a capital flight that would jeopardize the sustainability of universal-grant capitalism realized in this way. However, the fall in net wages together with the availability of a substantial unconditional grant may well depress the supply of labour and thus induce a rise in gross wages. In many cases, firms will react in the longer run by introducing labour-saving capital-using innovations.[28] But whether or not they do, their profits will have been negatively affected by the introduction of the universal grant. In other words, even though capital bears no tax burden, the tax incidence on capital income may well be considerable. Indeed, even if the tax burden on capital were negative (profits are subsidized out of taxes on wages), the overall incidence of a tax scheme that serves to finance a substantial universal grant may be strongly unfavourable to capital, and therefore conducive to a serious risk of disinvestment.[29]

The seriousness of this risk, however, depends on how much pressure the introduction of an adequate universal grant is going to generate on the labour market – a point on which we have already expressed our scepticism in the previous section, based on the massive unemployment that forms the background of our proposal. Moreover, whether profits suffer directly from increased taxation on capital income or indirectly via increases in labour costs, such negative effects may be offset for many firms by advantages of another sort. A universal grant system would further increase the stability of domestic purchasing power. It would provide a minimum level of financial security for every household, without which any significant increase of labour-market flexibility would be unachievable. It would strengthen the ground on which small businesses can be started and new ventures launched. And it may weaken resistance to the introduction of new technology.[30] The weight of these various advantages will of course vary enormously from one firm to another. And whether they balance the negative effects will very much depend on the exact nature of the tax scheme. Suppose for example that, as many advocates of universal grants recommend, transfer payments are no longer financed primarily by social-security premiums levied on labour, but instead by a tax on each firm's value added or on its energy consumption.[31] Labour-intensive firms may then stand to gain from the reform, all things considered, and have no incentive whatsoever to seek refuge in countries not haunted by the spectre of the universal grant. Here again, of course, relevant empirical evidence would be most welcome, but is unavoidably unavailable. All we have is very indirect, and not particularly alarming.[32] Given the considerable leeway provided by massive unemployment, it is hard to believe, as Carens (1986: 680–1) does, that the replacement of the current social-security net in advanced welfare states by adequate universal grants would dramatically damage profits (all things considered) and drive freely moving capitalists away.[33]

9.6 A political utopia?

Suppose now that we are right in believing that weak abundance has been achieved in some capitalist country, i.e. that the provision of an adequate universal grant can be durably secured by the country's government without needing to rely on forced labour or saving. (Whether or not this possibility is subject to keeping some residual elements of a conditional social-security system, to taxing labour and capital at different rates, to introducing the universal grant in a sufficiently large geographical area, etc., can be left open for our present purposes.) This does not turn universal-grant capitalism into more than a merely abstract possibility. For even if an adequate universal grant is sustainable, few people may be interested in its introduction or, even if many are, they may not have the power to overcome the resistance of those who are not. This issue of political feasibility was deliberately and explicitly left aside in chapter 8. But it has been taken up by most of our critics. And we would not like to dodge it entirely in this reply. Showing that this sort of proposal, if economically feasible, fits our intuitions about what a good society would be like and hoping that many people will come to share this view is obviously not enough. A cold-blooded analysis of naked self-interest and capacity to pursue it effectively cannot be dispensed with.

One interesting strategy for tackling this issue is suggested by Przeworski (1986: 703–5): so-called median voter models enable us to predict, given certain assumptions, how much redistribution a society of self-interested individuals will settle on under majority rule, taking both the pre-tax income distribution (its degree of skewedness) and the dynamic effects of redistribution (the deadweight loss) into account. The difficulty with this approach for the problem at hand is not so much that it has to rely, as Przeworski notes, on restrictive assumptions (for example, there is no majority equilibrium if progressive, and not just proportional, taxation is allowed) and rough estimates (for example of the labour-supply effects). The main problem is that our first transition does not raise the question of how much redistribution a majority will favour, given the central features of the redistributive structure, but rather the question of what sort of redistributive structure the majority wants. Whether the median voter prefers an adequate universal grant to an inadequate one, or to no grant at all, will be relevant when we come to talk of the second transition, but is of little interest in connection with the first one. What matters to the latter is whether the self-interest of a majority of citizens would be served by a shift from welfare-state capitalism's conditional social-security system to one based on an adequate universal grant.

One way of beginning to tackle this question consists in asking who would gain if current social-security systems were replaced by a system with a universal grant at the level of minimum social-security benefits for a single person (assumed to be *at most* sufficient to cover fundamental needs), while additional benefits are maintained for those currently receiving unemployment benefits and pensions in such a way as to bring up their total income from transfers to the level of their current entitlements. In a purely static perspective, gainers would be those currently with no personal income whatsoever (mainly housewives), those currently on welfare or unemployment benefits (in some cases – mainly claimants sharing a home – because of an increased income, but above all because of the 'right to work', the increased opportunities that the unconditionality of the universal grant has given them), part-time workers and, more generally, the low paid. The losers, of course, are income earners whose increased taxes are not compensated by their right to a universal grant. And pensioners would be at worst just as well off as before. Rough computations in typical welfare-state capitalist countries show that, when taxes are raised in such a way as to make the operation financially neutral, a significant majority of individuals would become better off as a result of introducing this sort of reform. And this result is even clearer if individuals are assumed to care about income and opportunities at the household level.[34]

Dynamic considerations might of course upset this result. But if the argument put forward in the previous two sections is sound, the deadweight loss would fall far short of what would be required to prevent the scenario described above from improving the majority's lot. On the other hand, part of that argument rested on the assumption of efficiency gains associated with the increased labour market flexibility (or 'deregulation') which the introduction of a universal grant would make possible. And although many workers may gain from this flexibility, especially among the more skilled and among those in the most precarious positions, many may also lose, notably among those in the middle range who owe the more-than-minimal security they enjoy to entrenched rights and collective bargaining agreements. This is, however, less an objection to the claim that a universal grant is in the self-interest of the majority than a warning to this majority that it should be most careful about what it lets in along with such a grant.[35]

9.7 A new social movement?

To be sure, political feasibility is not realized as soon as an abstract majority of voters would gain, all things considered, from a scheme. This majority needs to 'find itself', to shape the parties, associations, think tanks, lobbies through which its 'will' will be worked out and expressed – briefly, to rest on a *social movement*. If it does not, it will never manage to implement a scheme that would be in the interest of all its members, even in a situation in which no other force would attempt or manage to thwart its intentions if it actually tried to implement it. And even if Elster (1986: 709) is totally wrong, as argued earlier, when asserting that our proposal cannot be wedded to a conception of justice, he may still be right when claiming that 'it completely lacks the potential for being rooted in a social movement'.

Indeed, those who stand to gain most from the introduction of an adequate universal grant – housewives, the unemployed, those with precarious jobs – generally live under conditions which are far less favourable to collective organization than those who would lose from it. Many of them live in near isolation or with the feeling that their current situation will not last for long (thinking that they are just about to get a 'real job').[36] Moreover, not only do they have very limited material resources (just compare the lavish layout of a landlords' Union bulletin, generously financed by keen advertisers, with the shabby outlook of an unemployed Union newsletter!). They also tend to lack the human potential for organization because of the 'creaming off' of many of the ablest among them (if you can get a claimants' Union started, you can certainly find a good job), because of the heterogeneity of their statuses (how can you get excited about such objectives as an increase in benefits if, being a housewife, you do not receive any, or if your dearest hope is, by finding a job, to lose your entitlement to them?) and because of the stigmas attached to many of these (how can you identify with a situation that you must constantly give evidence of wanting to leave?). Of course, the labour movement, in its earlier stages, shared some of these difficulties. But at least the work performed in common in larger and larger factories provided workers with a shared experience and a natural opportunity to meet for which dole queues and cheap supermarkets are poor substitutes. And it would therefore seem that the sort of social movement that could back a universal grant system would be extremely difficult to get off the ground.

However, there is one major resource which the potential majority we are talking about possesses to a greater extent than the labour movement has ever done: time. Even with small amounts of material means, organizational skills, regained pride and stability, the abundance of this resource may provide enough ground for a resilient social movement to stand on, providing it can avail itself of more than purely defensive claims and mobilize around a coherent, positive aim, such as the universal grant claims to be. Numerous initiatives to organize welfare recipients in various West European countries suggest that this has already become much more than sheer speculation.[37] Whether such seeds grow strong enough to give bulk to the majority of people who would benefit from an adequate universal grant scheme will depend on a wide variety of factors.

One of them is the extent to which current social-security systems already include universal benefits, neither means-tested nor contingent upon past labour record or current willingness to work.[38] Universality is essential to attenuate stigmas, but also to give the needed stability to the status of a benefit receiver. Any step in the direction of more universal benefits is therefore a good thing, as far as our first transition is concerned, on two distinct counts: it brings welfare-state institutions substantially closer to a universal grant system and it enhances the political chances of an adequate universal grant by strengthening the potential for a powerful social movement supporting it. Another significant factor is the ease with which a progressive social movement without close ties to the established labour organizations can find a noticeable political expression, given the nature of the country's electoral system – a feat the German Greens achieved, but hardly anyone else.[39] Finally, the constitution of a strong social movement in favour of an adequate universal grant is of course also heavily dependent on the success of the ideological debate in convincing people that such a reform is desirable, most crucially in convincing social-democrats and feminists that it would not amount to a sell-out, to a poor compensation for giving up the struggle for the right to work.[40] This is one way in which the desirability issue, discussed earlier, feeds back into the feasibility issue. But there is another, which is equally important.

9.8 Will the popular will be thwarted?

We have assumed so far that gross income earners, whether workers or capitalists, simply adjust ('parametrically') to whatever tax and transfer scheme happens to be adopted by a democratic majority. But having observed that this majority (of low earners) needs to take the reactions of both workers and capitalists into account when determining which tax policy is in their best interest, why would workers or capitalists not choose to behave *strategically*, threatening to collectively reduce their income-generating activities more than would be individually rational for each worker or capitalist to do, in order to impose the choice of a policy that better suits them?[41] In other words, are not those with a low income, or with no income at all, who would most benefit from the introduction of an adequate universal grant, at the mercy of labour or capital strikes? Are those who own valuable resources not likely to organize and withdraw them in order to thwart – without trespassing their rights – the realization of a state of affairs that may be both economically feasible, in the sense that weak abundance ('parametrically' defined) is achieved, and politically feasible in the weak sense that most voters would be better off if it were implemented? Even if their preferences – in particular the value they attach to a high income – would lead each of them, taken individually, to work or save nearly as much, or just as much, or even more, under a universal-grant system than without, it may well be in their (strategic) interest to withdraw or export their labour or capital, or to threaten to do so, thus forcing the majority to cut its losses by giving up the attempt to introduce a universal grant, or by settling for a lower level of it. According to Wright (1986: 664–8), it is this sort of obstacle – politically motivated capital strike or coalition between capitalists and skilled workers – that shatters most fundamentally the feasibility of our proposal.

If this sort of coalition gets organized, let us be clear about this, we do not believe an adequate universal grant has a fighting chance under capitalist conditions. To curb the resistance of capital, one might attempt to impose narrow limits on the capitalists' freedom, such as an obligation to invest productively within a given period the major part of their profits. But we agree that this would 'begin to look much more like a compensation system for nationalized property' (Wright 1986: 666) that would, moreover, generate further resistance on the capitalists' part, in such a way that full-fledged socialism would soon be plainly superior to the resulting chaos. To curb the resistance of organized labour, on the other hand, no means is available that would not jeopardize at root the very freedom from toil that the universal grant prides itself on introducing. Determined, well-organized resistance by capitalists or well-paid workers or both means the collapse of universal-grant capitalism – *just as* the organized hostility of capital-managing bureaucrats or the workers' aristocracy or both would seal the fate of universal-grant socialism.

For universal-grant capitalism to have any future, it is therefore crucial to prevent the rise of such resistance. As far as capital is concerned, this means that profits must not be handled so roughly as to make organized resistance worthwhile. But it does *not* mean that any attempt to introduce a universal grant system must recoil from increasing to any extent the incidence of taxation on capital income (whether directly through higher taxes on profits or indirectly through higher labour costs). Firstly, because, as noted earlier, the new system may have other, less direct advantages for a sizeable proportion of firms (stabilization of consumer demand, flexibility, etc.) that may offset, or nearly offset, this negative incidence. And secondly because the negative impact will have to be quite massive and widespread before capitalists start doing more than mourn or threaten, manage to overcome their ever present free-rider problem, and decide to trigger off a process that may end up in chaos or nationalization. Thus, the threat of capitalist conspiracy does impose limits, but with the sort of room to manoeuvre which has accommodated the whole development of the welfare state thus far and – why not? – will accommodate this further step as well.

To prevent the rise of determined, organized, resistance of those well-paid workers who would lose out if an adequate universal grant were introduced, on the other hand, one can count on none of the items just mentioned in connection with the threat of a capital strike. But one can rely instead on a systematic discrepancy between what would be in these workers' self-interest and what they will actually decide to do. Whether workers will resist universal-grant capitalism does not just depend on whether their self-interest would be hurt by its introduction, but also on the extent to which they find it desirable, in the sense of being congruent with the *values* to which they are committed. For how far social groups will make strategic use of the power they have in order to further their interests partly depends on what they themselves, as well as society at large, regard as legitimate. (To successfully organize a strike aiming at a reduction of the tax burden, one needs to feel 'right' in a stronger sense than if one simply decides to work less in the face of a higher marginal tax rate.) If there is a general feeling that the universal grant is 'right', the skilled workers who resent the tax burden imposed on them to finance it will have no qualms about individually reducing their labour supply but will find it more difficult to use collectively the withdrawal of their labour power as a political weapon.[42] If only for this reason, the ethical discussion with which we opened this reply is crucially relevant to the present pragmatic discussion. The reason why we believe a universal-grant system to be feasible is (in part) that we believe it to be desirable and believe that many others will come to share this belief. For us, this desirability is in turn partly determined by one possibility such a system opens up: our more speculative 'second transition', with which the remaining sections are concerned.

9.9 Challenges to negative growth

Suppose now that the first transition is completed, i.e. that an adequate universal grant is viably secured. Do we then want to move on towards communism, defined as a situation in which every individual's income is made up entirely of this universal grant?[43] And, if so, can we? Whereas on the desirability of the first transition we could count on wide support among our critics, this support dwindles where the desirability of this second transition is concerned. Only Wright gives signs of wishing to come along. Przeworski and Elster do not take a stance on this issue, not even by implication.[44] But Carens (1986: 685) and Berger (1986: 693) object that our communism is incompatible with anyone satisfying more than fundamental needs, while Nove (1986: 677) complains that it rules out growth. Not only is such an austere picture very remote from Marx's rather more cheerful conception where communism and abundance go hand in hand; but, using our article's terminology, it also makes one wonder why anyone should want to drive taxation beyond the 'Rawlsian' maximum (where the universal grant is as high as possible), thus depressing not just average income, but *everyone's* income, even down to the ('communist') point where no one has the possibility of earning any net income above the universal grant.[45]

To this question – which arises, by the way, regardless of whether the move toward communism is supposed to operate in a socialist or in a capitalist context – we reply (in section 8.6 above) by stating that only communism thus defined guarantees that alienation, extrinsically motivated labour, is abolished, and we point out that the Marxian criterion, the maximization of the share of universal grants in total income, may not be best for equality, as soon as the distribution of income from the informal, untaxed sphere is taken into account. But this is no serious challenge to the Marxian criterion if the objective is not to eliminate inequality, but alienation. Carens (1986: 686), however, goes further and argues that taking the informal sphere into account shatters the equivalence between maximizing the relative level of the grant and minimizing alienation. Activities performed in the informal sphere cannot be equated with unalienated activities. Consequently, one *cannot* take it for granted that total labour (not just labour in the formal sphere) decreases as the tax rate goes up. With a high rate of tax, people may increasingly substitute poorly productive labour (even in the comprehensive sense, which takes the attractiveness of labour into account) conducted in the informal sphere for more productive labour in the formal sphere (think of car repairs, for example), with an overall *positive* effect on the volume of alienated activities.[46] Even statically and taking nothing but alienation into account, the pursuit of communism, construed as the use of the Marxian criterion (whether in a capitalist or a socialist context) hardly seems desirable.

Moreover, its feasibility is also most questionable. In chapter 8, section 8.6, we point out that taking immediate advantage of productivity gains to raise the tax rate as much as possible (under the constraint that the grant must cover fundamental needs) is dynamically counterproductive, because the negative growth of output this implies is most likely to slow down technical change or even bring it to a halt, and hence to make further progress toward communism extremely slow, if not altogether impossible. But political feasibility is even more dubious than economic feasibility. Why would a democratic society ever choose a level of taxation that gives *every one* of its members a lower income than is currently possible?[47] If the individual members of this society really wanted the levels of income and leisure induced by this collective choice, they would have chosen them at a lower rate of tax, where their freedom was greater (higher net wage *and* higher grant), rather than waiting to be forced into choosing them by prohibitive taxation. Thus, if such a collective choice is to make any sense, some externalities must be involved. This is precisely what we assumed when suggesting, in the same section, that only the pressure of ecological constraints could drive society into the 'Marxian' corner, thus turning 'a utopian dream into a historical necessity'. However, suppose there are stringent ecological constraints on growth. Could not any specified level of conservation of natural resources or of environmental protection be achieved more efficiently, and certainly at a lesser cost in terms of aggregate income, by specifically taxing the use of scarce natural resources and all major forms of pollution? The factor substitution that would result seems to be a much more appropriate response than the very gross strategy of discouraging production (in the formal sphere) altogether by taxing all income (or value added) undiscriminatingly or (even worse) by specifically taxing labour income. Hence, no pressure on the political process to discourage formal labour can be expected on this basis. And all that remains is the naked fact that ecological problems are a drag on productivity and therefore, whatever they do to the political feasibility of our second transition, erode its economic feasibility.

There are ways in which one could try to salvage this ecological argument for the political feasibility (or even necessity) of our second transition. For example, one might try to show that, under certain circumstances, specific measures for protecting the environment or conserving natural resources are hard to implement and that, therefore, only the rougher method – putting tax brakes on the whole growth process – is practicable. Or one might attempt to substitute one sort of externality for another, by arguing that reducing the time people spend in the formal economy through prohibitive taxation (a more supple and less oppressive tool for this purpose than uniform compulsory reduction of maximum working time) enables a society to redensify the 'home environment': neighbourhoods, villages, and towns would be turned back into places where people really live, availability for all sorts of voluntary mutual aid would thereby be enhanced, while crime and loneliness would be kept under check.[48] Such a hypothetical transformation is partly a public good, and it is therefore not ruled out that a democratic polity may be led by considerations of this type to impose on its members, through prohibitive taxation, levels of leisure and income that none of them would have chosen in its absence.

9.10 The way forward

However, we would not like to stake all the feasibility of our second transition on the probability that such conjectures may prove true. To vindicate the desirability and feasibility of our capitalist road to communism, we want to focus instead on another line or argument sketched in chapter 8, section 8.6. It was there suggested that the pursuit of communism as previously defined did not guarantee a development of the 'realm of freedom' in all its dimensions. True, one could expect a reduction in the length of (formal) working time and an improvement in its quality, up to the point where there would be no formal work left (full automation) or at least no formal work that would not be in itself (without any extrinsic reward) at least as attractive as time spent in the informal sphere. But this progress along the dimensions of length and quality of work might be achieved at the expense of a third dimension of the 'realm of freedom': the real freedom to live as one pleases in the *informal* sphere, as approximated by one's (formal) income. Hence the suggestion of an additional requirement for any desirable transition: that society's average income – its real standard of living, stripped of externalities – should rise, or at least not fall. Our second transition can then be conveniently pictured as a gradual move from an initial situation in which the universal grant, at a level covering fundamental needs, falls short of average income, to a notional end-point in which the universal grant has risen above (initial) fundamental needs to become equal to average income.

We are now in a much more comfortable position to answer our critics' objections to the *desirability* of our second transition. Even at the notional end-point of our second transition, where people have no income other

than their grant, each of them is able to satisfy much more than fundamental needs.[49] With no work whatsoever, average income is then at
least as high as it is now – and even considerably higher if in each period
productivity gains have been used not just to reduce toil but also to
increase output. This should be enough to assuage Berger's, Carens's and
Nove's fears on this count. Moreover, Carens's worry that our second
transition may not reduce alienation loses much of its plausibility. *If* the
gradual universalization of (formal) income is realized at the cost of a
falling average (formal) income, one can easily imagine that many people,
whose formal income is steadily decreasing, will move out of the heavily
taxed formal sphere, not to indulge in sound leisure or to engage in
spiritual quests, but to produce through domestic toil what their formal
income no longer enables them to buy. If, instead, average income
remains constant or indeed *increases* substantially, that objection loses its
bite. For why should people whose formal income increases – and these
would be the majority even if *average* formal income remained constant –
start toiling massively in the informal sphere, in such a way that alienated
activities (whether in the formal or informal sphere) would take up an
ever increasing proportion of their time? If this is not the case, our second
transition, as redefined, admittedly never abolishes alienation altogether
(the latter remains present in the informal sphere even at the end point),
but keeps reducing it through time.

Asking about our second transition's *economic feasibility* amounts to
asking whether, after an adequate universal grant has been introduced,
productivity in the formal sector keeps rising, in such a way that it
simultaneously makes room for a decrease in formal working time
(induced by a higher grant and higher taxation) and a growth (or at least
no fall) in formal output. If the reasoning we have used to argue for our
weak abundance claim holds water, then it also applies to the economic
feasibility of our second transition. Of course, this transition is likely to
proceed at a pretty slow pace. The rise of taxation must not be such as to
generate disinvestment, and thus threaten both current output and
continued productivity growth. Moreover, it is worth emphasizing that
the level of output that is not allowed to decline is the output that
actually contributes to the material welfare of the members of the society
concerned. It does not include, for example, those products that only
serve to cancel or reduce the nuisances generated by other parts of the
output, nor those parts that are given away outside the society concerned
in the form of foreign aid. Both ecological problems and an (unquestionably desirable) long-term redistribution of income on a world scale thus

appear as possible obstacles, which reduce the speed of economically feasible transitions by reducing the extent to which productivity increases can be used to raise the relative level of the universal grant under the stated requirement.

Political feasibility, finally, is far less problematic in this light than under the negative-growth interpretation of the second transition. If a desirable transition toward communism is construed as a rise in the relative level of the universal grant without a fall in average income, it becomes perfectly conceivable that the choice of increasing (without maximizing) the relative level of the grant be taken by a majority whose income would go up as a result.[50] However, the uncertainty surrounding the net effect of such a choice on individual income precludes that a firm majority will ever emerge as certain to gain from a higher relative level of the grant. Consequently, what the political feasibility of a gradual transition towards communism hinges on is whether, now and then, the majority's (or the democratically decisive group's) preference structure will be such – comparatively high importance to the opportunity for 'leisure' (or more fulfilling work), comparatively low importance to the opportunity to earn more income – that it will be willing to take the risk of increasing the level of the grant. Whether under (democratic) capitalist or under (democratic) socialist conditions, this political process, no doubt, will add a further time lag to the slowness with which the transition's economic feasibility will unfold. We have never believed, in any case, that our road to communism would be a speedway.

In both the previous chapter and in the present one, we have defended the idea of a capitalist transition towards communism. We do not claim that a socialist road to communism is ethically inferior or factually impossible. We started from the premise that the relative merits of transition proposals had to be judged in terms of their effectiveness at taking us closer to a state in which alienation is, as far as possible, abolished; and from the observation that the key material condition for such a process, productive development, was, if anything, more present under capitalism than under socialism. Of course, capitalism, by definition, subjects the pursuit of any collective purpose to the responses of private capital owners, just as any society that does not enslave its workers subjects the success of its pursuits to the responses of private owners of labour power and skills. Whether in connection with our first or second transition, much of our argument has attempted to show that, in the particular case of universal grants, this vulnerability of collective pursuits to private capital reactions was not so devastating as to offset entirely the *prima facie* advantage capitalism owes to its superior performance on the score of productivity.

This may, in actual fact, prove false. Even fairly modest levels of unconditional income may repeatedly generate lethally massive disinvestment, whether of a parametric or strategic nature. Maybe. And on our agenda too, socialism would then be back in top position.[51] But we are not that far yet. There is, in the meanwhile, only one way forward.

Notes

1 Nothing in this general definition precludes that part of this unconditional grant be given in the form of a health insurance package or of freely accessible public consumption goods (say, public parks and libraries).

2 That is: a significant degree of public ownership of productive capital and of democratic central planning, combined with extensive reliance on self-managed enterprises interacting on a market (see Nove 1983).

3 Among other articulate critics of our proposal on the Left, André Gorz, for example, adopts the Carens-Elster tack, while Gérard Roland (1988) joins in with Nove–Wright.

4 In practice, however, Carens might support a make-up guaranteed income (and even more, presumably, a work-and-household-size-conditional social-security system) if the choice is, because of cost constraints, between such a conditional system giving a decent income to the non-working poor and a universal system giving everyone a lower income guarantee. If the total volume of social transfers is taken as given, it is of course self-evident that the poor will receive more under a make-up system than under a universal system (where those transfers have to be shared with the rich). But taking such an amount as a constraint makes neither political nor economic sense. It does not make political sense because what taxpayers attach primary importance to is their *net* rate of tax, i.e. what is returned to them *as well as* what is taken away from them. And it does not make economic sense because what economic agents are primarily sensitive to is their net marginal reward, which can be the same with very different tax yields: a negative income tax scheme and a universal grant scheme, for example, may imply identical marginal rates of tax, even though the volume of transfers involved under the latter massively exceeds the volume required under the former. The relevant question, therefore, is not whether one should prefer a make-up guaranteed income to a universal grant with a given volume of transfers. It is rather whether one should prefer the former to the latter *if* it is (durably) possible to give the poor a higher income with the former than with the latter (which is not necessarily the case: see note 22 below). The answer given in chapter 8 is that it all depends on whether or not the income that can be guaranteed by the universal grant exceeds the level of basic needs. *If it does not*, we also prefer, along with Carens, a make-up scheme (providing of course the income it gives the poor is higher, but regardless of whether it is itself sufficient to cover basic needs). But *if it does*, we definitely favour a shift to a universal-grant scheme, not least for the sake of the non-working poor: such a scheme would reduce their numbers (no unemployment trap), it would allow them to supplement their guaranteed income with part-time work and it would free them from bureaucratic monitoring and means-testing. The distinction between these two cases is precisely what is involved in our emphasis on weak abundance as the key condition for the substitution of universal-grant for welfare-state capitalism.

5 Note, incidentally, that if Carens is really serious about (income) egalitarianism, his ideal income distribution should operate according to a universal principle and not with the

sort of selectivity that he proposes. For the most he could achieve with the latter is equality among full-time workers and people who would like to work full time but cannot.

6 Carens also challenges the desirability of universal-grant capitalism on the ground that, contrary to what we claim and what is taken on board by Nove and Wright, for example, introducing a universal grant would not lead to unpleasant work needing to be paid comparatively more and hence would not induce an improvement in the average quality of work nor move wages significantly in the direction of the 'old socialist ideal in which wage differences merely compensate for the relative disutilities of jobs' (Carens 1986: 681). In real-world capitalist systems, he argues, 'relative disutility has *much less impact* on relative scarcity, and thus on relative wages, than other factors such as differences in talents and skills, market imperfections, and luck'. And 'universal grants would not alter the factors determining the relative scarcity of different sorts of labour' (Carens 1986: 682, our emphasis). Further down, however, he undermines his own argument by asserting that 'capitalists already have *strong incentives* to make jobs more interesting whenever they can do so easily because that enables them to pay their workers less than comparably skilled workers performing less pleasant jobs' (Carens 1986: 682, our emphasis). If such 'strong incentives' exist, relative disutility *is* a major factor affecting wage differentials, contrary to what the earlier assertion implies. And because replacing the current welfare system by an adequate universal grant would amplify the play room of this factor – by removing the floor under the wages for attractive work as well as the compulsion to accept unattractive work on pain of starvation – our *ceteris paribus* claim is left unscathed. Note that Przeworski (1984: 701–3) too seems to be arguing against this 'dynamic claim' of ours. But there are two distinct statements that Przeworski labels this way: the statement that 'universal grants will result in an improvement of the quality of work', which is what we have just been talking about, and the more specific claim that the shrunken supply of labour for jobs with a high toil content (as a result of universal grants being introduced) 'will spur labour-saving investment in bad quality jobs'. The latter claim, Przeworski argues, cannot be substantiated because 'in the long run, the factor bias of technical change is indeterminate and unpredictable'. This is fine with us, because we only make the former claim: the quality of work may be increased by improving jobs at least as much as by suppressing them (a point strongly stressed by Carens, incidentally), and the dynamic claim we truly make, therefore, entails nothing about movements in the capital/labour ratio.

7 Take the analogous situation in which it is agreed that whoever gets the coffee ready for everyone *is entitled to two cups of coffee* instead of one (a crucial difference with the standard free rider case). If nobody is willing to make coffee under such conditions, it is simply impossible to give everyone the freedom to get a (full) cup of coffee without doing anything for it ('weak abundance' does not obtain). But if someone freely accepts the deal – because he enjoys drinking coffee more than others – why does the resulting distribution of burdens and advantages need to be unfair? The only circumstance under which it would fail to meet the minimum formal conditions for fairness is where the person who accepts to make coffee (however 'voluntarily', i.e. uncoerced by other) has no alternative, because he *needs* two cups of coffee. Hence the importance of an *adequate* universal grant, in the sense to be discussed below; everyone must have the real freedom not to work, even if not everyone must use it (due to differences in preferences, *not* in needs). Van der Veen (1991: section 6.3) discusses Elster's (1989: 215–16) response to this argument.

8 The important implications of this fact for class analysis in contemporary capitalist societies are developed in chapter 6 above.

9 We simply assume here, without having the space to argue in detail, that persistent

massive unemployment of this sort is inherent in advanced welfare-state capitalism as it is currently organized. This assumption does not rule out, as will become clear shortly, that there may be ways of tackling this unemployment problem that would not take us out of welfare-state capitalism into either universal-grant capitalism or socialism. For a brief critical discussion of these alternative strategies, see Van Parijs (1991b).

10 There are other ways in which one may try to justify an adequate universal grant, for example (along Paine–George–Steiner lines) as a rental on the use of commonly owned earth or (along Fourier–Nozick–Brody lines) as compensation for a welfare loss deriving from the private appropriation of natural resources, or again (along Bellamy–Liska–Aglietta lines) as a right of usufruct over social capital. (See Van Parijs (1992) for a comprehensive survey.) Each of these attempts raises serious conceptual difficulties (determination of 'value added' net of 'rent', identification of the relevant counterfactual 'state of nature', identification of what the current social product owes to 'society', respectively). Moreover, even if these could be solved, we do not believe that any of the attempts mentioned would justify an adequate universal grant. To put it in a nutshell, we believe that Paine–type attempts fail because the level of the universal grant they justify has little chance of being adequate (even under conditions where a more-than-adequate universal grant is actually viable). We believe that Fourier-type attempts fail because the level of the grant they justify varies with what people could fetch in the 'state of nature' (and hence would amount to a pittance for the least well endowed). Finally, Bellamy-type attempts do no more than make room for legitimate social control over a substantial part of the product, without specifically justifying redistribution in the form of universal grants.

11 The real freedom not to toil is of course only one real freedom among others, against which it may have to be traded off. In particular, the real freedom not to work (or to do enjoyable work) can only be introduced or increased at some price in terms of real freedom to consume goods and services. More money is given unconditionally to all, but less money is given to the fewer who bother to engage in paid activities. To use Hillel Steiner's (1986) illuminating way of phrasing the trade-off: 'the price (through forgone leisure and work quality) of satisfying preferences for goods and services' has to rise in order for 'the price (through forgone goods) of satisfying preferences for leisure and enjoyable productive activities' to fall. What is, Steiner asks, the moral justification for this price adjustment? Ultimately, our answer can only be that free disposal over one's time – which requires the availability of full-time leisure at a non-prohibitive price – is the 'central' component of freedom in the sense in which we are committed to the expansion of its realm. We shall briefly return to this answer (very much in need of elaboration) in connection with the second transition (section 9.9). This response is further discussed in van der Veen (1991: part 1); an alternative strategy is put forward in Van Parijs (1991c).

12 For typical Right-wing position, see e.g. Curtis (1968), Brody (1981) and, more cautiously, Becker (1980). For a typical official position of the social-democratic Left, see the justification given by the Dutch Labour Party for its principled opposition to the idea of a universal grant: 'According to democratic socialists, each person who is able to perform labour must do so.' (PvdA Congress resolution, April 1983, quoted by van Ojik (1983).) On the opposite side, see for example Offe (1985) and, more ambiguously, Gorz (1986).

13 As Hillel Steiner (1986) made us uncomfortably aware of, to spell out clear criteria and cogent arguments for such undesirability is no easy business.

14 Blocking the worker's-right-to-full-product argument is necessary but not sufficient to establish that every member of society is entitled to part of the worker's product. This is why the Bellamy approach discussed in note 10 will not do. Note, incidentally, that the argument does not hinge on any right violation having happened to prevent Calcutta barbers from invading Amsterdam (as in the sort of situation analysed by Hillel Steiner

204   Forward without socialism!

(1987)). If the income differential were due to the fact that Indian barbers hate Amsterdam or do not know about it, rather than to the fact that they are kept out of it, the claim that Amsterdam barbers are entitled to whatever the market gives them because they have 'created' the whole of the corresponding product would not become any more plausible as a result. See also the notion of citizenship exploitation discussed in chapter 7, section 7.2 above.

15 Again, this sort of argument may be sufficient to block an entitlement-based objection to any redistribution of income, but not to justify that this redistribution should take the form of universal grants. Hence the inadequacy of Fourier-type arguments mentioned in note 10.

16 Note, by the way, that being consequentialist does not prevent our argument from appealing to justice, nor indeed to autonomy (if freedom to run one's life as one pleases is part of it), which Elster (1986: 709) regards as characteristic of a non-consequentialist argument.

17 For a thorough and sophisticated attempt at making sense of the concept of needs in a way that turns out to be a variant of this approach, see Doyal and Gough (1991).

18 This test obviously needs refining (what is 'highly unpleasant'? what is 'full-time'?) and possibly revising (is equality with the grant the best specification of the wage level?). But it indicates what sort of stuff fundamental needs consist in, and also how these can vary from one individual to another: not just because of differences in objective contexts (for example, in the availability of cheap accommodation) and in abilities to spend (some people are much better at fulfilling their needs with a given amount of money), but also because of different trade-offs between leisure and income (in a given context and with a given ability to spend, different people will all take the job with a very small grant and turn it down with an infinite grant, but the level as from which they start turning it down may vary enormously). This variation by itself constitutes a problem. Taking as a benchmark the greediest individual with the worst spending ability in the worst possible context would in all likelihood pitch fundamental needs far above any country's per capita income – and hence leave weak abundance out of sight. Taking averages or medians instead is not altogether unreasonable or unfair (those with super-normal needs can endeavour to change context, enhance spending efficiency or reduce 'greed'). But we will probably want to be somewhat less harsh and define an *adequate grant* as one which covers fundamental needs as defined above in, say, 90 per cent of the cases (leaving out, e.g. those living in the most expensive area in town, those who tend to lose any cash they receive, as well as drug addicts). Another problem arises in connection with health needs. Hillel Steiner (1986: 6) asks: 'Does it make sense to say of a person who is suffering from some disability, or experiencing the general deterioration of ageing, or dying from some identifiable condition – all of which cannot be said to be irremediable with further knowledge and treatment – that s/he has (nonetheless) had her/his basic needs satisfied?' Strictly speaking, our test implies that it does.

19 The approach sketched above diverges from the one Przeworski (1986: 698) suggests insofar as it does not establish any *analytical* link between fundamental needs and per capita income. But it concurs with it insofar as it supposes that there is both an absolute and a relative element in the level of fundamental needs, and it is consistent with the view that (due to the absolute element) this level decreases in relative terms as per capita income rises.

20 This amounts to challenging what Przeworski (1986: 700) calls the 'strong version' of our weak abundance claim. The weak abundance claim we actually make is stronger still. We do not just claim that the level *of national income* dynamically induced by statically sufficient tax rates will not fall short of fundamental needs. We also claim that there are dynamically sufficient tax rates in the sense that the level *of the universal grant* (and *a fortiori* of national income) dynamically induced by these rates (necessarily greater than

statically sufficient ones) will not fall short of fundamental needs. We shall discuss both claims below, but not Przeworski's 'weak version' of our claim, which only applies to (non-existing) cases where the current tax level is sufficient to cover the universal grant (thanks to a reallocation of government expenditure).

21 The psychological perception may significantly differ, however. But this takes us to the issue of political feasibility to be discussed shortly. As Nove (1986: 676) elliptically suggests, it may be useful to distinguish between the 'disaffecting' and the 'disincentive' effect of taxation, which we understand to be closely linked to the feeling that some of one's money is being taken away by the tax authorities and to the reduction in one's post-tax marginal income, respectively. It would be quite wrong to suppose, however, that if the former disappears or is reduced (taxation being made less visible, e.g. by replacing income taxes by sales taxes or, as in socialist countries, by taxes on the enterprises' profits), the latter is also abolished or reduced. It is *not* true that 'the money actually received then has its proper incentive effect, and "Laffer" becomes irrelevant because invisible' (Nove 1986: 677). The same holds, *mutatis mutandis*, for negative income tax versus universal grant: the disaffecting effect of the former may be quite a bit smaller, but the disincentive effect can be expected to be identical.

22 To claim, as we have just done, that the increase in the gross earnings of people trapped in unemployment under a make-up system may *more than compensate* the decrease in the gross earnings of people facing a higher marginal rate of tax under a universal system, by no means commits us to claiming, as Carens (1986: 680) implies we do, that taxing the increased gross earnings of people freed from the unemployment trap would make it possible to avoid increasing the marginal rate of tax faced by other people and thereby to avoid a fall in their gross earnings. To expect this, we fully agree, is out of the question. If our claim holds, on the other hand, one *cannot* assert, as Carens (ibid) does, that 'for any given level of social expenditure on income transfers, we can provide a higher level of support for the most needy through a make-up guaranteed income than through universal grants'. Statically, this assertion is self-evident: if you transfer a given sum to the needy alone, they will have more than if they have to share it with others. But dynamically, it is false. Take the large amount needed to finance an adequate universal grant and use it all in the make-up fashion. Provided the 'needy' are not an overwhelming majority (in which case there would not be much difference between the two systems), the income awarded to each of them will then become far higher than the fundamental-needs level previously covered by the universal grant. But whoever earns less than this far higher income will lose any financial incentive to work. In all likelihood, aggregate income will collapse, leaving the needy much worse off than they would have been, had they shared the initial sum with everyone else. (For a numerical example and a somewhat more detailed discussion, see De Villé and Van Parijs (1985).)

23 See Wetenschappelijke Raad voor het Regeringsbeleid (1985). For a discussion of this proposal and an analysis of the economic and political conditions under which the 'partial' universal grant could be turned into a full one in the Dutch case, see van der Veen (1991: chapter 11).

24 This *prima facie* difference may be partly offset by another one. Whereas the supply of capital may well be more sensitive to tax rates, the supply of labour can be expected to be more sensitive to the availability of the grant. Given the very different shapes of the distributions of labour income and capital income, those whose income will rise as a direct result of the introduction of the universal grant are likely to push down the aggregate labour supply (due to their reduced need to earn wage income), while not being in a position to affect significantly the supply of capital.

25 This can happen even if all other countries tax both labour and capital income at an identical rate of 10 per cent. But since all countries are faced with the same asymmetry between labour and capital, it is most likely that each of them will tend to tax labour at a

higher rate than capital, thus further strengthening the constraints on capital income taxation elsewhere. Discussion of this sort is to be found in the literature on fiscal competition. See e.g. Mintz and Tulkens (1986).

26 For a lucid discussion of these issues, see Glyn (1986).

27 For a discussion of this sort of tax policy (which we assume in van der Veen and Van Parijs 1985), see Przeworski and Wallerstein (1982). As Przeworski (1986: 702) notes, whatever the rate at which consumption out of profits is being taxed, if invested profits are not taxed, the level of investment should not be affected – *but only provided* that gross wages are given and no choice of tax regimes allowed.

28 In an earlier article, Przeworski (1980: 146–9) argues that firms will not follow this labour-saving path – sadly, as far as freedom from toil is concerned – because the institutionalized guaranteed minimum forces them to pay for the labour displaced, which therefore they might as well keep putting to productive use. This would indeed be the case if each firm had to keep paying for the workers it laid off (or turned down). What happens, of course, is that it is society, not the firm concerned, that picks up the bill, to which each firm is asked to contribute, roughly (and to an extent that depends on whether social-security contributions or income tax are used to finance the guaranteed income) in proportion to the labour it still employs, not to the labour it has displaced. Rapid factor substitution is rooted at the very core of a guaranteed income system financed in this way. As such (i.e. abstracting from disinvestment induced by the high cost of labour) this need not involve the economy in a fatal spiral. True, labour-saving innovations reduce the use of the only (or main) factor that is being taxed. But they also increase its productivity. The burden on the remaining labour is heavier, but easier to carry.

29 Note that this dynamic effect, while worsening feasibility, enhances the ethical palatability of this sort of taxation scheme (though formally tax-exempt, capitalists bear part of the burden). At first sight, even the ethically less objectionable second variant (only reinvested profits are tax-exempt) does not have much to commend itself. As Ludo Cuyvers (1985) points out, both variants are equivalent in a world of abstemious power-mad capitalists who reinvest all their profits and live off their universal grant financed entirely out of labour income. However, this picture neglects the dynamic effects just mentioned. Why should we care about this apparent transfer from workers to capitalists if (1) dynamic efficiency is best served by the capitalist's restless search for maximally profitable investments, and (2) the introduction of the universal grant drives pre-tax wages upward (at the expense of profits) to such an extent that their post-tax incomes are higher than before despite the heavy taxation required to finance the grant?

30 For arguments along such lines, see e.g. Roberts (1984), Standing (1986) and Nooteboom (1986).

31 See, again, the Dutch proposals for financing a 'partial basic income': WRR (1985: 59) and Stroeken (1986).

32 For example, from the empirical literature they survey, Przeworski and Wallerstein (1986) conclude that there is no observed correlation between tax rates on the one hand, investment and growth on the other.

33 As Ian Gough pointed out to us, it would be interesting to compare our first transition, in this respect, to the 'Swedish road to socialism', as embodied in the Meidner plan.

34 These results are basically due (1) to the fact that, in Western Europe, the employed population typically constitutes less than half of the total adult population, and (2) to the fact that the individual loss of many of those employed is more than made up by increases in their dependants' own incomes. (Note, however, that such results are obviously very sensitive to the coefficient used to determine the level of a child's universal grant, as well as to any change in the tax regime occurring along with the introduction of the grant.) We are grateful to Paul-Marie Boulanger for supplying us with the relevant figures for Belgium.

35 One might object that it is not sufficient to show that a self-interested majority would prefer an adequate universal grant system to the current system. One must also show that it would be preferred by such a majority to any other feasible system, and in particular to some conditional social-security system (with means tests and/or willingness-to-work conditions) that could guarantee a higher minimum income. A universal grant will only be chosen if the income loss that may result in various ways from its unconditional nature is compensated (1) by a reduction in the cost of administration and control (the fewer conditions, the easier the implementation) and (2) by the importance given to the opportunity to take (unstigmatized, unbothered) leisure, as against the importance attached to a higher income.

36 Elster (1978: 139–49) himself usefully stresses elsewhere the importance of communicational distance and high rates of turnover as major obstacles to successful collective action.

37 See, e.g., Jordan (1973) and Maat & Co (1985) for first-hand reports on such initiatives.

38 Jordan (1986) suggests, e.g., that the reason why claimants' movements developed in the United Kingdom in the 1970s is that many more people were on social assistance (as opposed to social insurance) in the United Kingdom than in other European countries.

39 Van Parijs (1986) asserts the existence of potentially strong links between the Green movement, the unemployed and the demand for a universal grant. This link, however, does not stem from the fact that the universal grant provides a solution to structural unemployment that does not rely on growth, but rather from the fact that those willing to question growth as a central policy objective tend to be people who, given the nature of their preferences (comparatively much weight given to free time or to the quality of work), would gain from the introduction of a universal grant. Natural affinities, therefore, do not lie between Greens and the unemployed in general, but between radical Greens (willing to question growth as such) and the voluntarily unemployed. This point is further clarified in Van Parijs (1991a).

40 In this connection, we strongly object to Berger's (1986: 672) characterization of our proposal as the replacement of a right to work by a right to income. In advanced welfare states, the right to income exists. What our proposal does rather is give those with a transfer income the right to work, more precisely, the right to perform paid work without being punished for doing so through the loss of the transfer income which their 'idleness' entitled them to.

41 For a useful discussion of the distinction between parametric and strategic rationality, see Elster (1979: 117–23). We agree with Carens (1986: n. 4) that dealing with the strategic use of economic resources under the heading of political, as opposed to economic, feasibility can be misleading. One gets to 'political feasibility', in our terms, as soon as influences on collective decisions are taken into account.

42 In a capitalist context, of course, wage claims aimed at compensating increased taxation (of the sort that would be required if a universal grant were introduced) are directed against capitalists – thus leading to a profit squeeze or to an inflationary spiral, as analysed, for example, by Glyn and Sutcliffe (1972) or Bacon and Eltis (1976). And although the eventual outcome may be, via *non-strategic* disinvestment the failure of an adequate universal grant system that would have benefited society's poorest members, the fact that this struggle looks like one between labour and capital may lend considerable legitimacy to such strategic wage demands by the strongest fractions of the working class. This point is closely connected to Peter Jay's (1980) central argument for market socialism: getting rid of capitalist entrepreneurs will make it obvious that groups of workers are actually struggling against one another – and against non-workers – about the distribution of the social product.

43 For example, as a result of taxing away the whole of every firm's value added or the part of every firm's value added that is not reinvested, and redistributing it in the form of grants whose level varies only as a function of age and disability.

44 Under communism in this sense, there is, strictly speaking, no labour, and hence no one living off anyone else's labour, i.e. violating Elster's (1986: 719) 'widely accepted notion of justice'.
45 See Figure 8.2 in chapter 8 above.
46 One can admit that informal activities are and will always be, on average, less alienated than formal work – because of a lesser concern with productivity, a weaker grip of hierarchical structures, etc. It does not follow, even with a fixed total volume of activities, that any increase in the proportion of activities performed in the informal sphere would reduce alienation. For the effect of this increase on alienation may be more than offset by a simultaneous increase in the extent to which informal activities are alienated. A rise in the tax rate, for example, may induce households to substitute domestic drudgery for some outside employment.
47 In the terminology of chapter 8, why choose points lying on the prohibitive range of the Laffer curve, i.e. on the right of the 'Rawlsian' point, at which the income of the worst off (who rely solely on the universal grant) is maximized?
48 This vein of argument is suggested by Ivan Illich's or André Gorz's work, where the development of the 'autonomous' or informal sphere is favoured for reasons that do not all reduce to the objective of getting rid of alienation, as defined.
49 At least assuming that the level of fundamental needs itself does not increase at about the same pace as the universal grant. On the issue of how fundamental needs may evolve as average income grows during the second transition, see van der Veen (1991: section 4.2).
50 Not just compared to what it *was* in the previous period, when average income was lower than or equal to its current level, but also compared to what it *would have been* without that choice, and hence in the presence of a *higher* average income (assuming that the latter is negatively affected by the tax rate).
51 We go along with Wright's analysis on this point. Obviously, we do not need to wait for socialism to be on the political agenda, before we start exploring as rigorously as possible the implications of introducing an attractive form of socialism. It would be useful, for example, to get a more precise picture of the functioning of market socialism with an adequate universal grant. See Yunker (1977), which takes off from Oskar Lange's idea of a universal grant as a dividend on socialized capital.

References

Bacon, Robert and Walter Eltis. 1976. *Britain's Economic Problem: too few producers*, London: Macmillan.

Becker, Lawrence C. 1980. 'The obligation to work', *Ethics* 91, 35–49.

Berger, Johannes. 1986. 'The capitalist road to communism: groundwork and practicability', *Theory and Society* 15, 689–94.

Brody, Baruch. 1981. 'Work requirements and welfare rights', in P. G. Brown, C. Johnson and P. Vernier, eds., *Income Support. Conceptual and Policy Issues*, Totowa, NJ: Rowman and Littlefield, 247–57.

Carens, Joseph. 1986. 'The virtues of socialism', *Theory and Society* 15, 679–87.

Curtis, Thomas B. 1968. 'The guaranteed opportunity to earn an annual income', in J. H. Bunzel, ed., *Issues of American Public Policy*, Englewood Cliffs, NJ: Prentice-Hall, 120–5.

Cuyvers, Ludo. 1985. 'De kapitalistische overgang naar het communisme: commentaar op van der Veen en Van Parijs', *Contactgroepen Humane en Politieke Wetenschappen 1984*, Brussels: Nationaal Fonds voor Wetenschappelijk Onderzoek, 682–7.

De Villé, Philippe and Philippe Van Parijs. 1985. 'Quelle stratégie contre la pauvreté? Du salaire minimum garanti à l'allocation universelle', *La Revue Nouvelle* 81, 361–72.

Doyal, Len and Ian Gough 1991. *A Theory of Human Need*, Basingstoke: Macmillan.

Elster, Jon. 1978. *Logic and Society*, London: Wiley.

1979. *Ulysses and the Sirens*, Cambridge: Cambridge University Press.

1986. 'Comment on van der Veen & Van Parijs', *Theory and Society* 15, 709–22.

1989. *Solomonic Judgements*, Cambridge: Cambridge University Press.

Glyn, Andrew. 1986. 'Capital flight and exchange controls', *New Left Review*, 155, 37–49.

Glyn, Andrew and Bob Sutcliffe. 1972. *British Capitalism, Workers and the Profit Squeeze*, London: Penguin Books.

Gorz, André, 1985. 'L'Allocation universelle: version de droite et version de gauche', *La Revue Nouvelle* 81, 419–28.

1986. 'Qui ne travaille pas mangera quand même', *Partage* 27, 8–11.

Jay, Peter. 1980. 'The workers' cooperative economy', in A. Clayre, ed., *The Political Economy of Cooperation and Participation*, Oxford: Oxford University Press, 9–45.

Jordan, Bill. 1973. *Paupers. The making of the new claiming class*, London: Routledge and Kegan.

1988. 'Basic incomes and the claimants' movement', in A. G. Miller, *Proceedings of the First International Conference on Basic Income*, London: Basic Income Research Group; Antwerp: Basic Income European Network, 257–68.

Maat & Co 1985. *Heel eigenwijs. Nieuwe sociale bewegingen rond arbeid en inkomen*, Utrecht: Commissie Oriënteringsdagen.

Mintz, Jack and Henry Tulkens. 1986. 'Commodity tax competition between member states of a federation. Equilibrium and efficiency', *Journal of Public Economics* 29, 133–72.

Nooteboom, Bart. 1986. 'Basic income as a basis for small business', *International Small Business Journal* 5 (3), 10–18.

Nove, Alec. 1983. *The Economics of Feasible Socialism*, London: Allen and Unwin.

1986. 'A capitalist road to communism: a comment', *Theory and Society* 15, 673–8.

Offe, Claus, 1985. 'He who does not work shall nevertheless eat', *Development* 2, 26–30.

Przeworski, Adam. 1980. 'Material interests, class compromise and the transition to socialism', *Politics and Society* 10, 125–53.

1986. 'The feasibility of universal grants under democratic capitalism', *Theory and Society* 15, 695–708.

Przeworski, Adam and Michael Wallerstein. 1982. 'Investment policies and their political determinants', University of Chicago: Department of Political Science.

1986. 'Popular sovereignty, state autonomy and private property', *Archives Européennes de Sociologie* 27, 215–59.

Roberts, Keith V. 1984. 'Basic income schemes: advantages for business and industry', London: Basic Income Research Group.

Roland, Gérard. 1988. 'Why basic income needs socialism, why socialism needs basic income', in A. G. Miller, ed., *Proceedings of the First International Conference on Basic Income*, London: Basic Income Research Group; Antwerp: Basic Income European Network, 94–105.

Standing, Guy. 1986. 'Meshing labour flexibility with security: an answer to mass unemployment?', *International Labour Review* 125, 87–106.

Steiner, Hillel. 1986. 'Comment on van der Veen & Van Parijs's Reply', paper presented at the 1986 meeting of the September Group, unpublished.

   1987. 'Exploitation: a liberal theory amended, defended and extended', in A. Reeve, ed., *Modern Theories of Exploitation*, London: Sage, 132–48.

Stroeken, Jan. 1986. 'Socialistische politiek voor de sociale zekerheid', *Maandschrift Economie* 50, 50–60.

van der Veen, Robert J. 1984. 'From contribution to needs: a normative-economic essay on the Critique of the Gotha Programme', *Acta Politica* 19, 463–92.

   1991. *Between Exploitation and Communism. Explorations in the Marxian Theory of Justice and Freedom*, Groningen: Wolters-Nordhoff.

van der Veen, Robert J. and Philippe Van Parijs. 1985. 'Capitalism, communism and the realm of freedom: a formal presentation', Université Catholique de Louvain: Départment des Sciences Economiques, Working Paper 8501.

van Ojik, Bram. 1983. 'Basisinkomen en arbeidstijdverkorting', *Socialisme en Democratie* 10, 25–30.

Van Parijs, Philippe. 1986. 'L'Avenir des écologistes: deux interpretations', *La Revue Nouvelle* 83, 37–47.

   1991a. 'Impasses et promesses de l'écologie politique', *Esprit* 171, 54–70. (Also in F. De Roose and P. Van Parijs, eds., *La Pensée écologiste*, Bruxelles: De Boeck Université, 135–55.)

   1991b. 'Basic income: a green strategy for the new Europe', in Sara Parkin, ed., *Green Light on Europe*, London: Heretic Books, 166–76.

   1991c. 'Why surfers should be fed. The liberal case for an unconditional basic income', *Philosophy and Public Affairs* 20, 101–31.

   1992. 'Introduction: competing justifications of basic income', in P. Van Parijs, ed., *Arguing for Basic Income. Ethical foundations for a radical reform*, London and New York: Verso.

Wetenschappelijke Raad voor het Regeringsbeleid (WRR). 1985. *Safeguarding Social Security*, The Hague: Staatsuitgeverij, Report 26.

Wright, Erik O. 1986. 'Why something like socialism is necessary for the transition to communism, *Theory and Society* 15, 657–72.

Yunker, James A. 1977. 'The social dividend under market socialism', in *Annals of Public and Cooperative Economy* 48, 91–133.

10. In defence of abundance

Every single day, every newspaper in the world carries some further evidence as to how limited the earth's resources are.[1] Every single day, therefore, we should grow more deeply convinced that the notion of abundance has become hopelessly irrelevant and can safely be shelved forever. Or so it seems. In the final section of this chapter, I shall defend the opposite view: that growing awareness of the limits of our resources should make the notion of abundance, suitably (though still plausibly) defined, more and not less relevant to our pursuits. Whether or not this defence turns out to be successful, I hope this chapter will go some way towards clarifying this notoriously elusive notion, as well as its no less elusive and no less important antonym: scarcity.

10.1 Abundance in Eve's orchard

Let us first focus on a highly simplified one-person economy; define, in that context, an intuitively adequate notion of abundance, and explore what it does and does not imply. The economy is called Eden. Its one member is called Eve. Eve's welfare is affected by only two factors – in addition to the nature of her tastes. It increases with the amount of fruit she consumes – up to a point where any further fruit consumption leaves her indifferent. And it decreases with the amount of time she spends picking fruit – but only as from a certain threshold below which she is indifferent between doing more or less fruit picking. I shall call Eve's *satiation set* the set of combinations of fruit consumption and fruit picking which Eve weakly prefers to any other.[2] Of course, the amount Eve can consume is finite, and it is, moreover, dependent on the amount of time she spends picking fruit. Let us call Eve's *feasible set* the set of combinations of fruit consumption and fruit picking that are actually possible,

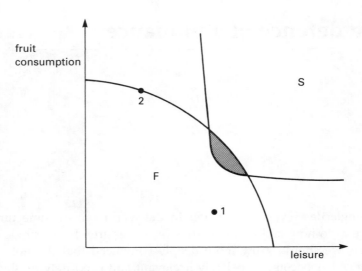

Figure 10.1   Abundance in Eve's orchard

given the location, yield and shape of the fruit trees, as well as Eve's picking skills. By definition, I submit, Eden is an *abundant* economy if Eve's satiation set S and her feasible set F intersect (see Figure 10.1). Abundance prevails, in other words, if and only if Eve can consume as much as she cares to consume without having to do anything she minds doing, however slightly.[3]

Let us briefly focus on some key features of this definition. First, note that abundance, thus defined, constitutes a *capacity*, a potential of the economy, which may or may not be actualized. An economy is here being characterized as the conjunction of its member's *tastes* – which determine the shape of the satiation set – and of its material and human *resources* – which determine the shape of the feasible set. Suppose that tastes and resources in Eden are such that abundance can be said to obtain. It does not follow that Eve, its sole member, is satiated, i.e. consumes as much as she cares to consume while doing no work she minds doing. For all abundance means is that such satiation is *possible*. This potential may fail to be realized for two distinct types of reasons. First, Eve may make an inefficient use of available resources – for example, she has overlooked a couple of magnificent trees, from which fruit is particularly easy to pick (point 1 in Figure 10.1). Second, though using resources efficiently, Eve may select a combination of leisure and consumption which does not optimally fit her preferences – for example, God obliges her to spend sixteen hours a day picking fruit (point 2 in Figure 10.1). Neither Eve's failure to find the magnificent trees nor God's cruel command prevents abundance from prevailing in Eden. For what abundance means is not that Eve is not short of anything she wants (whether fruit or leisure), but that it is *possible* for her not to suffer any such shortage. And the possibility of satiation only implies satiation under the further assumption of fully rational behaviour.[4]

It follows that abundance can be characterized as the negation of *scarcity*, understood as the impossibility for Eve to satisfy all her material wants while working no more than she fancies. But – and this is the second feature I want to stress – abundance remains consistent with 'scarcity' in two more demanding senses. (1) There can be abundance even if it is the case that, however hard Eve works, the fruit available for her to consume will always be in finite supply. Abundance, in other words, does not entail unlimited resources. (2) There can also be abundance even though it is the case that, without any work on her part, Eve cannot possibly get enough fruit to satisfy her wants, or even simply to survive. Abundance, in other words, does not entail the possibility of idleness.[5] As long as there is scarcity in this last sense, i.e. as long as the satiation of material wants requires that some work be done – even work that one does not mind doing in the least[6] – it remains as relevant as ever to allocate correctly one's time and other resources. Abundance does not make economic calculation obsolete. Scarce means still need to be wisely allocated.[7]

Third, what is the relation between abundance and *gratuity*? For Eve, as her situation has been described so far, both goods she cares for have a price in the following sense. Assuming she makes an efficient use of available resources (i.e. her choice lies on the frontier of her feasible set), if she wants to take more leisure, she has to cut down on her fruit consumption. And if she wants to eat more fruit, she has to work more. Increased access to either good has an opportunity cost in terms of the other.[8] This follows directly from the downward shape of the curve which expresses production possibilities, itself in this case the reflection of the very fact that it makes sense to distinguish work and leisure. (Nothing would count as work if there was nothing Eve could do to increase the amount of some goods she cares for.) Of course, as long as she moves inside her satiation set, this opportunity cost, expressed as the quantity of the other good which has to be given up, is no real cost to Eve. For it follows from the definition of the satiation set that giving up this quantity does not make her welfare any lower than it would be if she did not have to give it up.

This brings us to a fourth and final remark, which concerns Marxists' central use of the concept of abundance, i.e. to the relation between abundance and *communism*. Let us define a communist society as a society which inscribes not just on its banners, but in its actual functioning, 'From each according to his capacities, to each according to his needs,' and interpret this formula, for the time being, as follows: people provide their labour spontaneously, for no pay, while all their material wants are satisfied, thanks to the free provision of all the goods they care for. What would communism look like in Eden? For communism to be realized, Eve's fruit picking must no longer give her access to increased fruit consumption (paid labour has been abolished) and, conversely, an increase in Eve's fruit consumption must no longer be paid for by the giving up of some of her leisure (gratuity now obtains). In other words, the trade-off, or opportunity cost, described in the previous paragraph no longer applies to the economy's sole agent, even though it still holds, of course, for the economy as such. And yet, enough fruit gets picked for everyone's desire for fruit to be satiated.[9] Is communism, thus characterized, possible in abundant Eden? Not without some strengthening of the condition of abundance. For if Eve is told that she can choose to consume and (independently) to pick as much or as little fruit as she wishes, she can be relied upon to choose a point in her satiation set, but there is no guarantee that this point will also be in Eden's feasible set. Indeed, as inspection of Figure 10.1 readily shows, even if she were told to display some moderation by choosing first any level of consumption and next the highest level of fruit picking that would leave her satiated (or, conversely, by choosing first any amount of leisure and next the lowest level of consumption that would satiate her wants), there would still be no guarantee that her choice would be feasible.[10]

However, only a mild strengthening of abundance is required in order to make communism possible. For communism, as defined, can be implemented as follows. First, society chooses some level of consumption consistent with Eve's satiation (say, C_1 in Figure 10.1). Next, Eve decides to do the maximum amount of fruit picking (L_1 in Figure 10.1) that she does not mind doing (or to enjoy the minimum level of leisure that does not jeopardize her satiation), given the unconditionally promised level of consumption C_1. Eve is thus given her satiation bundle of fruit free of charge and supplies her work for no pay – Eden has turned communist. But this can only be guaranteed to be possible if in addition to abundance one assumes that Eve is willing to choose the lowest of the levels of leisure among which she is indifferent. If she were not, the lifting of the pressure (and guidance) of opportunity costs, as entailed by the very definition of communism, would constantly lead Eve to make choices incompatible with the constraints of production which (as we have seen) even an abundant society cannot ignore. Mildly strengthened along these lines,[11] abundance can thus also be characterized as the following dispositional property of the society concerned: abundance obtains in a society if and only if it is (economically) possible to introduce communism into it, i.e. to leave work unpaid and provide goods free of charge, without generating shortages.[12]

Put differently again, abundance is not just the potential to fully satisfy the demand for goods, for excess demand can always be removed through the price system, say by making Eve pay a sufficiently high price (in foregone leisure) for the fruit she wants. Nor is abundance just the potential to satisfy the demand for goods under conditions of ample leisure, for the latter may have nothing to do with satiation and simply reflect poor labour productivity, i.e. the fact that the price (in foregone leisure) to be paid for increased material satisfaction soon becomes prohibitive.[13] Abundance, as defined, is more than this. It is the potential to satisfy the demand for goods in the absence of any quid pro quo, i.e. the potential to simultaneously avoid shortages and dispense with prices.

10.2 Many goods, many people

Most of what has been said so far generalizes easily when there is more than one good Eve cares for (in addition to her leisure). Suppose Eve does not only like to eat fruit, but also to drink water, which needs fetching from a well. Both the feasible set and the satiation set are now made up of four-dimensional points (combinations of amounts of fruit, water, fruit picking and water fetching), and abundance can again be defined by the existence of a non-empty intersection between these two sets.[14] Such abundance does not imply actual satiation, nor an unlimited supply of both fruit and water, nor the possibility of satiation without any picking or fetching, nor the absence of opportunity cost (more water, for example, means less fruit and/or less leisure). What it does imply is the possibility of communism, i.e. gratuity without shortage, providing some more specific guidance is given by society to its single agent than in the one-good case. Society must not just select amounts of fruit and water consistent with Eve's satiation and made available to her free of charge. It must also instruct Eve about which combinations of fruit picking and water fetching – among those between which she is indifferent – she should perform, if society's production and consumption plans are to be consistent. Whatever the number of goods involved, abundance implies that demand for them can be met even at zero price. But the more numerous the goods – whether final, intermediate or capital goods –, the more differentiated the required productive activities, and hence the more detailed the instructions society will have to make available to Eve.

Let us now return to the one-good orchard, while letting Adam in. Abundance, in this enlarged society, can be analogously defined as the existence of a non-empty intersection between the social feasible set and the social satiation set. But we must be very careful about how these two sets are defined. Neither the social feasible set nor the social satiation set can be viewed as sets of combinations of aggregate amounts of fruit and aggregate amounts of leisure. This is obvious enough for the satiation set. A given combination of total fruit and total leisure can lie inside or outside the satiation set depending on how fruit and leisure are distributed among Eve (who, say, loves eating apples) and Adam (who, say, loves picking them).

That distribution matters is somewhat less obvious, but no less true, for the feasible set. First, Eve's and Adam's fruit-picking skills are not necessarily equal. When they differ, how total leisure is distributed between Eve and Adam obviously affects the total amount of fruit picked. Hence, whether a given combination of total fruit and total leisure is feasible, cannot be determined as long as the distribution of leisure is left unspecified. Second, how much fruit picking Adam and Eve are willing to do will generally depend on how much fruit each of them is entitled to consume. This is the case both because how good one is at picking fruit may depend on how well one eats, and because how keen one is to pick fruit may depend on how much fruit one expects to get (or to retain) as a reward for the picking one does. As a consequence of such efficiency considerations (in a broad sense that covers both capacity and incentive effects), whether a given combination of total fruit, Eve's leisure and Adam's leisure is feasible, cannot be determined as long as the distribution of fruit consumption is left unspecified.

It follows that both the social satiation set and the social feasible set must be defined as sets of pairs of combinations of fruit consumption and leisure (one combination for each individual), and abundance obtains if and only if there is at least one such pair that lies in both sets. Note that abundance, thus defined, may be attained when Adam joins Eve even if it could not be attained by both of them separately, indeed even if it could not be attained by either separately. This is due, *first*, to the possibility of

redistribution – constrained, but not abolished, by the efficiency considerations mentioned above. If abundance prevails for Eve, but not for Adam,
when taken separately, it may prevail for both when they come together,
even if their productivity is not enhanced by the change. Some of the
fruit that (more productive or more austere) Eve does not mind picking,
may be available for redistribution to (clumsier or greedier) Adam,
without such redistribution jeopardizing Eve's own satiation. *Second*,
society's production possibilities may of course be affected by interaction
between Eve and Adam. The effect on productivity may be negative
(Adam now picks some of the most accessible fruit), but it may also be
positive (Eve can now carry Adam on her shoulders). In the former case,
the social feasible set is strictly smaller than the set of pairs of individually
feasible combinations. In the latter case, it is strictly larger, and may
therefore include a pair of individually inaccessible combinations that lie
in Eve's and Adam's respective satiation sets. *Third*, interaction between
Adam and Eve may also affect their preferences. As a result of coming
together, they may become more difficult to satiate (chatting has become
an attractive substitute to fruit picking) or easier to satiate (eating fruit,
they realize, was a poor *Ersatz* for making love). In the former case, the
social satiation set is strictly smaller than the set of pairs of individually
satiating combinations. In the latter case, it is strictly larger, and may
therefore include a pair of feasible but individually non-satiating combinations, thereby turning two separate scarcities into one joint abundance.

This concept of abundance for a two-person world can easily be
extended to the general case of any number of people. Both the social
feasible set and the social satiation set are then sets of n-tuples of
fruit–leisure combinations. And abundance obtains if and only if there is
at least one such n-tuple that belongs to both sets (bearing in mind the
three caveats mentioned in the previous paragraph). A society has
reached abundance, in other words, if and only if there exists a feasible
allocation of fruit and leisure among its members, such that none of these
prefers any other fruit-leisure combination to the one s/he has under that
allocation. This more general concept possesses properties closely analogous to those mentioned in the single-agent world. In particular, it does
not imply that anyone is actually satiated, nor that fruit is available
without limits, nor that material wants can be satisfied without anyone
working, nor that an increase in one agent's consumption has no cost in
terms of consumption possibilities for the others.

What requires closer analysis at this stage is the relation between
communism and abundance. In this more crowded world, the possibility

of communism (which now becomes less of a misnomer) means that the social product – the fruit picked by all, whether alone or in cooperation – can be distributed free of charge, irrespective, that is, of each person's contribution to fruit picking, without this generating a shortage of fruit or requiring a compulsion to work. Here again, of course, abundance alone does not strictly guarantee the possibility of communism. For if each individual is left to choose any combination of (free) fruit consumption and (unpaid) fruit picking inside his/her satiation set, the odds are that shortages will set in. Even if society selects, for each individual, some level of consumption consistent with his/her satiation, and next asks him/her to work as much as is compatible with remaining satiated (the straight extension of the requirement that sufficed in the one-person case), there is still no guarantee that the end result will lie in the aggregate feasible set.

To make sure that enough will be produced for everyone to be satiated, one must not only ask people to keep the lower frontier of their satiation set (they could not be satiated with less leisure and no more fruit or with less fruit and no more leisure), but also to select exactly that point of this frontier at which the surplus available for redistribution is maximized (or the deficit to be made up by redistribution minimized). At this point, their marginal productivity is equal to their marginal disutility from work (working any more would produce less fruit than what would be needed as a result to keep them satiated). And this they will have to be instructed to do, since no specific incentive will make them make such choices: working less than this would cost them nothing in terms of fruit consumption, and if they chose to work more, they could fully compensate this increased effort by consuming more. Thus, no self-sacrifice is required of communist (wo)man. For abundance allows him/her to fully satisfy all his/her material wants, as well as all his/her taste for free time. In order for this potential to be actualized, however, some willingness to follow the planner's guidance will in general be indispensable. Not only will all agents have to give the planner adequate information about their tastes and productivity. But among the various combinations in their satiation set (all individually accessible to them, since they have no budget constraint, and all equivalent in their eyes, since they are all sufficient for satiation), they will have to choose the one the planner directs them to choose.

This conclusion is of course even more true if we combine the two complications introduced in this section – many goods and many people. All abundance means is that the set of n-tuples which satiate the n agents' preferences has a *common intersection* with the set of feasible *n*-tuples. (Each element of each *n*-tuple is itself an *m*-tuple of amounts of the *m* goods and activities that affect the agents' welfare.) It is only if abundance meant something far more demanding, namely *inclusion* of the former set in the latter, that compliance with the planner's instructions could be dispensed with. For then the agents' preference of less consumption to more and of more labour to less (as from a certain point) would keep the agents' decentralized choices within the feasible set. Abundance as here defined is sufficient for communism, not for decentralized communism.[15]

One final word on the relation between abundance on one side, *conflict* and *class* on the other. It is often said that conflict only makes sense on the background of scarcity, and that abundance, therefore, would put an end to all conflicts.[16] Under abundance, to use Tartarin's (1981: 248) telling formulation, the equilibrium is not just Pareto-optimal – it is impossible to make someone better off without making someone else worse off – but also *Marx-optimal* – it is impossible to make someone better off even by making someone else worse off. Moreover, in so far as classes are defined in terms of differential access to assets – land, wealth, skills, jobs, etc. – which affect people's incomes, or their income-leisure bundles, or their material welfare, it can also be said, it seems, that an abundant society is bound to be a classless society: no one's material welfare could possibly go up as a result of a redistribution of assets, i.e. of a redistribution of whatever determines material welfare.

Let us not forget, however, that abundance is just a potential. It means that some allocation of resources (to various uses and various people) can generate the satiation of everyone's wants, but not that the way in which resources are allocated has no impact on the level and distribution of material welfare. Given that mismanagement, spiteful behaviour or random events may jeopardize their access to satiation, it can therefore be rational for individuals and groups to struggle over the control of resources even though abundance would seem to make this pointless. Furthermore, acute conflict and sharp class divisions (in a correspondingly broadened sense) can also persist under abundance because income or material welfare is not all that matters to people. Power, for example, may matter for its own sake. And even when everyone's material wants are actually satiated, people may still meaningfully fight over the distribution of power-conferring assets.[17] Finally, there are many conflicts – between two parents about how to educate their children, for example, or between fundamentalists and liberals about the nature of a good society – which are not reducible to class conflicts even in this broad sense. There is of course no reason why we should expect them to disappear, or even to become any less acute, as abundance sets in. For these three distinct reasons, nothing prevents an abundant society from being a class society, and even less from being conflict-ridden.

10.3 Neither unfairness, nor inefficiency

Despite all these cautionary remarks about what it does not entail, abundance, as defined, still represents a rather grandiose state of affairs of which it is uncontentious enough to say that it is not within our current reach – and will never be. There are, however, two general ways in which one can conceive of getting closer to it: through an upward expansion of the aggregate feasible set and through a downward expansion of the aggregate satiation set. The former is a matter of developing the productive forces, of increasing productivity.[18] The latter is a matter of containing wants, of inducing more austere preferences.[19] It is of course the former that has traditionally been given most emphasis in the Marxist tradition.[20] But it has come under attack from various quarters. From Veblen (1899) and Goblot (1925) to Baudrillard (1972) and Hirsch (1977), or Girard (1962) and Dumouchel (1979), many authors have analysed and/or denounced the dynamics of wants which fatally undermines current attempts to satisfy these wants through the expansion of industrial production. The more radical inference from such analyses is that the only way of getting closer to (or back to) abundance is the second one mentioned above – want containment – in the form of some modern analogue of, say, Buddhist character building – as advocated by Schumacher (1973) or Kolm (1982) – or of the moulding of ambition by gender – as suggested by Illich (1983) or Sachs (1988). The more moderate inference, which I shall endorse in the remainder of this chapter, is that productive progress remains relevant to the pursuit of abundance, *providing that* the dynamics of wants can somehow be curbed.

Of course, even assuming that this condition is fulfilled, technical progress only has the potential to take us nearer to abundance, not to make us reach it in one stroke. For those who find communism an attractive ideal and are unwilling to wait (forever) until the condition for its full realization is met, it is therefore worth asking whether and how this ideal might be realized gradually, as the process leading up to abundance develops. If abundance has not been reached for all people, for all goods and at any level of want satisfaction, it may still have been reached for some people and/or for some goods and/or at some level of want satisfaction, thus making it possible to introduce a correspondingly partial form of communism. Of the three paths thus suggested, the first two do not make much sense, for two contrasting reasons.

It is most probably the case that abundance restricted to some sub-set of the total population is already with us. It would be possible to let a small number of people consume (free of charge) a satiating amount of all the goods they wish, without requiring them to do any work. This might be viewed as a very partial realization of communism, to be developed into a fuller version as more and more people can be allowed to indulge all their material desires thanks to enhanced productivity. If each of the privileged 'communists' is (successfully) asked to choose a bundle on the lower frontier of his/her satiation set, such partial materializations of communism can be efficient (there is no way of improving some people's lot without worsening that of some others). But they are, no doubt, unacceptable on grounds of gross unfairness. Even on purely utilitarian grounds, a reallocation of resources away from the lucky few to some of the non-satiated is certain to commend itself (assuming decreasing marginal utility of consumption). And anyone caring for fairness or equality over and above what they contribute to aggregate welfare would of course be even more adamant in calling for such reallocation.

If it does not make sense to move towards communism person by person, can we not conceive of moving towards it good by good, as some have actually proposed.[21] One could, for example, provide water, salt, bread, electric power, housing, etc. free of charge and at satiation level to all, while still making people pay for any other good. People would thus have to keep making trade-offs between the amounts of these other goods they choose to consume, as well as between their total consumption and their leisure, while being given as much as they wish (but no more) of a selected few items. This might again be viewed as a very partial realization of communism, to be developed into a fuller version as more and more goods can be made available free of charge thanks to enhanced productivity. The trouble, here, is no longer unfairness, but inefficiency. For if one assumes, as is plausible, that the consumption of any particular good yields decreasing marginal utility, it follows that the resources required to achieve everyone's satiation for one good are inefficiently allocated: unless these resources could not have been used for the production of any other welfare-enhancing good (which is utterly unlikely as soon as they include some human labour), gratuity (without rationing) for some goods is bound to be inefficient, in the sense that everyone could be made better off as a result of abolishing it.[22] Inefficiency, of course, need not be a lethal sin. But it must be justified as a by-product of pursuing some other value, equality or fairness, for example, and no such justification is available in this particular case.

The two strategies explored so far have twin defects. By realizing communism for some people or some goods, they mobilize resources to guarantee abundance for those people or for those goods, thereby worsening scarcity for other people – which is unfair – or for other goods – which is inefficient. This leaves us with the third strategy. *All* people now keep being faced with trade-offs – i.e. with a budget constraint or opportunity costs – for the full satisfaction of their wants for *all* goods. But a certain *level* of satisfaction of material wants is given to all at no cost – i.e. without quid pro quo in terms of leisure forgone – in the form of an unconditional income. Again, this may be viewed as a partial realization of communism, to be developed into a fuller version, as the height of the income that can be unconditionally provided to all rises, due to enhanced productivity, up to the point where it is sufficient to enable everyone to buy a satiating bundle of goods.[23] The objection of gross unfairness no longer applies, since the income is given to all.[24] Nor does the objection of gross inefficiency, since what each good costs in resources can keep affecting the allocation of resources, via the prices faced by consumers.

10.4 Three concepts of abundance

Thinking of this third path towards full communism naturally suggests a different notion of abundance, considerably weaker than the one explored so far but arguably present in many current uses of the term. For along this path, there is a point which is admittedly rather tricky to locate with precision but whose existence is nonetheless hard to question: the point as from which the level of people's want satisfaction provided by the unconditional income is such that their *needs* can be said to be satisfied. It is no part of the purpose of this chapter to work out a defensible notion of need.[25] On any defensible account, however, I regard it as certain that need satisfaction will fall far short of satiation, and that the income needed to reach it may vary considerably from one individual to another, though only to reflect some objective differences for which the individuals concerned cannot be held responsible. Hence, long before its productive development makes it achieve abundance as defined so far, a society may reach a point at which it could durably provide everyone of its members with an unconditional income, possibly differentiated to take objective differences into account, sufficient to cover her/his needs.[26] I shall call this point abundance in the weak sense or, for short, *weak abundance*, to contrast it with the earlier concept, which I shall henceforth refer to as *absolute abundance*.

One way of characterizing the relation between these two concepts is as follows. Whereas absolute abundance means that it is possible to sustainably satisfy everyone's material *wants* without anyone *toiling* (i.e. working more than s/he fancies), weak abundance means that it is possible to sustainably satisfy everyone's material *needs* without anyone *having to* toil. This characterization suggests a further, intermediate concept, which I shall refer to as *strong abundance*: strong abundance obtains when it is possible to sustainably satisfy everyone's *needs* without anyone *toiling*.[27] To express the contrast differently, weak abundance amounts to the sustainability of (i) an adequate universal grant, i.e. an unconditional income sufficient to cover everyone's needs; strong abundance to the sustainability of (ii) an adequate universal grant absorbing the whole social product; and absolute abundance, as we have seen, to the sustainability of (iii) communism.[28] Under both (i) and (ii) but not (iii), only need-level consumption is available to those who perform no labour. Under both (i) and (iii) but not (ii), (most) people can consume more goods than is required to satisfy their needs. Under both (ii) and (iii) but not (i), work is left unpaid, and toil, therefore, has disappeared. Weak abundance, in other words, means the possibility of giving people the *individual* freedom not to toil (i.e. the bearable option, for each of them taken separately, to give up the sort of work they would not do for no pay). Strong abundance means the possibility of giving them the *collective* freedom not to toil (i.e. the freedom to simultaneously stop toiling). And absolute abundance means the possibility of giving them the collective freedom both not to toil and to indulge all their material wants. But in all three senses, abundance is consistent with the impossibility of giving people the collective freedom not to *work*, i.e. the freedom to simultaneously give up any form of productive activity.[29]

The relation between the three concepts of abundance can be further clarified with the help of Figure 10.2. Along the horizontal axis, t represents the proportion of the total product that is distributed in the form of a universal grant, i.e. irrespective of contributions. Along the vertical axis, $G1$, $G2$, and $G3$ represent the maximum sustainable absolute level of the grant as a function of t, for three levels of productivity. (The downward sections of the curves reflect the 'supply-side' assumption that high levels of t have a negative impact on incentives.) N and W represent the levels of income sufficient to cover everyone's needs and wants, respectively (both

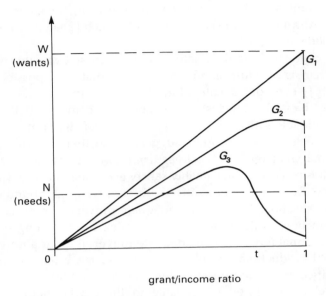

Figure 10.2   Three concepts of abundance

assumed to be homogeneous across individuals, for the sake of simplicity). Weak abundance is achieved if there is at least one value of t such
that $G(t) \geq N$, i.e. such that the corresponding sustainable level of the
grant is adequate. This is the case with $G1$, $G2$ and $G3$. Strong abundance
is achieved if $G(1) \geq N$, i.e. if people's incomes could (sustainably) remain
adequate to their needs even if they were entirely distributed irrespective
of people's contributions to production. This is the case with $G2$ and $G3$.
Finally, absolute abundance is achieved if $G(1) \geq W$, i.e. if people's
incomes could (sustainably) remain sufficient to satiate their wants even
if they were entirely distributed irrespective of people's contributions to
production. This is the case with $G3$ only.[30]

Of these three concepts of abundance, the last one – absolute abundance – is clearly relevant to the normative ideal of communism, but is
hopelessly utopian. The second one – strong abundance – still remains
highly utopian, and is anyway hardly relevant to any defensible ideal.
For realizing the potential it consists in – distribution according to needs
and no more – means forgoing the possibility of making everyone better
off (by opting for a lower level of t in Figure 10.2), at least under the
plausible assumption that reducing net pay for the labour performed has
a significant impact on the level of output as long as the level of the grant

falls far short of satiation.[31] The third concept – weak abundance – is of course the least demanding and, therefore, the least utopian of the three. Moreover, realizing the potential it consists in – by introducing a universal grant at a level at least sufficient to cover needs – does not lend itself to the normative objection just mentioned. For those who find full communism an attractive ideal and are not willing to wait for absolute abundance before beginning to realize it, the introduction of such a subsistence grant is an obvious way to start. And weak abundance is the first thing they must check on if they want to assess the feasibility of such a programme.

10.5 Weak abundance and the limits to growth

This is not the place to discuss the claim that weak abundance has now been achieved.[32] I want instead to conclude this chapter by returning to my opening claim that growing awareness of the limits of our resources makes the notion of abundance, suitably (though still plausibly) defined, more and not less relevant to our pursuits. The notion of abundance I there had in mind was of course weak abundance, as it has now been defined. Though far less extravagant than absolute abundance, which no doubt fits some uses of the term, it can still be regarded as a plausible understanding of the way the term is often used, typically by twentieth-century advocates of the introduction of some version of a universal grant.[33] But why should growing awareness of the limits of our resources make this admittedly weak notion of abundance more and not less relevant to our pursuits? I would like to suggest the following link.

Concern with the depletion of natural resources and environmental destruction has prompted appeals to stop economic growth, or at the very least to slow it down in the most advanced industrial countries. Low rates of output growth, however, are most likely to fall short of the rate at which labour productivity increases, due to technical progress. As a consequence, we need less and less labour to achieve the level of production we think is desirable, and unemployment is bound to expand. There is nothing like massive unemployment to generate a broad social consensus around pro-growth policies. As a consequence, whether or not they are bothered by the unemployment problem as such, environmentalists who mean business must find a way of tackling the unemployment problem through means other than the fostering of economic growth. This is where the idea of an unconditional income comes in. For by giving every citizen an unconditional income, whether or not s/he makes any contribution to the gross national product (i.e. to the magnitude whose increase constitutes, by definition, growth), one reduces people's incentive to make such contribution, i.e. to work or invest in the formal, recorded sphere. And one increases instead the part of their lives which they will be able and keen to spend either producing nothing at all or, possibly, engaging in informal, unrecorded production – which can be trusted to be on average far less polluting and less natural-resource-intensive than formal production.[34] Of course, for the introduction of a universal grant to have a significant impact along these lines – and for it to be an acceptable alternative to prevailing social policies in advanced industrial countries –, the level of this grant must not be shockingly low. This leads us straight to the question whether an adequate universal grant is sustainable, i.e. precisely to the question of whether weak abundance obtains.

The link thus suggested rests on two main premises: (1) awareness of the limits of what the Earth can provide, or of what the environment can take, tends to induce policies which generate unemployment, and (2) the universal grant provides an appropriate solution to the unemployment thus generated. I am not claiming that a fully compelling case can be made for both of these premises.[35] But their *prima facie* plausibility is sufficient to dispel the paradoxical appearance of the claim I made at the outset of this chapter. It is the growing awareness of the limits of our resources – and hence of how inaccessible absolute abundance is – that prompts us to look for a type of brake on the growth process that does not give rise to massive unemployment. If a decent universal grant provides such a brake, the question of its viability becomes of central importance. And weak abundance is just another name for what is at stake in this question.

Notes

1 So at least I feel confident enough to infer, on the basis of casual observation of an admittedly unrepresentative sample.

2 That is, combination C is in Eve's satiation set if, for any combination X, either Eve strictly prefers C to X, or she is indifferent between C and X. Note that satiation is not bliss and that, on some absolute scale of happiness, satiation may still leave Eve pretty miserable.

3 This definition and much else in this section are largely inspired by Tartarin's (1981: 247–54) illuminating formal discussion. Phelps' (1987: 7) characterization of the 'economy of plenty' expresses a closely related notion, even though it makes abundance a matter of satiation, not just of potential satiation: 'Everyone would work to the point where working longer would not be enjoyable, so all available job satisfactions would be completely realized. And thanks to those efforts, the technology, and the plentifulness of natural and capital resources, everyone's desires for the outputs produced would also be completely satisfied.'

4 It may be objected to both examples that they should be construed as illustrating the

absence of abundance (as defined), rather than the coexistence of abundance and non-satiation. For since satiation, by definition, is preferred by Eve to any feasible alternative, and since abundance, by definition, implies that satiation is feasible, Eve's ending up with less than satiation must mean that abundance was not really present: in the first example, because Eve lacks the skill which would have enabled her to notice the magnificent trees (her actual feasible set is smaller than was assumed); in the second example, because Eve has a taste for not angering God (her actual satiation set is smaller than we thought). I trust, however, that the examples lend themselves to a more refined description which enables them to meet such objections, as long as those who raise these allow for the possibility of irrational behaviour, and hence for the possibility that what is both feasible and (unanimously) preferred may fail to materialize, even in a one-person world.

5 Of course, abundance entails both unlimited resources and the possibility of idleness in the special case in which Eve *only* reaches satiation with an *infinite* amount of fruit and *no* fruit picking whatever. But this is, precisely, no more than a special – and most implausible – case, even though it is one that is commonly assumed to obtain: see e.g. Debreu's (1959: 46) insatiability axiom, which states for each consumer that 'no matter what his consumption is there is another one which [he] prefers'. Gérard Roland has objected that although satiation is conceivable for some finite amount of any good or service, it is not conceivable for any finite amount of human time. Though people may not want to work a lesser proportion of a day or life of given length (there is satiation for leisure, in the sense that no further substitution of leisure for labour would yield any additional utility), they will always want (with the rare exception of suicidal cases) to have more time available to them (human time is radically scarce, its marginal utility is – almost – never zero). I am not sure, however, that there is a fundamental difference here. For given how tired we are at the end of the day (or how decrepit we are likely to be at the end of our lives), most of us would not care for a bit of extra time, unless it came along with a matching dose of physical and mental rejuvenation. But in that case, where lies the difference with the consumption of goods? Would we not care indefinitely for more cake or more opera music if it came along with some physical or mental improvement that enabled us to digest the former or enjoy the latter? Satiation for leisure no less than for goods is always relative to one's personal features. (One implication is the fact [see note 2] that satiation need not amount to bliss.)

6 Work is standardly defined, and contrasted with leisure, in at least three distinct ways: (1) by reference to the utility of the activity's product; (2) by reference to the disutility of the activity itself; and (3) by reference to the payment to which the activity gives rise. It is the first definition, which equates work and production (of goods or services), that has been used so far and will be used throughout this chapter. By definition, therefore, leisure is totally unproductive and idleness means that there is no production at all. By no means does it follow, of course, that one cannot be highly productive or make most useful things without toiling (i.e. while indulging in leisure according to the second definition) or while being 'off work' (i.e. while indulging in leisure according to the third definition).

7 See Tartarin (1981: 251–5), who points out that 'economic calculation could only disappear completely if all goods entering consumption were available without production in amounts that saturate wants'. The opposite view, which closely associates abundance and the end of economics – is expressed, among many others, by Ernest Mandel (1969: 185), Alec Nove (1983: 5) and Edward Phelps (1985: 9). In Phelps' formulation, economics studies the economy of scarcity, i.e. situations where unfilled wants for the economy's goods press the economy to the limits of some of its resources, leaving wants still unfilled. The point is that even if all wants are filled – and they can be, by definition, when abundance obtains – economic calculation has been necessary (except under the

far stronger condition spelled out in the quotation from Tartarin) to make sure that resources are so allocated that this result is indeed achieved. On the other hand, as pointed out to me by Philippe Mongin, Tartarin's condition, though sufficient, is not a necessary condition for the pointlessness of economic calculation. If the supply of goods entering consumption were insufficient for satiation but allowed for no trade off between them (which entails, in particular, the absence of production) – think of fixed amounts of various types of manna – there would no doubt be room for distributive decisions, but not for economic calculation. Scarcity, therefore, is neither necessary (Tartarin's point) nor sufficient (Mongin's point) for economic calculation to make sense.

8 Economists usually refer to this 'technical' opportunity cost as the rate of transformation of one good into another, and reserve the term 'opportunity cost' to the welfare opportunity cost to be introduced below.

9 This agrees, for example, with Lenin's (1917: section V.4) canonic description of the higher stage of communism, where no norm of consumption is socially imposed and everyone just takes according to her/his needs.

10 This is the case because all abundance requires is that the satiation set should intersect the feasible set, not that it should be interior to it. If the latter were the case, i.e. if some feasible combination of leisure and consumption were such that no unfeasible combination would be at least as good as it, no social coordination would be required to select it. This is, however, a far stronger assumption than our condition of abundance, and one, therefore, which would be even more difficult to justify. (One can of course point out that Eve might get bored if she did not do some fruit picking and that the fruit she would thus pick might be at least as much as her stomach could cope with. But this still falls far short of what is needed to substantiate the stronger assumption: the fact that the satiation set does not contain the infinite point is a necessary but not sufficient condition for its being interior to the feasible set.)

11 Strictly speaking, all we need is a propensity to choose some satiating level of leisure in the feasible set, not the lowest among them. But it would be hard to provide this weaker assumption with a plausible rationale which would not also hold for the stronger one.

12 Along similar lines Nove (1983: 15–17) defines abundance as a 'sufficiency to meet requirements at zero price'. Elster (1985: 231) too establishes a connection between abundance and communism: 'Abundance, in the sense of suppression of scarcity, means that all goods under communism would be free goods, that is that demand for all goods would be saturated. When everyone had taken from the common consumption stock, there would be something of each good left over.' But he imposes requirements which are too strict on two counts. First, what is required is that there should be enough, *not* more than enough, for the desire for each type of good (including leisure) to be satisfied. Second, abundance is a potential. It does not mean that the demand for all goods is saturated, but that it *could* be.

13 This point invalidates the inference commonly made, in the wake of Sahlins (1972), from stone-age leisure to stone-age abundance.

14 Three-dimensional points, with leisure as the third good (in addition to fruit and water), would be insufficient, because different work activities may bear differently on people's welfare. Abundance may fail to obtain even though Eve does not mind working for longer than the time required to produce her satiation bundle of water and fruit: for example, if she does not mind picking fruit all day long but hates fetching even one handful of water.

15 The planning, assessment and information work required by centralized communism is then of course among the activities which, under abundance, it must be possible for people not to want to do any less of, while doing enough of them for all material wants to be satisfied.

16 See, for example, Nove (1983: 15): 'Abundance removes conflict over resource allocation,

since by definition there is enough for everyone, and so there are no mutually exclusive choices, no opportunity is forgone, and therefore no opportunity cost', and Phelps (1985: 7): 'Thus, an economy without scarcity would have no opposing conflicts, no bones of contention.'

17 The underlying concept of class is spelled out and defended in chapter 6 above.

18 Since what matters is the per capita productive potential, one variant of this first strategy in a world with scarce natural resources consists in negative population growth. In most of what follows, however, I shall concentrate on the standard variant of technical progress (including productivity-enhancing capital accumulation).

19 This second strategy would be ruled out if it were the case, as Phelps (1985: 7) claims, that 'not even monks and mystics have enough – not as long as they could meditate longer or better with the help of more land or capital or the assistance of others. To have run out of uses for additional rewards is to suffer from a failure of the imagination.' The point, however, is that satiation is not defined as the fulfilment of any want one *might have*, but of those one *actually has*. It denotes the fact that 'all have access to whatever is needed to realize their ends' (Levine 1984: 34), not the fact that all have access to whatever is needed to realize whatever ends they *might* have, and is therefore crucially different from, and significantly less ambitious than, what might be called *full* real freedom. Whereas curbing the 'imagination' is, at best, ineffective as far as the latter is concerned, it is not irrelevant to the pursuit of the former.

20 Marx himself displays some interest in the latter approach in some of his early writings, but unambiguously dismisses it later on. For a useful discussion and textual evidence, see Elster (1985: 71, 231). Some later Marxists have not followed this lead, including Lenin (1917: section V.4), when he insists that reaching the higher stage of communism 'requires the disappearance of today's average man who takes pleasure in wasting public wealth and in demanding the impossible'.

21 One classic instance is Lange (1937: 42): 'if the price is already so low, and incomes so high, that the quantity consumed of those commodities is equal to the saturation amount, free sharing can be used as a method of distribution ... It is quite conceivable that as wealth increases this sector increases too, and an increasing number of commodities is distributed by free sharing until, finally, all the prime necessaries of life are provided in this way, the distribution by the price system being confined to better qualities and luxuries. Thus Marx's second phase of communism may be gradually approached.' A similar line is taken by Ernest Mandel (1969: 156), Howard Sherman (1972: chapter 23) and some Soviet theoreticians quoted by Tartarin (1981: 244–5).

22 See Tartarin (1981: 250–1). There are, however, three types of circumstances under which this does not hold: (1) the competitive process too would lead to a zero price, due to the absence of a genuine opportunity cost (think of a subject – say, philosophial logic – which a few people, who know it well, are so keen on, that they would gladly teach it for free, while nearly everyone else finds it so utterly boring that even in the absence of any fee they would never dream of enrolling for a course in it); (2) the administrative cost of making people pay according to their consumption more than offsets the loss stemming from overconsumption (think of Nove's example of water supply in Scottish towns – which must be the sort of example Lange had in mind in the passage quoted in the previous footnote); (3) positive external effects justify that consumption should be encouraged by lowering the price, possibly all the way to gratuity (think of vaccination against contagious diseases or basic education). The relevant question is not whether under such circumstances some categories of goods should be provided free of charge, but whether it makes sense to expand the number of goods provided free of charge beyond these three categories, as a way of gradually realizing communism.

23 See van der Veen (1984), Van Parijs (1985) and chapter 8 above. This *may* also be the transition Nielsen (1985: 285) has in mind when writing: 'Ideally, as a kind of ideal limit

for a society of wondrous abundance, a radical egalitarianism would go beyond that [equal resources for the satisfaction of needs] to a similar thing for wants ... An egalitarian starts with basic needs, or at least with what are taken in the cultural environment in which a person lives to be basic needs, and moves out to other needs and finally to wants as the productive power of the society increases.'

24 This does not mean that no other, more refined, objection of unfairness applies. Along with Elster (1986), e.g., one could argue that even though everyone receives the same unconditional income, the outcome of introducing the latter is that some able-bodied people will become unfairly entitled to live off the labour of others. This is not the place to examine this sort of objection with the care it deserves. For an inchoate reply, see section 9.2 above and, for a more rigorous treatment, Van Parijs (1991a).

25 For some recent work, see Hagenaars and Van Praag (1985), Braybrooke (1987), Doyal and Gough (1991). See also section 9.3 above.

26 By speaking of 'durably provide', I mean (1) that the granting of this income must not be achieved at the cost of running down the capital stock, and (2) that the possibility of granting such an income must be preserved, once it has been fully anticipated by the agents. The impact of such anticipation can of course vary greatly, depending, for example, on whether the means of production are privately or collectively owned. But this does not imply that whether or not a society is abundant (in this weak sense, *as well as* the earlier one) depends on its (*currently*) being capitalist or socialist: abundance has been reached in a given (capitalist or socialist) society when resources and tastes are such that under *some* institutional arrangement (whether capitalist or socialist), each could be durably given an unconditional income covering all her/his needs (or wants).

27 Weak and strong abundance coincide with what is thus labelled in sections 8.4 and 9.3 above. Strong abundance provides a possible interpretation of the 'world of extensive abundance' which Nielsen (1985: 283; 291) views as the key condition of possibility for the 'ideal of equality' to be turned into a 'right to equality'.

28 There are, of course, more austere definitions of communism (including the one used in chapter 8) which make strong abundance, rather than absolute abundance, equivalent to the sustainability of communism. See, e.g. the pre-World War II Soviet theoretician S. G. Strumilin, who insists that at the highest stage of communism goods should be distributed to match 'scientifically assessed needs' (Tartarin 1981: 242–3).

29 The distinction between individual and collective freedom not to toil is parallel to, and inspired by Cohen's (1983) distinction between individual and collective freedom to leave the proletariat. Note that the collective freedom not to toil which can be given under strong (and hence absolute) abundance is not also a collective freedom not to work, whereas the individual freedom not to toil which can be given under weak (and hence strong or absolute) abundance is also an individual freedom not to work.

30 In a language suggested by Nove (1983), weak, strong and absolute abundance can equivalently be characterized as the sustainability of (i) uncompelled supply exceeding subsistence demand; (ii) zero-price supply exceeding subsistence demand; and (iii) zero-price supply exceeding zero-price demand. Or, if P means sustainability, while Ni, Wi, Gi and Xi refer to the needs, wants, unconditional income and total income of individual i, they can also be defined as (i) P (for all i, $Gi \geq Ni$); (ii) P (for all i, $Gi = Xi \geq Ni$); and (iii) P (for all i, $Gi = Xi \geq Wi$). Note, furthermore, that even weak abundance – P (for all i, $Gi \geq Ni$) – is still far stronger than what could be called *distributive sufficiency*, or the potential to generate and distribute income in such a way that everyone's needs are covered – P (for all i, $Xi \geq Ni$) – and *a fortiori* than *aggregate sufficiency*, i.e. the potential to generate an aggregate income larger than aggregate needs – P ($\Sigma Xi \geq \Sigma Ni$).

31 This makes the 'Marxian point' in chapter 8 very hard to defend on substantive grounds – as timidly conceded in section 8.6 and rightly stressed by some of our critics (see section 9.9) – quite apart from its being hard to square with the bulk of Marx's own statements on the matter.

32 See Przeworski (1986: 696–9; and 1991: chapter 3) for relevant discussions, which suffer, however, from the lack of a clear distinction between weak abundance and distributive sufficiency as defined in note 30 above.

33 From Major Douglas' Social Credit movement – whose Newsletter happens to be called *Abundance* – and the supporters of Jacques Duboin's 'économie distributive' – whose organization used to call itself 'le mouvement français pour l'abondance' – to Yoland Bresson's 'participat' (see esp. Bresson and Guilhaume 1987: 34, 48, 83, 88). In the Marxist tradition too, some related uses of the term can be found. Cohen (1978: 307), for example, emphasizes that 'the promise of abundance is not an endless flow of goods but a sufficiency produced with a minimum of unpleasant exertion'. The stress on 'sufficiency' makes the notion Cohen here uses weaker than absolute abundance. And reference to 'a minimum amount of unpleasant exertion' (rather than no unpleasant exertion at all) makes it weaker than strong abundance, too.

34 More or less explicit versions of this argument linking ecological concerns and basic income can be found in Johnson (1973: 181), Stoleru (1974: 306–8), Cook (1979: 6), etc.

35 I have explored a number of sore spots in the arguments behind these claims in Van Parijs (1991b).

References

Baudrillard, Jean. 1972. *Pour une économie politique du signe*, Paris: Gallimard.

Braybrooke, David. 1987. *Meeting Needs*, Princeton: Princeton University Press.

Bresson, Yoland and Philippe Guilhaume. 1987. *Le Participat*, Paris: Chotard.

Cohen, G. A. 1978. *Karl Marx's Theory of History. A defence*, Oxford: Oxford University Press.

   1983. 'The structure of proletarian unfreedom', *Philosophy and Public Affairs* 12, 3–33.

Cook, Stephen. 1979. *Can a Social Wage Solve Unemployment?*, Birmingham: University of Aston Management Center, Working Paper 165.

Debreu, Gérard. 1959. *Theory of Value. An axiomatic analysis of economic equilibrium*, New Haven and London: Yale University Press, 1971.

Doyal, Len and Ian Gough. 1991. *A Theory of Human Needs*, London: Macmillan.

Dumouchel, Paul. 1979. 'L'Ambivalence de la rareté', in P. Dumouchel and J. P. Dupuy, *L'Enfer des choses: René Girard et la logique de l'économie*, Paris: Le Seuil.

Elster, Jon. 1985. *Making Sense of Marx*, Cambridge: Cambridge University Press.

   1986. 'Comment on van der Veen and Van Parijs', *Theory and Society* 15, 709–22.

Geras, Norman. 1984. 'The controversy about Marx and justice', *Philosophica* 33, 33–86.

Girard, René. 1961. *Mensonge romantique et vérité romanesque*, Paris: Le Livre de Poche.

Goblot, Edmond. 1925. *La Barrière et le Niveau*, Paris: PUF, 1967.

Hagenaars, A. J. M. and B. M. S. van Praag. 1985. 'A synthesis of poverty line definitions', *Review of Income and Wealth* 32, 139–54.

Hirsch, Fred. 1977. *Social Limits to Growth*, London: Routledge and Kegan Paul.

Illich, Ivan. 1983. *Gender*, London: Marion Boyars.

Johnson, Warren. 1973. 'The guaranteed income as an environmental measure', in H. E. Daly, ed., *Toward a Steady-State Economy*, San Francisco: Freeman, 175–89.

Kolm, Serge-Christophe. 1982. *Le Bonheur-Liberté. Bouddhisme profond et modernité*, Paris: PUF.

Lange, Oskar. 1937. 'On the economic theory of socialism. Part II', *Review of Economic Studies* 5, 123–42.

Lenin, Vladimir I. 1917. *State and Revolution*, in *Selected Works*, London: Lawrence and Wishart, 1969.

Levine, Andrew. 1984. *Arguing for Socialism*, London: Routledge and Kegan Paul.

Mandel, Ernest. 1969. *Traité d'économie marxiste*, vol. 4, Paris: UGE.

Marx, Karl. 1885. *Das Kapital*, vol. 2, Berlin: Dietz, 1962.

Nielsen, Kai. 1985. *Equality and Liberty. In defence of radical egalitarianism*, Totowa (NJ): Rowman and Allanheld.

Nove, Alec. 1983. *The Economics of Feasible Socialism*, London: Allen and Unwin.

Phelps, Edmund S. 1985. *Political Economy*, New York: Norton.

Przeworski, Adam. 1986. 'The feasibility of universal grants under democratic capitalism', *Theory and Society* 15, 695–708.

——— 1991. *Democracy and the Market*, Cambridge: Cambridge University Press.

Roland, Gérard. 1989. *L'Economie politique du système soviétique*, Paris: L'Harmattan.

Sachs, Wolfgang. 1988. 'The gospel of global efficiency. On Worldwatch and other reports on the state of the world', *IFDA Dossier* 68, 33–9.

Sahlins, Marshall. 1972. *Stone Age Economics*, Chicago: Aldine.

Schumacher, Fritz. 1974. *Small is Beautiful*, London: Abacus.

Sherman, Howard. 1972. *Radical Political Economy*, New York: Basic Books.

Stoleru, Lionel. 1974. *Vaincre la pauvreté dans les pays riches*, Paris: Flammarion.

Tartarin, Robert. 1981. 'Gratuité, fin du salariat et calcul économique dans le communisme', in Marie Lavigne, ed., *Travail et monnaie en système socialiste*, Paris: Economica, 233–55.

van der Veen, Robert J. 1984. 'From contribution to needs. A normative-economic essay on the transition towards full communism', *Acta Politica* 19, 463–92.

Van Parijs, Philippe. 1985. 'Marx, l'écologisme et la transition directe du capitalisme au communisme', in Bernard Chavance, ed. *Marx en Perspective*, Paris: Ecole des Hautes Etudes en Sciences Sociales, 135–55.

——— 1991a. 'Impasses et promesses de l'écologie politique', *Esprit* (Paris), 171, 54–70. (Also in F. De Roose and P. Van Parijs, eds., *La Pensée écologiste*, Brussels: De Boeck Université, 1991.)

——— 1991b. 'Why surfers should be fed. The liberal case for an unconditional basic income', *Philosophy and Public Affairs* 20, 101–31.

Veblen, Thorstein. 1899. *The Theory of the Leisure Class*, London: Allen and Unwin, 1970.

Envoi: the greening of Marx?

Marxism has gone bust, ecologism has triumphed: contestable reading of two incontestable, massive, irreversible facts which are shaping the history of our planet as this century comes to a close – the collapse of so-called communist regimes and the explosion of environmental awareness. Whether or not one endorses this reading, whether or not one wishes to connect the two phenomena, this is a good opportunity to reflect on the substantive links between the two great traditions of anti-capitalist critique: the old one and the new one, socialism and ecologism. In the following pages, I shall briefly contrast and relate what socialist and ecologist alternatives have to offer by way of analysis of our society and conception of its future. This is a huge topic, which I cannot hope to exhaust in such a short space, but I shall endeavour to go to its core.

The paroxysm of productivism

At first sight, the gap that separates the two analyses is enormous. To start with, one would have the greatest trouble finding in Marx, who wrote at a time the Far West had hardly been conquered, anything like an acute awareness of the risk of depletion of natural resources. His work, from this angle, even makes for a regression relative to his predecessor David Ricardo, whose 'law of the tendency for the rate of profit to fall' (reinterpreted by Marx in an altogether different way) precisely expressed the fact that growing production would force us to make do with increasingly unsuitable natural resources. Moreover, the destruction of the physical and human environment, whose horror Marx occasionally describes, is in his view only one of the many sufferings experienced by the proletariat – and no more than an unavoidable by-product of the

233

accomplishment by capitalism of its historical task. To lament this process would amount to displaying a reactionary attitude which Marx relentlessly fought.

This point is of fundamental importance. For historical materialism, the Marxian theory of history, the history of mankind is above all the history of the development of its productive forces. What Marx calls modes of production – primitive communism, slavery, feudalism, capitalism, socialism – appear and disappear according to whether or not they are able, at a given moment, to develop as much as possible society's productive power. Marx's condemnation of capitalism, for example, does not appeal to the fact that under capitalism workers are exploited or oppressed. It rests on the claim that, as from a certain stage, capitalism is unable to adequately promote the development of the productive forces. And if socialism – based on public ownership of the means of production – is to replace capitalism – based on the private ownership of the means of production – this will be because, given the level of productive development already achieved, socialism becomes better suited to further boost this development.

It is this theory of history which enables Marx and Marxists to interpret class struggles and revolutions, legal structures and ideologies. It is this theory of history which enables them to explain the past, situate the present and anticipate the future. But what is this theory but the purest, most impassioned expression of what ecologists call productivism, voiced more clearly than any liberal thinker has ever dared to. The horizon ascribed to mankind – as both desirable and unavoidable –, the objective towards whose realization the workers' movement and other forces are working, whether consciously or not, is nothing but the unfettering of the productive, nature-transforming power of mankind! At first sight at any rate, we could not be further from ecological thought.

The abolition of work

And yet there is in Marx another dimension, which he happens to share with those of his contemporaries whom he scornfully called 'utopian socialists'. And this other dimension, which may seem very hard to reconcile with the one recalled above, is as likely to attract ecologists as the previous one was to put them off.

Both in his early writings – such as the *1844 Manuscripts* – and in his late writings – such as the 1875 *Critique of the Gotha Programme* – though not in his magnum opus *Capital* (whose only finished volume appears in 1867),

Marx repeatedly expresses the idea that the development of productive forces, and hence in particular the transition to socialism, far from being ends in themselves, are but means for the sake of achieving the genuine aim: access to the ultimate stage which he sometimes calls the 'communitarian mode of production'. What characterizes this stage is the full liberation of mankind, its full *disalienation*, in the sense that the activities of men and women would then no longer need any external constraint or material stimulation. As Marx put it, society could then, without risking a catastrophe, write on its banners: 'From each according to his capacities, to each according to his needs.'

Various remarks spread around Marx's work indicate that there are in his view two complementary ways of gradually moving towards this 'ultimate stage', whose full achievement is forever out of reach. One consists in reducing working time, in increasing the share of 'autonomous' activities relative to the share of people's lives that is being spent in the sphere of 'work'. The other consists in improving the quality of work, its intrinsic attractiveness to workers, so as to reduce the need to motivate them by external constraints and rewards. Disalienating human activity involves, at the same time, the shrinking of the sphere of work and the improvement of its quality. Put differently, it consists in abolishing work along two converging routes: by giving work an ever smaller place in life and by making it less and less like work.

Productivity, zero growth and the environment

But for Marx – and we are now back to the first dimension mentioned above – one fundamental condition must be met if this abolition of work, this liberation from an age-old alienation and slavery, is to become less and less utopian: this is precisely the development of the productive forces. For such a claim to make sense, however, it is clear that this development cannot be understood as output growth – quite the contrary. What *is* indisputably required, if working time is to be reduced and its quality enhanced, is an increase in labour productivity in a broad sense. One needs to introduce production techniques and patterns of work organization which make it possible to produce the necessary goods with less and less work, and/or with work that is increasingly attractive. There would be no point, as far as the stated objective is concerned, in reducing the quantity of work required by proportionally worsening its quality.

Thus, productivity growth (in this broad sense) is a necessary condition of the gradual abolition of work. But it is not a sufficient condition. For it is obvious that were this growth to translate entirely into output growth, life would not at all be freed from the grip of work. More goods would be produced, but work would remain as long and irksome as before. It is here that ecological concerns come to the rescue of the great emancipatory ideal of disalienation conceived in the nineteenth century by all brands of socialists. The insuperable obstacles encountered by continuous growth – the depletion of natural resources, pollution, international tensions, financial chaos – turn their utopia into a survival condition. It is no longer unrealistic today to beg people to stop wanting ever more. It is no longer unrealistic to request that productive growth be used to massively reduce the length and irksomeness of work, rather than to increase the mass of goods produced. To ask this, to demand something like 'zero growth' has become a pressing necessity. However dismal this necessity may sometimes seem, it feeds hope: the hope that the gluttony of the 'ever more' will stop annihilating the emancipatory, disalienating potential of technical progress.

That one should do something does not imply that one will. That a limitation of global growth is necessary does not imply that each nation, each individual (or even only every rich individual of every rich country) is ready to accept it. This is where another central ecological theme comes in: environmental protection. For what makes unacceptable a reduction, or even only a stagnation of 'real income', especially when accompanied by an increase of free time, is precisely the physical and human degradation of the environment. If you live stuck between an express way and a rubbish dump, how could you be attracted by the prospect of having more free time at your disposal if you do not also have the prospect of a greater income and hence of the means to escape (physically and/or mentally) from the debilitating environment in which you live?

Neither productivism nor collectivism

Thus, a lucid look at the old emancipatory ideal which Marx shares with utopian socialists, leads one to emphasize three fundamental conditions. The disalienation of mankind, construed as the gradual abolition of work (not, of course, of all activity) demands an increase in productivity, understood as a decrease in the human suffering needed to produce a given output. It also requires that the limits imposed to output growth should force mankind to use this increase, not to swell the flow of goods, but to reduce the length and irksomeness of work. Finally, if people are to find it bearable that the flow of goods should stop growing, it requires that the living environment be dramatically improved. Hence, the warnings and exhortations of today's ecologists can be interpreted from within the framework of the critique of industrial society that took shape over a hundred years ago and of the emancipatory project it generated.

In one sense, therefore, the ecologists' fundamental project is no different from Marx's. But it is important to add at once that the means Marx thought most adequate to realize this project – and on which, after him, the various socialist traditions have tended to focus, sometimes to the point of losing sight entirely of the ultimate objective – are not those ecologists view as most appropriate.

Firstly, it is to them absolutely clear that the 'development of productive forces' required by the scenario can by no means be assimilated – as it has so often been in the socialist tradition – to the growth of production or the accumulation of capital. As sketched above, the development of productive forces must be interpreted as an increase in the productivity of human effort in the broadest sense, which takes account of both the length and the irksomeness of work, and also of the nuisances caused to neighbouring communities and future generations. According to ecologists, in other words, the development of productive forces, on which the hope of realizing the great project of disalienation relies, need not be understood in a productivist sense.

Moreover – and this is for them no less important – ecologists find it very far from obvious that the collective ownership of the means of production, by which socialism or collectivism is usually defined, provides the best means to increase productivity in the sense indicated above. Whether one looks at technological innovation (which makes it possible to reduce working time) or at the development of self-management (which provides a way of improving its quality), historical experience casts the greatest doubts on the superiority of planned economies over market economies. According to ecologists, in other words, it is by no means ruled out that a duly modified form of capitalism may be far more efficient than real (not imagined) socialism as a means of increasing productivity in the sense indicated, and thus – providing growth is kept under check and the environment looked after – of making true the old emancipatory dream of utopian socialists and of Marx himself.

Neither productivism nor collectivism! Had he been alive today, Karl Marx would no doubt have had some trouble in condoning the conclusions thus sketched. But it cannot be taken for granted that his analytical powers and his sense of history would not have had the upper hand. It cannot be taken for granted that he would not have abandoned the dearest convictions of his most devout heirs and taken up, in the very name of his most fundamental political project, the heretic theses of the great green thinkers, from Schumacher to Gorz, from Illich to Bahro. It cannot be taken for granted that he would not have devoted to the setting up of a Green International some fragments of his immense energy – at least if any was left, at night, after a day spent working (half-time) at the British Museum, planting pumpkins on his allotment in Hampstead, cycling through the countryside with his three daughters or playing concertino at the neighbourhood fair.

Index of names

Index of subjects

justice
  and basic income: 178–81, 191, 195, 204
    n. 16, 230 n. 24
  and exploitation: 103–5, 108 n. 18
  entitlement conception of: 105, 108
    n. 17, 204 n. 15
  patterned conceptions of: 103, 108 n. 17
  Ricardian-socialist conception of: 104–5,
    108 n. 18
  Roemerian conception of: 105
  unpatterned conceptions of: 104

Keynesian mechanism: 54–5, 65 n. 33, 82
    n. 3

labour
  distribution according to: 156–7, 173
    n. 17, 179
  movement: 110, 192, 194
Laffer curve: 166–8, 208 n. 47
Left: 1, 155, 172 n. 1, 180, 201 n. 3, 203 n. 12
libertarianism: 89, 105–6

Marxism
  analytical: 4
  neoclassical: 70, 78–81
  orthodox: 2, 17, 78, 155, 161
Marxist
  causation: 20, 32
  economics: 37, 62, 78, 81
  ethics: 140–1, 143, 148
  regimes: 2–3
  tradition: 1–4, 20, 132 n. 3, 140, 142, 220,
    231 n. 33
Marx-optimality vs. Pareto optimality:
    219
methodological
  foundations: 79
  individualism: 84 n. 25
  rationalism: 80–1, 83 n. 21, 84 n. 25
microfoundations: 3, 17, 29, 75, 79–81, 83
    n. 20, 84 n. 25
migration
  of capital: 140–1, 144–50
  of people: 140–1, 143–50
modes of production: 12, 17, 112, 120, 234
  precapitalist: 17, 49
  (*see also*: capitalism, socialism)

natural resources: 64 n. 5, 159, 197, 203
    n. 10, 211, 233
natural selection: 81
necessity
  causal: 52, 55, 75
  functional: 51–2, 55, 75
  historical: 172
  of a fall in the rate of profit: 37, 45–8,
    61, 81 n. 1

needs
  basic (or fundamental): 156, 164–5, 171,
    176, 182, 196, 204 nn. 18, 19, 208 n. 49,
    222–32, 229 n. 21
  collective: 157
  differences in: 202
  distribution according to: 156–7, 161–2,
    170, 173 n. 17, 214, 222, 228 n. 9,
    235
negative income tax: 184–5, 201 n. 4, 205
    n. 22
neoclassical
  economics: 73, 78, 83 n. 19, 136 n. 30
  Marxism: 70, 78–81
Netherlands: 137 n. 43, 186, 203 n. 12, 205
    n. 23, 206 n. 31

OECD: 183–4
overdetermination: 9

positivism: 17 (*see also*: empiricist fallacy)
Prisoners' dilemma: 72, 82 n. 3
productive forces
  definition of: 33 n. 1
  development of: 10–15, 20–33, 157–8,
    220, 234–5, 237
  fettering of: 158–60, 173 n. 8
productivism: 234, 236–7
profit squeeze: 44, 64 n. 14

rationality
  and abundance: 213, 227 n. 4
  and historical necessity: 172
  and Marxist economics: 79–80
relations of production
  definition of: 33 n. 1
  explanation of: 9–17, 20, 33,
  see also: capitalism, socialism, mode of
    production)
revolution: 11, 15, 141
Right (the): 180, 203 n. 12
right
  to one's job: 124, 126
  to the product of one's labour: 104, 181,
    203 n. 14
  to work: 191, 193, 207 n. 40

September Group: 4–5
social credit movement: 231 n. 33
socialism
  and basic income: 187–8, 194, 208 n. 51
  and democracy: 148
  and historical materialism: 10–11
  and motivation: 177
  as a road to communism: 4, 141, 155–60,
    200–1, 237
  bureaucratic: 122
  centrally planned: 122, 129, 159